Knox Press
www.knoxpress.com

First edition, first printing
Copyright © 2021 by American Battlefield Trust
Washington, D.C.

Printed in the United States of America
BOOK DESIGN by Steven Stanley
TEXT by Kristopher D. White
MAPS by Steven Stanley

Library of Congress Control Number: 2021902642
ISBN: 978-0-9988112-4-6
Published by: Knox Press Princeton, New Jersey

The paper in this book meets the guideline for performance and
the durability of the Committee on Production Guidelines for
Book Longevity of the Council on Library Resources.

COVER PHOTO: Doug Menuez
COVER DESIGN: Jeff Griffith

BATTLE MAPS OF THE AMERICAN REVOLUTION
MAPS FROM THE AMERICAN BATTLEFIELD TRUST — VOLUME 3

FOREWORD

*"I just love those maps you guys send to me.
Could you put them into a book for members?"*

BACK IN 2000, AS THE NEW DIRECTOR OF MEMBERSHIP AND DEVELOPMENT FOR THE AMERICAN BATTLEFIELD TRUST, then known as the Civil War Preservation Trust, my first campaign was to raise funds to save the Cross Keys battlefield in Virginia. As I prepared that first appeal letter to our members, I knew a good map of that Civil War battlefield would be immensely helpful in allowing our members to visualize what we trying to do.

A well-crafted map would not only show how Confederate Gen. Stonewall Jackson's army held off Union forces at the small Shenandoah Valley village but would highlight the parcel of land that the Trust intended to save, which is known as the Widow Pence Farm. In one captivating presentation, our members would see how the Widow Pence farm was in the heart of the battlefield and visualize the intense fighting that took place there and how important it was to save this land.

You, our loyal and generous members, let us know right away how much you enjoyed and appreciated that map. As my friend and mentor, our President Emeritus Jim Lighthizer, recalled: "It changed everything. . . . And we paid that property off in 90 days."

Ever since that first map of Cross Keys, our battle maps, expertly drawn by cartographer and graphic designer Steven Stanley in close consultation with our battlefield preservation experts, have played an important role in our preservation campaigns. And right from the start, you started collecting them. They were such a hit that we began issuing binder notebooks and added punch holes to the maps so members could collect them as they received each new map in the mail with our appeal letters describing our latest efforts to save hallowed ground.

After countless requests over the years, we published our first volume of maps in late 2019: *Battles of the Eastern Theater of the Civil War*. We ran through our modest first printing in less than a month and have now sold more than 7,000 copies of Volume 1. That resounding success led us to print a second book: *Battle Maps of the Civil War Volume 2: The Western Theater*, which was also wildly popular and is currently in its third printing.

Now, you hold in your hands Volume 3 of that series, which spotlights the battlefields of the Revolutionary War, reflecting the Trust's expansive mission to preserve America's battlefields.

I'm excited by the scope of coverage in our new volume, with maps of almost 40 battlefields of the Revolutionary War.

From the clashes at Lexington and Concord, with the British advance and withdrawal graphically delineated on the map, to the final triumphant siege at Yorktown, where Cornwallis's British army was pinned into submission by land and sea, the book provides a comprehensive review of the battlefields where a new nation was forged in the bravery and fortitude of America's first soldiers—the young combatants of George Washington's Continental Army. We'll have the maps of the most famous battles, from Brandywine in Pennsylvania to King's Mountain on the North Carolina/South Carolina border, as well as ones showing lesser-known fights, such as Fort Ann in New York and Kettle Creek in Georgia.

This book functions as the only atlas of the Revolution that not only shows the battle lines and the ebb and flow of the fighting, but also pinpoints what land on the battlefield has been saved, who has saved it and what still needs to be preserved. These graphic features help you understand both the past and the present in one glance and reminds us here at the Trust of our ongoing duty to save hallowed ground wherever it may be.

Based on your enthusiastic support, which we deeply appreciate, we know you feel the same personal connection with our mission when you study our maps. It's the nature of our mission that any book of maps showing battlefields as they relate to preservation will be outdated soon after it is printed, since we save dozens of new properties each year. So, I'm sure many of you will be like me and still keep those binders handy to collect the latest maps with the newest preservation opportunities and successes.

I am grateful to all of the members of the Trust staff who have worked to create these first three volumes, but want to especially note Deputy Director of Education Kristopher White, who wrote the stellar text (it is wonderful to have a published author on staff), GIS Specialist Jon Mitchell, who oversaw the maps and offered key initial project management, and Deputy Director of Development Amanda Murray, who somehow gets everything printed and delivered on time and on budget, and you can't forget Steven Stanley and his outstanding maps.

But most of all, I am thankful for you, our members, and how loyal you have been over these many years. The popularity of our battlefield maps have no doubt been reflected by your generosity in supporting our ever-growing mission of preservation.

David

David N. Duncan
President
American Battlefield Trust

AMERICAN BATTLEFIELD TRUST ★ ★ ★

PRESERVE. EDUCATE. INSPIRE.

WHAT GOES INTO MAKING A "NEW" MAP?

By Steven Stanley

THIS IS A TOPIC THAT COULD BE THE BASIS FOR AN ENTIRE BOOK in and of itself. Map creation is a topic that fascinates many history buffs. So much so that I have an entire 45-minute talk and PowerPoint presentation dedicated to how I create my battle maps. In a nutshell, the process is straightforward, but it's also labor and research intensive, while being wildly rewarding.

The first thing I do is actually find the battlefield. This might sound silly, but it is easier said than done for the majority of the battles I map. Granted, most people can locate Gettysburg, Vicksburg and Antietam, but do they know where the Natural Bridge Battlefield is located? I didn't either when I was first assigned the task of creating a battle map for land the Trust was preserving. I'll give you a hint, the battlefield is located in the Sunshine State.

Once I have located the battlefield, I then start pulling together all of the source materials I can find. For some battles, the list of materials is extensive; for others, not so much. I use primary sources first—letters, diaries, books—and then gather contemporary sources, too. After this step, I try to locate any existing maps; these are in the form of both primary and contemporary sources.

The existing maps help to get me started on locating the troops on the battlefield proper. Some of these maps are right on the money, and some are not. Now that I have this wealth of material spread across my office desk and floor, my wife knows that I am getting deeply involved in creating a new map by the mess around me.

Next, I will locate the oldest topographical (Topo) map of the battlefield. This topographical map gives me a better sense on how the battlefield looked around or at the time of the battle. As we all know, the topography of battlefields can change greatly after 150 or more years due to man and Mother Nature.

Using the old topographical map as a base, I then overlay a modern United States Geological Survey (USGS) map over the historical map. Before USGS reworked its modern Topo maps to be more user-friendly, I used to hand draw each and every Topo line on the maps. The Virginia Peninsula battles weren't too bad to draw because the terrain is fairly flat, but for the Shenandoah Valley battles you have mountains to contend with. Some maps take a couple of hours to hand draw, whereas others take a couple of days.

Using the historical and contemporary maps as guides, I start adding in the historical and modern roads, using different symbols for each. Sometimes the historical and modern roads coexist, which makes my job slightly easier. Then on to adding in the water features. They could be just small streams that were there at the time of the battle to huge rivers, bays, and sometimes, the Atlantic Ocean. After adding in the water, it is now time to add in historical features such as houses, commercial buildings, churches and other elements that make up the battlefield. Finally, I add in the historical treeline.

Once the base map is complete, I can truly add in the location of the troops. Using the sources I have collected, I add in where a unit entered the battle, and then follow the said unit's subsequent movements during the battle. The primary and contemporary resources I have collected get the troops moving in the correct direction.

After I feel I have the troops in the correct positions and moving the correct way, I send the maps to a historian for that battle and have them check my work. I will take any and all suggestions or corrections to heart and adjust the maps accordingly.

Once all the adjustments and corrections are made to the map, I deliver it to the American Battlefield Trust, which, in turn, delivers it to supporters and preservationists such as yourself.

INTRODUCTION

"WE FIGHT, GET BEAT, RISE, AND FIGHT AGAIN," DECLARED GEN. NATHANAEL GREENE. In many ways, Greene's quote encapsulates the Patriot experience during the American War for Independence. Time and again Patriot forces met with disaster at places like Brooklyn Heights, Brandywine, Charleston, and Camden. Yet, time and time again the American's picked themselves up, rallied to the cause of liberty, and stood against the most powerful army and navy in the world. Patriot victories at Trenton, Saratoga, Kings Mountain, Cowpens displayed the resilience of American colonists, paved the way for an alliance with Bourbon France, and gave credence to the Declaration of Independence.

The match that struck the long slow burning fuse of rebellion in thirteen of Britain's American colonies was ignited more than a hundred years earlier. From the time of the founding of the colonies, the Crown took a very passive approach to governing their North American holdings and subjects. Each colony sprung up at a different time, for different reasons, and sometimes were created by different nations. A land deed to pacifist Quakers gave birth to Pennsylvania. The Dutch founded the city of New Amsterdam (New York City), a lost colony at Roanoke placed European settlers in North Carolina for the first time. Trade companies and those persecuted for the religious beliefs established other colonies. And in the end, the thirteen colonies that eventually gave birth to the United States were formed. All with their own government, economies, infrastructures, and identities.

History does not happen in a vacuum, and while the British Crown turned a blind eye to events in North America a civil war erupted at home, the ruling house transitioned from the House of Stuart to the House of Hanover, mercantilism took root, and the many wars of empire raged across the globe. The greatest 18th century war for empire erupted in the backcountry of Western Pennsylvania and spread across the globe like a wildfire. The French and Indian War (the Seven Years War in Europe) gripped the world and involved some of the most powerful nations of the age—France, Russia, Prussia, Spain, Great Britain, and more—and by its conclusion had morphed into a world war, with Great Britain standing as the victor. French Canada, Spanish Florida, and other land holdings now came under British control. While victorious on paper, the war was costly to the Crown in terms of money, and the good will of the American colonists. The war forced the Empire to station large numbers of regular troops on North American soil for the first time. While British soldiers had come and gone since 1676, rarely did the Crown offer major military assistance to their North American colonies. The Seven Years War changed all of that, and to maintain the newly won peace, it would take a force of regular soldiers to ensure that harmony.

War is an expensive venture, and the annual cost of this "peace keeping force" alone was £22,000 (nearly £4.5 million in modern British pounds), and this was just the tip of the iceberg. The national debt of the British Empire nearly doubled due to the war, skyrocketing from £74 million in 1756, to roughly £133 million by 1763 (a little more than £27 billion in modern British pounds). With citizens in the British Isles being the most heavily taxed in the world and given that the Crown spent substantial time and resources securing their North American holdings, it seemed only fair to those in Parliament that the colonies pay their share in taxes. Unfortunately, the colonists did not agree with this assessment.

Many colonists were disgusted by the way the Crown treated them during the war. Colonial militia, who had spent decades defending their hearth and home, were treated as second class citizens by regular officers. At first, Col. George Washington of the Virginia militia was only allowed to hold the rank of captain while serving under the command of British regulars, a fact that hurt his ego and eventually set him at odds with regulars who never served in the North American backcountry. Draconian British punishments were doled out to men like Daniel Morgan—500 lashes—a death sentence for most men, for striking an officer. Advice from men such as Washington or Benjamin Franklin was disregarded. And the headstrong militia were many times treated as laborers rather than soldiers. By 1763, many colonials had grown tired of the British way of war and only the intervention of men such as William Pitt the Elder, Secretary of State for the Southern Department, who understood the colonists, soothed the ruffled feathers by allowing militia officers to retain their rank above captain, furnished militia with arms and equipment, and even promised to take colonial grievances to Parliament. Unfortunately, politics and egos reared their ugly heads. Pitt resigned from his office shortly after King George III assumed the throne, and events spiraled out of control. Prime Minister and Chancellor of the Exchequer George Grenville assumed the reins of government in 1763. Grenville implemented a series of direct and indirect taxes upon the American colonies. The Stamp and Sugar Acts, and the enforcement of the Molasses Act of 1733 proved to be unwelcomed taxation on colonists who believed in home rule. Colonists, too, were angered by the fact that colonial interests were not represented in Parliament. Simply put, it was "taxation without representation." Boycotts of paper products were implemented in many of the colonies, and the smuggling of goods increased. In the lead to rebellion, the homes of Crown officials in American were looted or burned, and some unlucky government agents were tarred and feathered. Somewhat taken aback by the actions of their colonists, Parliament repealed the Stamp Act and eased up on the Sugar and Molasses Acts.

Still seeking to pay war debts and to get their fair share out of the American Colonists, more taxes and acts were imposed on the Colonists, leading to more unrest. The Townshend Acts and the Tea Act of 1773 drew the ire of Whigs in North America. In response to the Townshend Acts, an angry mob of Bostonians gathered in front of the State House in March of 1770. A shot rang out and then a ragged volley. When the smoke cleared, five colonists lay dead, and colonial propaganda dubbed the incident the "Boston Massacre." In 1773, the Sons of Liberty boarded ships in Boston Harbor and dumped some

340 chests of tea into the harbor. In response Boston Harbor was closed, and the King's troops acted as an occupation force. Colonists tarred and feathered British agents, homes of officials were ransacked, and boycotts of British good abounded. Committees of Correspondence were formed, a Continental Congress convened, and a petition was sent to King George. War was far from inevitable, but neither side was ready to back down. And the two belligerents came to blows in April of 1775.

Few could have imagined in 1775 that the American Revolution would last for eight long years. Fewer still could have imagined that a group of colonists could successfully stand against the British Empire and gain their independence. What started as an uprising morphed into a small-scale war for empire when France entered on the side of the Americans, and Spain and the Netherlands, supported the French and their own interests abroad.

As the clouds of war streaked across the sky, it was clear that British subjects on both sides of the Atlantic Ocean did not understand one another. Some in London felt that they should allow their American cousins to break away, while others staunchly refused to give in to the colonists demands. What emerged was a war of outposts against insurgents who were underestimated by the Crown, Parliament, and the military. Elements of 58 British regiments served in the war in North America, supplemented by some 29,000 Hessian auxiliaries (dubbed mercenaries in the Declaration of Independence), and roughly 39 loyalist regiments. Scores of British war ships roamed the American coast. Yet this impressive 18th century show of force could not subjugate a ragtag group of ill supplied, ill prepared, and sometimes ill led colonists.

Even with all their advantages in manpower, finances, alliances, and even possessing the imposing Royal Navy, the British high command could never settle upon a coherent strategy for their war in North America. Politicians in London were out of touch with the wants, needs, and desires of their own colonists. They lacked the knowledge of the geography of the new world and underestimated just the vastness of their own colonial holdings. Coordinating campaigns across more than 3,000 miles of ocean in the time of wooden ships and sail, was daunting. Military leaders allowed egos to get in the way of their duty, washing themselves in personal glory at times trumped what was best for the Empire. Some leaders were halfhearted in their prosecution of the war. Campaigns in various theaters worked at cross purposes against their cause. And at every turn they woefully underestimated their enemy. Like a football team who should dominate a game, the British high command allowed the scrappy upstarts to stay in the contest and ultimately best them on the world stage.

In the end, war is a political act. When the Continental Congress approved the Declaration of Independence, they showed the world (especially France and Spain) that the American colonists were willing to fight to secure their inalienable rights—life, liberty, and the pursuit of happiness. Thus, it was up to Washington, Greene, Israel Putnam, and tens of thousands of American colonists to take up arms and to translate the enduring beliefs, values, and political ideals of the colonists and revolution into victory on the battlefield. When the delegates affixed their names to the document, they were essentially signing their death warrants. It was treason in the face of King and country, there was no turning back. The plucky Americans showed a resilience that few could have predicted. Washington did not allow the British to destroy his army—the true center of gravity of the American cause. The colonists lost many battles and even their capital, but they never lost their core of Continentals, and the symbol of the rebellion, the Continental Army. They were resilient, too, on the political front, and perhaps shrewd. Turning to England's perennial enemy, the French, for assistance. It was French assistance—men, money, arms, ships, material, and friendship—that ultimately helped to secure American independence, and which sadly helped to bankrupt their country in 1789 and led to one of the greatest revolutions in human history—the French Revolution.

The importance of what happened on the battlefields of the American Revolution cannot be understated. Without the Declaration of Independence, we would not be who we are as a people. And without out battlefield victories we would not be the United States. To that end—now more than 30 years ago—the American Battlefield Trust was created to preserve the battlefields associated with the Revolutionary War, War of 1812, and the American Civil War. Over the last three decades, the Trust and its members have preserved more than 53,000 acres of hallowed battlefield land in 24 states. And the Trust's hallmark in land preservation has been our battle maps. Due to the sheer number of battlefields in the Revolutionary War, we cannot tell the story of every battle, and we cannot fit every map that we have ever created into this work. Thus, we have focused on some of the most significant actions and campaigns of the conflict.

As in our other volumes of this series, the battle maps are the real "star" of this work. We have provided the reader with some brief overview text to bring them up to speed on the battle action and then allowed the maps to tell the rest of the story.

It is our sincere hope that this collection of maps will give you a better understanding of the American War for Independence. And an appreciation for the tens of thousands of acres of hallowed ground our members have helped to preserve over the last three decades.

Please visit our website www.battlefields.org for more maps and more information about America's defining conflicts.

Authors Note: The ranks and titles of the various high commands have been simplified throughout this work. Ranks differ greatly in the British Army between modern day and 1783. For example, Lt. Gen. Thomas Gage was colonel of the 22nd Regiment of Foot, while Lt. Gen. Charles Cornwallis, who commanded the King's troops in the south, was also colonel of the 23rd Regiment of Foot. Lieutenant Colonel Barry St. Leger was also referred to a brigadier or brigadier general, a rank that only existed in war time. Some officers were knighted in the midst of the war or after the war, and some only held a certain rank in North America as the war raged but did not hold the same rank at home. For the sake of continuity and to avoid confusion, any general officer's rank is simply referred to as general. For field grade and line officers (and there can be some confusing cases here as well), we used their respective ranks of colonel, captain, lieutenant, etc.

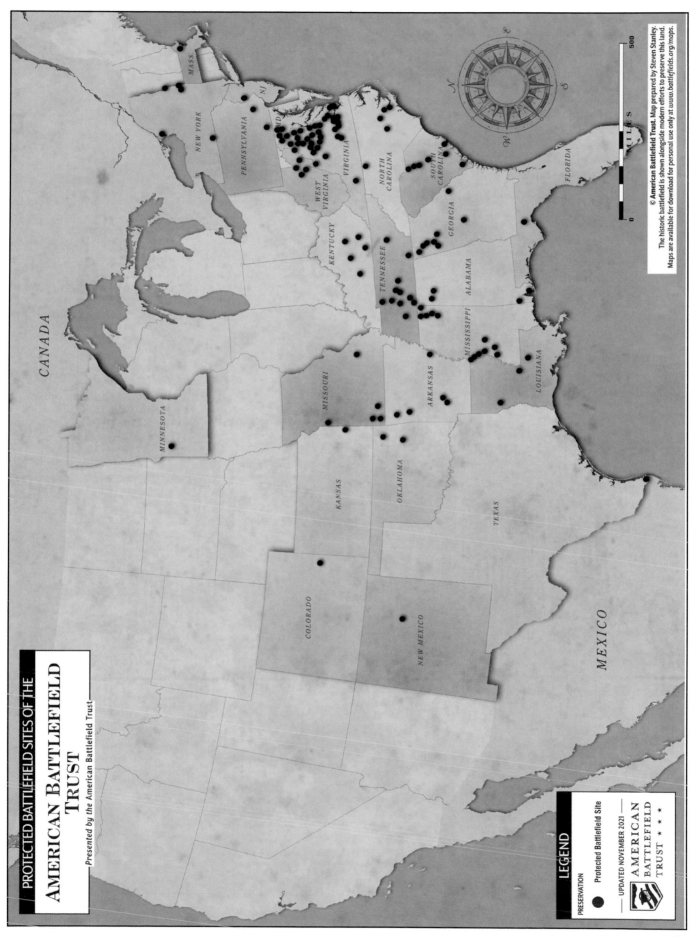

PRESERVATION BATTLEFIELD SITES OF THE
AMERICAN BATTLEFIELD TRUST

Presented by the American Battlefield Trust

LEGEND

PRESERVATION

● Protected Battlefield Site

— UPDATED NOVEMBER 2021 —

AMERICAN BATTLEFIELD TRUST ★ ★ ★

LEXINGTON *and* CONCORD

APRIL 19, 1775

A RAGGED VOLLEY OF MUSKET FIRE RIPPED THROUGH THE COOL MORNING AIR as the American colonists unleashed the "Shot Heard 'Round the World." The slow-burning fuse on the powder keg that was the Massachusetts Colony, which had been lit years earlier, finally reached its zenith, exploding into open rebellion. On Wednesday, April 19, 1775, years of protests among the American colonists, triggered by proclamations issued by Parliament and King George III, gave way to open rebellion.

Authorized by the King's cabinet to quell the seeds of the growing rebellion by capturing its ringleaders, the commander-in-chief of the British Army in North America and military Royal Governor of Massachusetts, Gen. Thomas Gage, dispatched some 800 men west from Boston to capture arms and munitions stockpiled by the rebels. The expedition, led by Col. Frances Smith and Maj. John Pitcairn, set out on their march near 10 p.m. on April 18. Word of the movement was spread across the countryside to the rebels by William Dawes, Paul Revere, and Dr. Samuel Prescott.

The King's troops strode into the small town of Lexington around 5:00 a.m. More than 70 militia commanded by Capt. John Parker aligned on Lexington Green to meet them. "Damn you!" declared Pitcairn as he admonished his fellow subjects to lay down their arms. The vanguard of the British force rushed forward upon the town green, and Parker immediately ordered his company to disperse. A shot rang out. And then the nervous British soldiers fired a volley, killing eight and wounding ten militiamen. The British column then moved on toward Concord.

Arriving in Concord around 8:00 a.m., Smith and Pitcairn ordered about 220 troops to secure the North Bridge across the Concord River and then continue on another mile to the Barrett Farm. By the time the British arrived at the North Bridge, a force of some 400 militia from Concord and the surrounding towns had gathered on the high ground overlooking the bridge. From their vantage point on the hill, they could see smoke rising from Concord, the result of British burning some supplies they had uncovered. Thinking the town was being put to the torch, Lt. Joseph Hosmer shouted, "Will you let them burn the town down?" As the rebels marched across the bridge, the King's soldiers opened fire. "For God's sake, fire!" shouted a militiaman and the minutemen replied with a volley of their own.

Smith and Pitcairn soon ordered a return to Boston, which devolved into a rout as thousands of minutemen patriots descended on the area. Swarms of angry minutemen attacked the British from all sides along what is now known as Battle Road. When the soldiers reached Lexington, John Parker and his men had their revenge, firing on the British regulars from behind cover. For the next 12 miles, minutemen continually ambushed the British by shooting from behind trees, rock walls, and buildings.

The British conducted a running fight until they could get under the cover of British guns in ships anchored in the waterways surrounding Boston. By 8:00 p.m., it was clear that the day had been a disaster for the British. Conflict had erupted that would change the world forever.

✳ ✳ PRESERVATION ✳ ✳

To date, the **American Battlefield Trust** has saved **one acres** at Lexington & Concord.

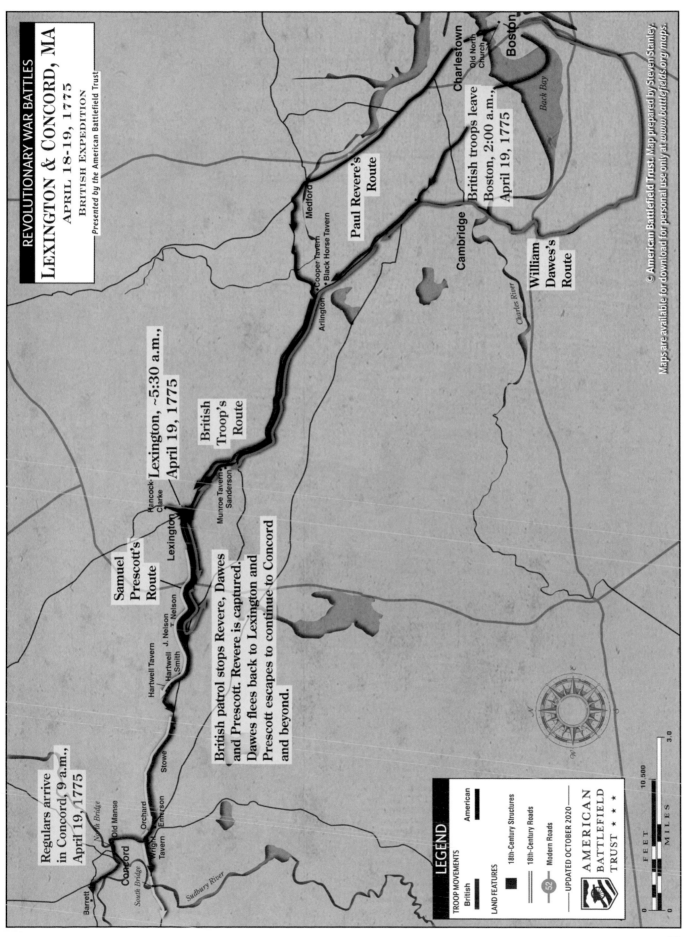

REVOLUTIONARY WAR BATTLES
LEXINGTON & CONCORD, MA
APRIL 18-19, 1775
BRITISH EXPEDITION
Presented by the American Battlefield Trust

Paul Revere's Route

British troops leave Boston, 2:00 a.m., April 19, 1775

William Dawes's Route

Charlestown

Old North Church

Boston

Back Bay

Charles River

Cambridge

Medford

Cooper Tavern
Black Horse Tavern

Arlington

British Troop's Route

Lexington, ~5:30 a.m., April 19, 1775

Hancock-Clarke

Munroe Tavern
Sanderson

Lexington

Samuel Prescott's Route

British patrol stops Revere, Dawes and Prescott. Revere is captured. Dawes flees back to Lexington and Prescott escapes to continue to Concord and beyond.

J. Nelson
T. Nelson

Hartwell Tavern

Hartwell
Smith

Stowe

Regulars arrive in Concord, 9 a.m., April 19, 1775

North Bridge

Old Manse

Orchard

Emerson

Wright Tavern

Concord

Barrett

South Bridge

Sudbury River

LEGEND
TROOP MOVEMENTS

British ▬▬ American ▬▬

LAND FEATURES

▪ 18th-Century Structures

—— 18th-Century Roads

52 Modern Roads

—— UPDATED OCTOBER 2020

AMERICAN BATTLEFIELD TRUST ★ ★ ★

FEET 0   10,500

MILES 0   3.0

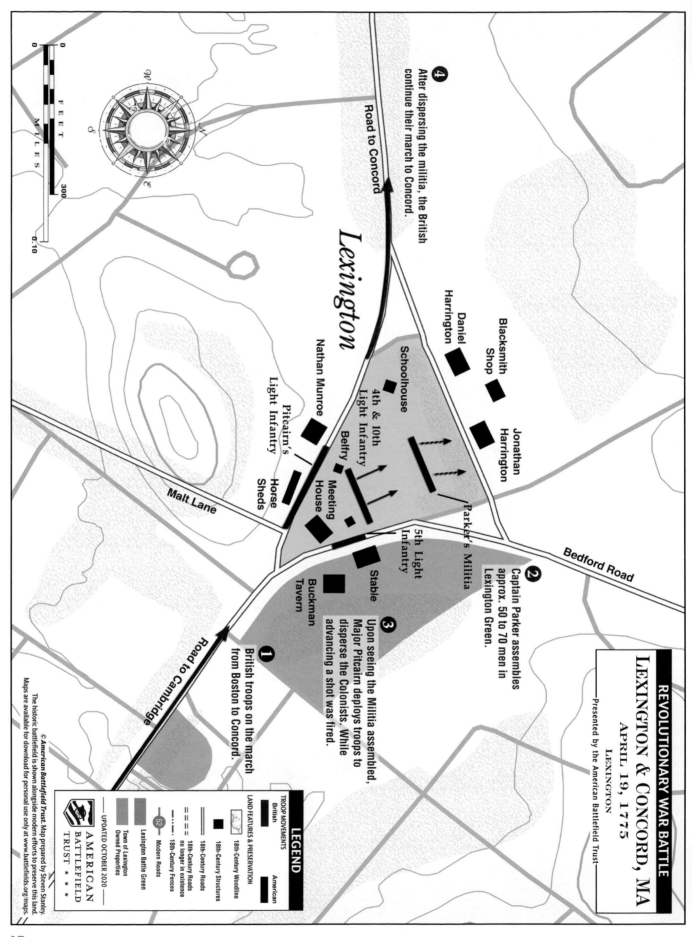

REVOLUTIONARY WAR BATTLE

LEXINGTON & CONCORD, MA
APRIL 19, 1775
LEXINGTON
—Presented by the American Battlefield Trust—

Lexington

Road to Concord

Road to Cambridge

Malt Lane

Bedford Road

Daniel Harrington

Blacksmith Shop

Jonathan Harrington

Schoolhouse

4th & 10th Light Infantry

Nathan Munroe

Pitcairn's Light Infantry

Belfry

Horse Sheds

Meeting House

Parker's Militia

5th Light Infantry

Stable

Buckman Tavern

4 After dispersing the militia, the British continue their march to Concord.

1 British troops on the march from Boston to Concord.

2 Captain Parker assembles approx. 50 to 70 men in Lexington Green.

3 Upon seeing the Militia assembled, Major Pitcairn deploys troops to disperse the Colonists. While advancing a shot was fired.

0 FEET 300
0 MILES 0.10

LEGEND

TROOP MOVEMENTS
- British
- American

LAND FEATURES & PRESERVATION
- 18th-Century Woodline
- 18th-Century Structures
- 52 Modern Roads
- 18th-Century Roads
- 18th-Century Roads no longer in existence
- 18th-Century Fences
- Town of Lexington Owned Properties
- Lexington Battle Green

UPDATED OCTOBER 2020

AMERICAN BATTLEFIELD TRUST ★★★

© *American Battlefield Trust*. Map prepared by Steven Stanley. Maps are available for download for personal use only at www.battlefields.org/maps.

The historic battlefield is shown alongside modern efforts to preserve this land.

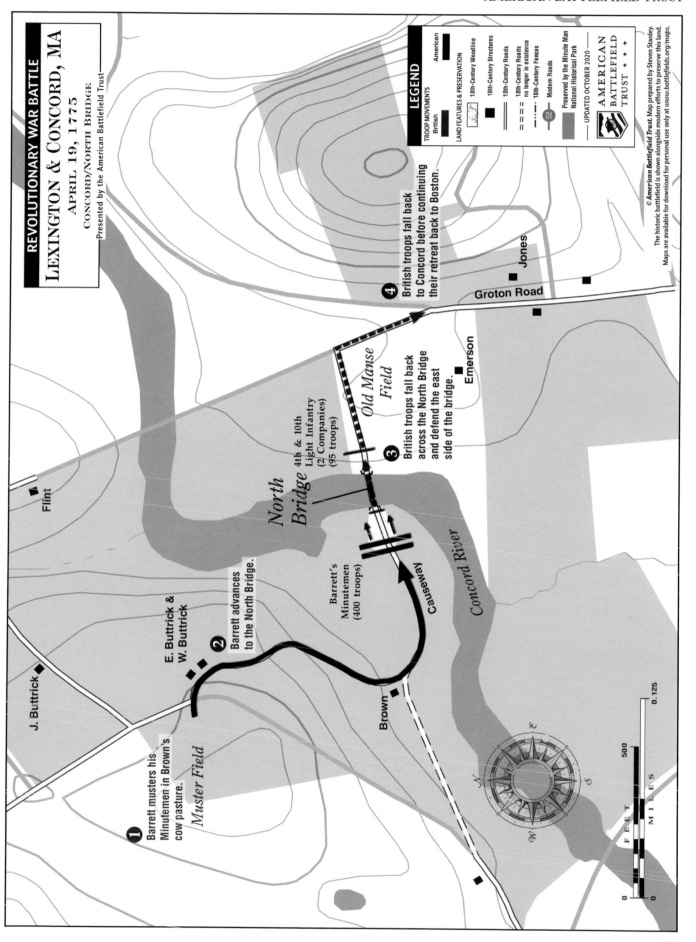

REVOLUTIONARY WAR BATTLE
Lexington & Concord, MA
APRIL 19, 1775
CONCORD/NORTH BRIDGE
Presented by the American Battlefield Trust

LEGEND

TROOP MOVEMENTS

British ▮   American ▮

LAND FEATURES & PRESERVATION

- ▨ 18th-Century Woodline
- ■ 18th-Century Structures
- ═══ 18th-Century Roads
- ═ ═ ═ 18th-Century Roads no longer in existence
- ·─·─· 18th-Century Fences
- 52 Modern Roads
- ▨ Preserved by the Minute Man National Historical Park

— UPDATED OCTOBER 2020 —

AMERICAN BATTLEFIELD TRUST ★ ★ ★

© *American Battlefield Trust.* Map prepared by Steven Stanley. The historic battlefield is shown alongside modern efforts to preserve this land. Maps are available for download for personal use only at *www.battlefields.org/maps.*

① Barrett musters his Minutemen in Brown's cow pasture.

Muster Field

J. Buttrick ◆

Flint ▪

E. Buttrick & W. Buttrick ◆◆

② Barrett advances to the North Bridge.

North Bridge

4th & 10th Light Infantry (2 Companies) (95 troops)

Barrett's Minutemen (400 troops)

Brown ▪

Causeway

Concord River

③ British troops fall back across the North Bridge and defend the east side of the bridge.

Old Manse Field

Emerson ▪

④ British troops fall back to Concord before continuing their retreat back to Boston.

Groton Road

Jones ▪

FEET 0 — 500
MILES 0 — 0.125

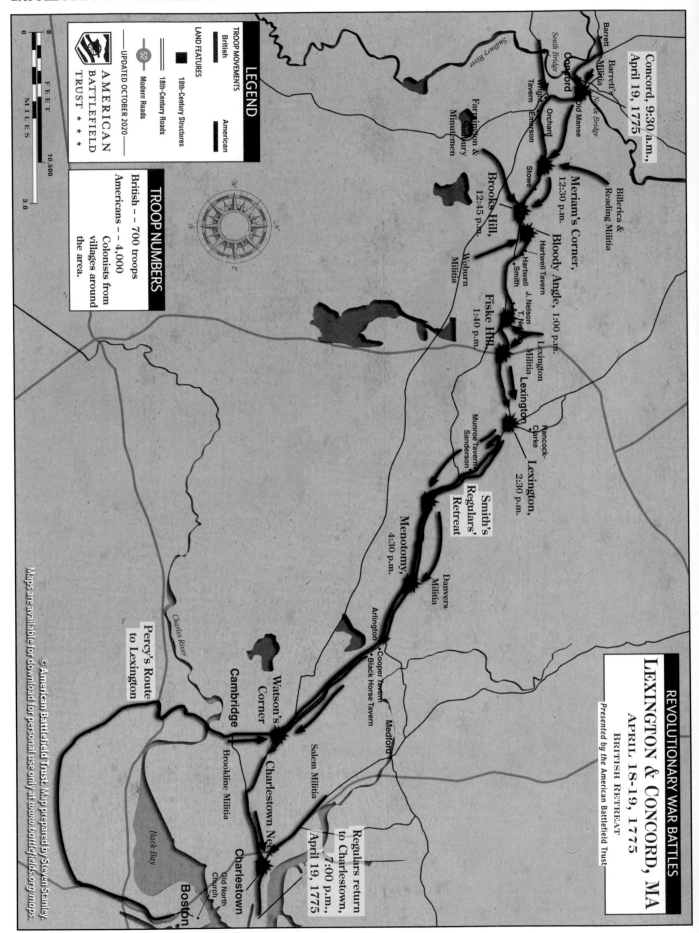

REVOLUTIONARY WAR BATTLES
LEXINGTON & CONCORD, MA
APRIL 18-19, 1775
BRITISH RETREAT
Presented by the American Battlefield Trust

LEGEND

TROOP MOVEMENTS
British
American

LAND FEATURES
18th-Century Structures
18th-Century Roads
52   Modern Roads
UPDATED OCTOBER 2020

AMERICAN BATTLEFIELD TRUST ★ ★ ★

FEET   0   10,500
MILES 0   3.0

TROOP NUMBERS

British ~ 700 troops
Americans ~ 4,000 Colonists from villages around the area.

Concord, 9:30 a.m., April 19, 1775

Barrett's Militia
South Bridge
Sudbury River
Concord
North Bridge
Old Manse
Wright Tavern
Emerson
Orchard
Farrington & Sudbury Minutemen
Stowe
Billerica & Reading Militia
Meriam's Corner, 12:30 p.m.
Brooks Hill, 12:45 p.m.
Bloody Angle, 1:00 p.m.
Hartwell Tavern
Hartwell
J. Nelson
Smith
Woburn Militia
Fiske Hill, 1:40 p.m.
T. Nelson
Lexington Militia
Lexington
Hancock-Clarke
Lexington, 2:30 p.m.
Munroe Tavern
Sanderson
Smith's Regulars' Retreat
Menotomy, 4:30 p.m.
Danvers Militia
Arlington
Cooper Tavern
Black Horse Tavern
Medford
Salem Militia
Percy's Route to Lexington
Charles River
Cambridge
Watson's Corner
Charlestown Neck
Brookline Militia
Regulars return to Charlestown, April 19, 1775
Back Bay
Charlestown
Old North Church
Boston

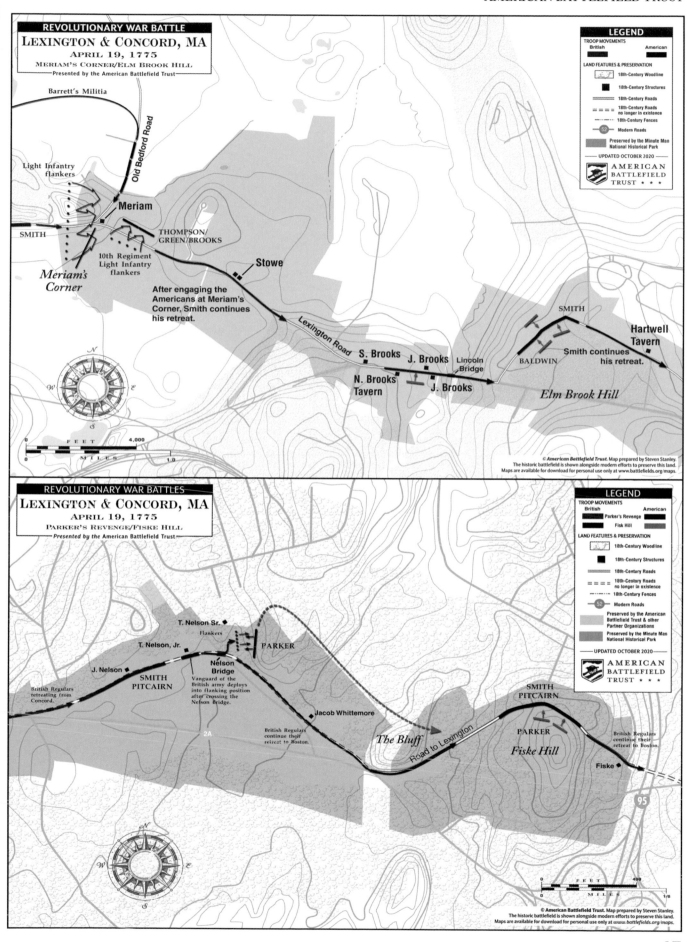

BATTLE *of* FORT TICONDEROGA

MAY 10, 1775

SITUATED AT THE CONFLUENCE OF LAKE CHAMPLAIN AND LAKE GEORGE, Fort Ticonderoga controlled access north and south between Albany, New York, and Montreal, Canada. In the early days of the American colonies, the lakes and rivers of the countryside acted as the highways and byways of North America. Lake Champlain and Lake George combined to form a superhighway of sorts between New York and Canada. The lakes offered an attacker an avenue of advance, while a defender could fortify strategic points along the waterways.

In 1755, the French began construction on a fort at the confluence of Lakes Champlain and George, Fort Carillon, to protect the approach to Canada via Lake Champlain. By 1757, a formidable star-shaped stone fort had sprung to life. In 1758, the British and the French engaged in heavy combat at the Battle of Fort Carillon during the Seven Years' War (French and Indian War), with the French winning the day. A year later, the British finally seized the fort and dubbed it Fort Ticonderoga. The name "Ticonderoga" comes from an Iroquois word meaning "it is at the junction of two waterways."

After the Seven Years' War, the map of North America changed dramatically. With Canada now part of the British Empire, the strategic significance of Fort Ticonderoga waned—that was, until May of 1775.

Against the better wishes of the Continental Congress, which only wanted to act defensively at this point of the war, both Connecticut and Massachusetts dispatched forces to capture the fort. A force commanded by Col. Ethan Allen represented Connecticut, unexpectedly met up with the Massachusetts force led by the haughty but capable

Col. Benedict Arnold's force on May 9, 1775, near the fort. There had been no coordination between either colony, and the arrival of the respective forces was a shock to both officers. Nonetheless, the two men decided to work in concert to take the fort.

On May 10, 1775, the American force silently rowed across Lake Champlain from present-day Vermont and captured the fort in a swift, late-night surprise attack. In reality, the fort had fallen into disrepair, and the undersized garrison of some 45 British officers and men were taken wholly by surprise. The capture was the first offensive victory for American forces and secured the strategic passageway north, opening the way for the American invasion of Canada later that year.

Allen received the lion's share of the credit for the victory and quickly moved on to capture nearby Crown Point. Between the two installations, the Americans secured seventy-eight cannon, six mortars, three howitzers, eighteen thousand pounds of musket balls, and some thirty thousand flints. The "Gibraltar of North America" gave Gen. George Washington the advantage he needed in firepower to force the capitulation of the British at Boston. Colonel Henry Knox oversaw the extraction and delivery of Ticonderoga's guns to the American siege lines at Boston. Traveling through snow, over frozen rivers and lakes, Knox and his men delivered the guns in 40 days rather than his estimated sixteen or seventeen days. Regardless, this logistical feat lives on in the annals of American military history.

✳ ✳ **PRESERVATION** ✳ ✳

The **American Battlefield Trust** has not saved any land at Fort Ticonderoga Battlefield.

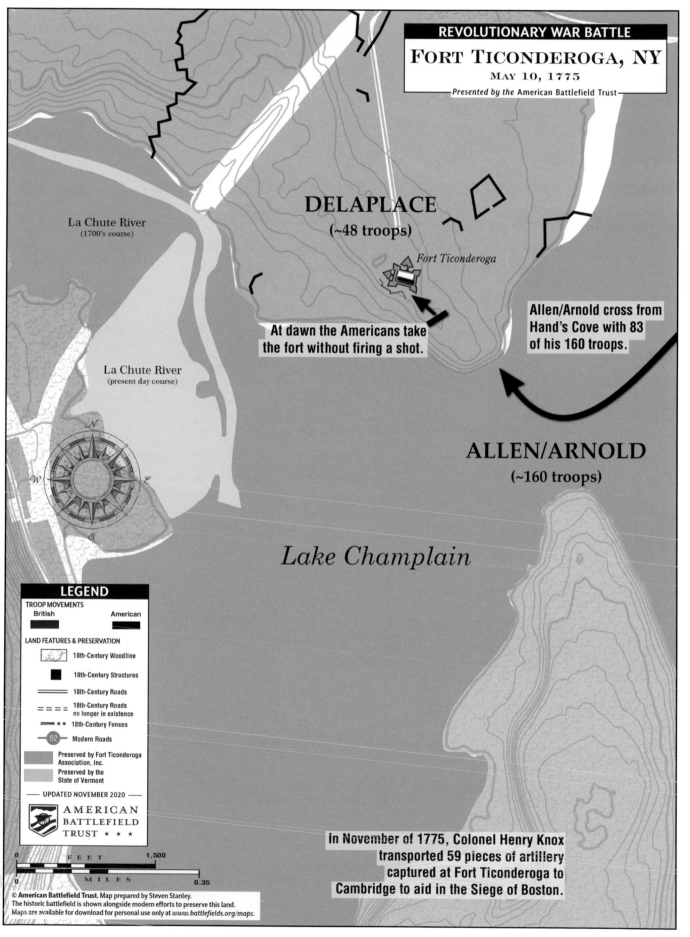

REVOLUTIONARY WAR BATTLE

FORT TICONDEROGA, NY

MAY 10, 1775

Presented by the American Battlefield Trust

DELAPLACE
(~48 troops)

Fort Ticonderoga

La Chute River
(1700's course)

At dawn the Americans take
the fort without firing a shot.

Allen/Arnold cross from
Hand's Cove with 83
of his 160 troops.

La Chute River
(present day course)

ALLEN/ARNOLD
(~160 troops)

Lake Champlain

LEGEND

TROOP MOVEMENTS
British   American

LAND FEATURES & PRESERVATION

18th-Century Woodline

18th-Century Structures

18th-Century Roads

18th-Century Roads
no longer in existence

18th-Century Fences

52 Modern Roads

Preserved by Fort Ticonderoga
Association, Inc.

Preserved by the
State of Vermont

— UPDATED NOVEMBER 2020 —

AMERICAN
BATTLEFIELD
TRUST ★ ★ ★

0   FEET   1,500

0   MILES   0.35

in November of 1775, Colonel Henry Knox
transported 59 pieces of artillery
captured at Fort Ticonderoga to
Cambridge to aid in the Siege of Boston.

© **American Battlefield Trust.** Map prepared by Steven Stanley.
The historic battlefield is shown alongside modern efforts to preserve this land.
Maps are available for download for personal use only at *www.battlefields.org/maps.*

BATTLE *of* BUNKER HILL

JUNE 17, 1775

THE DAY AFTER GEORGE WASHINGTON'S APPOINTMENT TO COMMAND THE CONTINENTAL ARMY, the American and British forces engaged in one of the bloodiest battles of the Revolutionary War. Washington was still in Philadelphia preparing for his journey to Boston when the armies of Gen. Artemas Ward and Gen. Thomas Gage engaged in the Battle of Bunker Hill.

The American force outside of Boston grew in size and strength in the weeks following the Battle of Lexington and Concord. Militiamen from Connecticut, New Hampshire, Rhode Island, and what would later become the state of Vermont streamed into the vicinity of Boston. While the quality of the American soldiers was questionable at best, their sheer numbers troubled Gage. Flush with reinforcements and new subordinates, Gage held a council of war with three officers who played key roles in the war in North America and all of whom failed time and again to quell the rebellion: Gens. William Howe, Henry Clinton, and John Burgoyne. The problem that lay before them was that the Americans assumed a position on a peninsula of land (the Charlestown Peninsula) bordered by the Mystic and Charles Rivers and which was only accessible to the British via an amphibious landing.

The Americans, for their part, had decided to fortify two of the three high points on the west side of the peninsula: Bunker and Breed's hills. As Breed's Hill sat closer to the British (and at an elevation about 40 feet lower in height), the Americans chose to fortify Breed's Hill first followed by Bunker Hill.

Gage and his subordinates debated the situation, with Clinton advocating for a landing in the rear of the rebels where they could smash them from behind and isolate them on the peninsula. Howe advocated for a direct assault, with the King's soldiers attacking the unsecure Rebel left, outflanking the enemy from their position. Howe's proposal won the day.

The rebels did not play to the British tune. General John Stark from New Hampshire recognized that the left flank was exposed along the south bank of the Mystic River. He and his men assembled a makeshift split-rail barricade to blunt any flanking action employed by the British.

On the sultry afternoon of June 17, 1775, Gage and his commanders ordered British regulars and grenadiers to be transported across Boston Harbor and disembarked in lower Charlestown. Howe led King George's troops in the assault, but the situation had changed since the officer advocated his plan. The American left was not open, and the flanking column of eleven companies of light infantry was stopped cold as it made its way along the narrow beach. A second attempt was made to dislodge the fence defenders in concert with a frontal assault on the main redoubt atop the hill. This attack, too, failed.

A third attack against the American fortifications atop Breed's Hill finally carried the day for the British. Once again marching head-on into musket fire, British tenacity and a lack of ammunition on American side finally carried the day for Gage and Howe. "A dear bought victory," Henry Clinton declared, "another such would have ruined us." British losses amounted to roughly one-third of the men engaged. Within weeks, Washington arrived to assume command of his army, and undertake siege operations. For now, Patriot forces held the advantage in New England.

✳ ✳ PRESERVATION ✳ ✳

The **American Battlefield Trust** has not saved any land at Bunker Hill Battlefield.

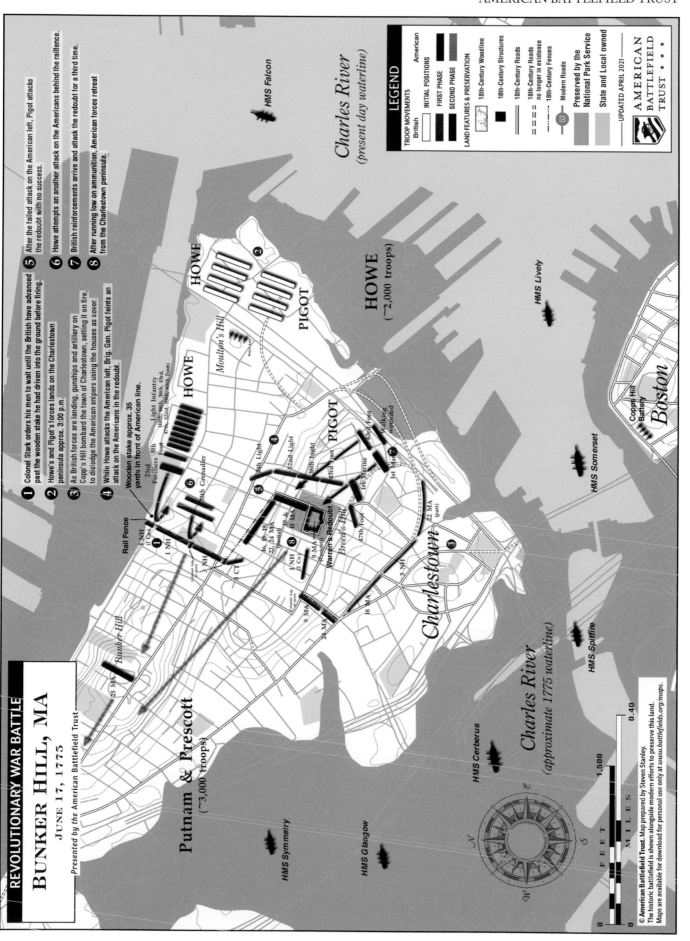

REVOLUTIONARY WAR BATTLE
BUNKER HILL, MA
JUNE 17, 1775

Presented by the American Battlefield Trust

1. Colonel Stark orders his men to wait until the British have advanced past the wooden stake he had driven into the ground before firing.
2. Howe's and Pigot's forces lands on the Charlestown peninsula approx. 3:00 p.m.
3. As British forces are landing, gunships and artillery on Copp's Hill bombard the town of Charlestown, setting it on fire, to dislodge the American snipers using the houses as cover.
4. While Howe attacks the American left, Brig. Gen. Pigot feints an attack on the Americans in the redoubt.
5. After the failed attack on the American left, Pigot attacks the redoubt with no success.
6. Howe attempts an another attack on the Americans behind the railfence.
7. British reinforcements arrive and attack the redoubt for a third time.
8. After running low on ammunition, American forces retreat from the Charlestown peninsula.

LEGEND

TROOP MOVEMENTS
British · American
- INITIAL POSITIONS
- FIRST PHASE
- SECOND PHASE

LAND FEATURES & PRESERVATION
- 18th-Century Woodline
- 18th-Century Structures
- 18th-Century Roads
- 18th-Century Roads no longer in existence
- 18th-Century Fences
- Modern Roads

Preserved by the
- National Park Service
- State and Local owned

—UPDATED APRIL 2021—

AMERICAN BATTLEFIELD TRUST ★ ★ ★

Charles River
(present day waterline)

HMS Falcon
HMS Lively
HMS Somerset
HMS Spitfire
HMS Cerberus
HMS Glasgow
HMS Symmetry

Boston
Copp's Hill Battery

Charlestown

Bunker Hill
25 MA

Rail Fence
1 NH
1 Co.
1 NH
3 NH
3 CT
Colonial Army (2 guns)
9 MA
3 MA
18 MA

HOWE
HOWE
HOWE
HOWE (~2,000 troops)
PIGOT
PIGOT

Light Infantry
(10th, 18th, 38th, 43rd, 47th, 52nd, 59th, 63th Foot)
5th Foot
23rd Fusiliers
35th Grenadier
4th Light
52nd Light
38th Light
43rd Foot
63rd Foot
1st Marine
King's wounded
1st Marine

Moulton's Hill

Warren's Redoubt
16, 18, 19 MA
22, 24 MA (partial)
10 & 11 MA
9 MA
1 NH (1 Co.)
47th Foot
22 MA (part)
Breed's Hill (Redoubt)

Putnam & Prescott (~3,000 troops)

Charles River
(approximate 1775 waterline)

FEET 1,500
MILES 0.40

© American Battlefield Trust. Map prepared by Steven Stanley.
The historic battlefield is shown alongside modern efforts to preserve this land.
Maps are available for download for personal use only at www.battlefields.org/maps.

SIEGE *of* BOSTON

APRIL 19, 1775 – MARCH 17, 1776

FOLLOWING THE DEBACLE AT LEXINGTON AND CONCORD, the British army took positions in and around Boston. The true strength of British arms lay in Boston Harbor with the ships of the Royal Navy. As thousands of militiamen men flocked to Boston from the countryside and nearby colonies, Thomas Gage and his soldiers, sailors, and marines always had a means of escape—the sea—even if they could not break out of Boston via a land route.

Meantime, the Continental Congress met in Philadelphia in an effort to assess the situation and to put the colonies on a war footing. Money was borrowed, powder was purchased, and on June 15, a Virginia planter named George Washington was promoted to the rank of general and given "command [of] all the continental forces, raised, or to be raised, for the defense of American liberty." In New York and Massachusetts, events were picking up speed. The Americans controlled the land approaches to Boston— Charlestown Neck and Boston Neck—but lacking a navy, were unable to blockade the harbor. In May, Allen and Arnold's force of militia seized Fort Ticonderoga and its arsenal of weapons.

By June, the British had received enough reinforcements to attempt a breakout from Boston. Their plan was to occupy Bunker Hill to the North and Dorchester Heights to the South, using both as a base of operations against the American fortifications— resulting in the Pyrrhic British victory at Battle of Bunker Hill. Between his lackluster administration of the Massachusetts Colony and his failure to quell the rebellion, Gage was relieved of command, and he departed for England in October of 1775. Gage was replaced by Gen. William Howe (later Sir William Howe).

On July 2, Washington arrived and assumed command of the American forces, now officially dubbed the Continental Army. American reinforcements also arrived from New England, the Middle Colonies, and Virginia. Washington, however, lacked heavy artillery, and could neither dislodge the British nor risk the losses of a direct assault. The British likewise could not attack the American position without risking heavy losses. Washington feared that inaction would lead to the wholesale desertion of the militia gathered for the siege. On the waters, American privateers harassed British traffic in and out of Boston, threatening Gage's lifeline. On land, Washington bolstered his firepower. He ordered Col. Henry Knox to retrieve the guns captured at Fort Ticonderoga and bring them to Boston. By March, these cannon were in position on the heights around the besieged city. On March 2, the Americans began their cannonade, with the British responding in kind.

On the night of March 4, Washington made the critical decision to fortify Dorchester Heights. With cannon frowning down on them, and with backing from the cabinet, Howe, decided to abandon Boston. His soldiers stripped the city of any war materials that would benefit the rebels, and he even went as far as authorizing the burning of the city. It did not come to that, and the British withdrew to Halifax, Nova Scotia, on March 17. Boston remained in American hands for the rest of the war, as Washington prepared to move south and defend the next logical target, New York City.

✳ ✳ **PRESERVATION** ✳ ✳

The **American Battlefield Trust** has not saved any land at Boston.

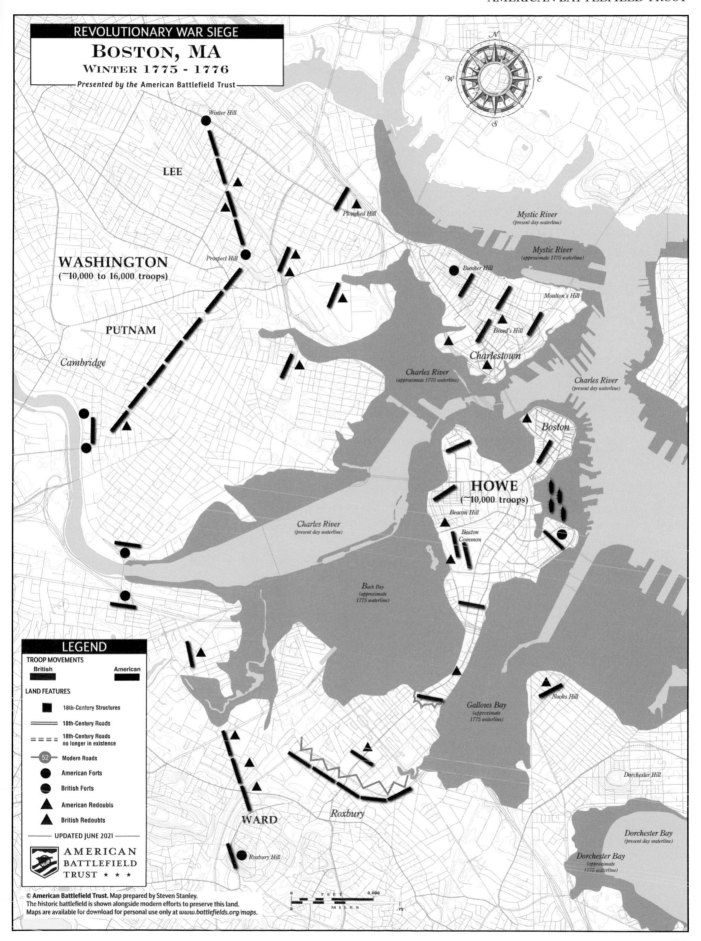

REVOLUTIONARY WAR SIEGE

BOSTON, MA
WINTER 1775 - 1776
Presented by the American Battlefield Trust

LEE

Winter Hill

Ploughed Hill

Mystic River
(present day waterline)

Mystic River
(approximate 1775 waterline)

WASHINGTON
(~10,000 to 16,000 troops)

Prospect Hill

Bunker Hill

Moulton's Hill

PUTNAM

Breed's Hill

Cambridge

Charlestown

Charles River
(approximate 1775 waterline)

Charles River
(present day waterline)

Boston

HOWE
(~10,000 troops)

Beacon Hill

Charles River
(present day waterline)

Boston Common

Back Bay
(approximate 1775 waterline)

LEGEND
TROOP MOVEMENTS

British   American

LAND FEATURES

■ 18th-Century Structures

18th-Century Roads

= = = = 18th-Century Roads no longer in existence

52 Modern Roads

● American Forts

● British Forts

▲ American Redoubts

▲ British Redoubts

Gallows Bay
(approximate 1775 waterline)

Nooks Hill

Dorchester Hill

— UPDATED JUNE 2021 —

AMERICAN BATTLEFIELD TRUST ★ ★ ★

WARD

Roxbury

Dorchester Bay
(present day waterline)

Roxbury Hill

Dorchester Bay
(approximate 1775 waterline)

FEET   3,000

MILES   .75

BATTLE *of* GREAT BRIDGE

DECEMBER 9, 1775

WHILE MUCH OF THE TROUBLES OF 1775 WERE **FOCUSED IN NEW ENGLAND,** and specifically Boston, there were uprisings throughout all thirteen colonies. In Virginia, disputes between whigs and tories were reaching a boiling point. These two political parties were the predominant forces in 18th-century British politics and were carried over into the colonies. Before the Revolutionary War became patriots against loyalists, American colonists were still British citizens of these political parties vying against one another. The Whigs were the liberal force against taxation, while the Tories supported the Parliament in which they held the majority.

The Royal Governor of Virginia, John Murray, Earl of Dunmore, under threat of local militia turning out against him, ordered Royal Marines of the HMS Magdalen to confiscate the gunpowder held at the magazine in the capital city of Williamsburg. Word quickly spread, and militia from several counties in Virginia formed for action.

Governor Dunmore moved his family and took refuge aboard a Royal Navy ship in the York River before departing for Norfolk, Virginia, where he began raising Tory forces. Among the new recruits flooding to the King's colors were escaped slaves who were promised their freedom by Dunmore if they took up arms against their Whig masters. Dunmore formed them into the "Ethiopian Regiment." Meantime, Dunmore's position was reinforced by Tory militias as well as two companies of the 14th Regiment of Foot, adding a backbone of regulars to his mostly untested troops.

The main land route out of Norfolk crossed over the Elizabeth River at Great Bridge. Dunmore ordered detachments of the 14th Foot and Ethiopians to construct a stockade on the Norfolk side of the bridge, which was named Fort Murray. At the same time, the Whig leaders ordered a detachment of the 2nd Virginia Regiment with a detachment of the Culpeper Minutemen to destroy the Tory force on the far side of the river and proceed to Norfolk.

The Whig force arrived at the far side of the bridge on December 7, 1775, On the 9th, Dunmore decided to drive the militia back from the approach to Norfolk. The tories fired two cannon into the Whig breastworks. Moments later, an approaching column in red pressed toward the militia. As soon as they came in range, the British soldiers opened fire by platoons, alternating advancing while being covered by another platoon, eventually reaching the bridge, which they could cross while formed six men abreast.

At this point, the whigs opened fire. Both company commanders within the 14th went down, and the bridge was scattered with the dead and dying. The British again charged across the bridge, with several men reaching the Whig earthworks before being shot dead.

With casualties mounting the Regulars and tories withdrew into Fort Murray. At 7:00 p.m., the tories spiked their cannons and left the field. Within the next few days, the whigs entered Norfolk, and Lord Dunmore left Virginia. The incipient revolution continued to spread.

✳ ✳ PRESERVATION ✳ ✳

To date, the **American Battlefield Trust** has saved **0.66 acres** at Great Bridge Battlefield.

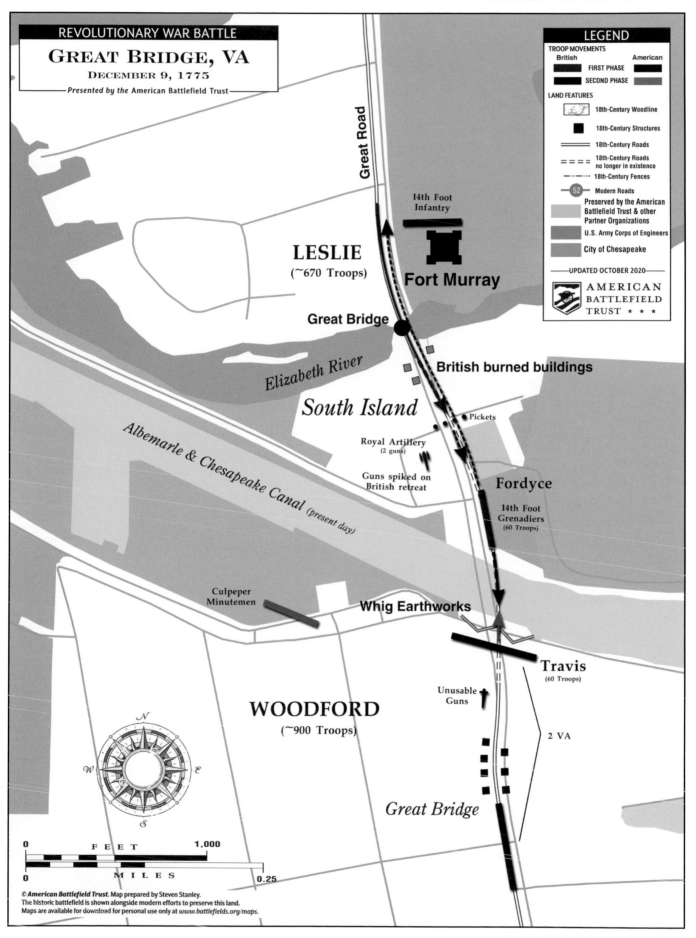

REVOLUTIONARY WAR BATTLE
GREAT BRIDGE, VA
DECEMBER 9, 1775
Presented by the American Battlefield Trust

LEGEND

TROOP MOVEMENTS
British   American
FIRST PHASE
SECOND PHASE

LAND FEATURES
18th-Century Woodline
18th-Century Structures
18th-Century Roads
18th-Century Roads no longer in existence
18th-Century Fences
52 Modern Roads
Preserved by the American Battlefield Trust & other Partner Organizations
U.S. Army Corps of Engineers
City of Chesapeake

UPDATED OCTOBER 2020

AMERICAN BATTLEFIELD TRUST ★ ★ ★

Great Road

14th Foot Infantry

LESLIE
(~670 Troops)

Fort Murray

Great Bridge

Elizabeth River

British burned buildings

South Island

• Pickets

Royal Artillery
(2 guns)

Guns spiked on British retreat

Fordyce

14th Foot Grenadiers
(60 Troops)

Albemarle & Chesapeake Canal (present day)

Culpeper Minutemen

Whig Earthworks

Travis
(60 Troops)

Unusable Guns

2 VA

WOODFORD
(~900 Troops)

Great Bridge

N
W   E
S

FEET   1,000
0
0   MILES   0.25

© *American Battlefield Trust*. Map prepared by Steven Stanley.
The historic battlefield is shown alongside modern efforts to preserve this land.
Maps are available for download for personal use only at *www.battlefields.org/maps*.

BATTLE *of* QUEBEC

DECEMBER 31, 1775

THE SUCCESSFUL CAPTURE OF FORT TICONDEROGA ON MAY 10, 1775, by Allen and Arnold steeled the officers' resolve to press north and invade Canada. The Continental Congress reluctantly agreed to allow an invasion of Canada if it would benefit the American cause. They made overtures to the Canadians in an effort to have them join the growing rebellion. The overture fell on deaf ears. By late summer, American forces were pressing north toward Canada.

One group, headed by Gens. Phillip Schuyler and Richard Montgomery, advanced on Montreal. A second effort led by Col. Benedict Arnold took a route through modern-day Maine toward the bastion city of Quebec. Both campaigns were fraught with setbacks. Schuyler became ill and turned command over to Montgomery, who was plagued by foul weather and supply shortages. Eventually, Montreal fell to the Americans, which was a hollow victory for the overstretched combatants. Montgomery then set his eye on a rendezvous with Arnold.

Meantime, Arnold's force took a path through an unrelenting wilderness, fighting the elements and the currents of numerous rivers, while at times having to carry their boats rather than ride in them. The supply situation grew dire, and enlistments were set to run out at the end of the year. Still, the Americans persevered, and Arnold and Montgomery met up on December 2 outside of Quebec.

British General and Governor of Quebec Guy Carleton organized the defense of the city. Although Carleton had powerful enemies in the British government, he was an experienced officer. Carleton gathered some 2,000 men and further fortified the city. With fewer than 1,000 men, no heavy artillery, enlistments about to expire, low stocks of supplies, and local Canadians that had turned against rather than for the American cause, Arnold and Montgomery were running out of time. They could not besiege the city, and they could not wait for spring.

Near 2 a.m. on the morning of December 31, 1775, Montgomery led a coup de main assault against the city utilizing the cover of a snowstorm. The plan was for the Americans to assault two portions of the lower city simultaneously, combine forces once they breached the walls, and force the capitulation of its defenders. Montgomery led his column around the walls of the city and attacked the city via the less secure coastal shore areas of the Saint Lawrence River. However, during the first assault, a blizzard decreased visibility and served to create disorganization among the Continentals. Additionally, a small group of Canadians spotted the lanterns used by the Americans to guide the men and promptly opened fire at close range. With the bells of the city ringing in the early morning air calling out its defenders, the American assault was doomed. Montgomery's column was blasted by grapeshot and small arms fire and the general fell dead; his men (including Aaron Burr) withdrew in disorder.

Arnold's group met with a similar fate, although his men penetrated deeper into the lower city. The future traitor was wounded in the fighting and commanded devolved to Capt. Daniel Morgan, a tough-as-leather leader of Virginia and Pennsylvania riflemen. Brutal street fighting raged in the lower city, but Morgan's men were outnumbered, and the weather began to foul their weapons. Near 9 a.m., Morgan and upwards of 400 Americans surrendered.

Arnold managed to hold what was left of his force together outside of the city until May 6, 1776, when he was finally forced to withdraw. The failure to capture Quebec ended the American campaign in Canada and failed to garner support among the Canadians.

✳ ✳ PRESERVATION ✳ ✳

The **American Battlefield Trust** has not saved any land at Quebec Battlefield.

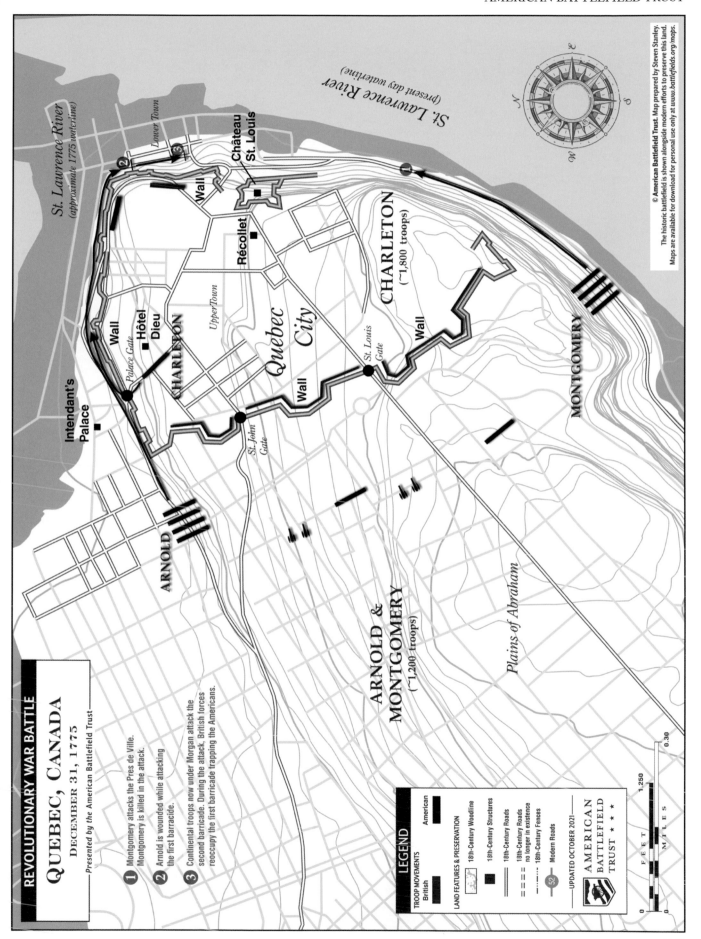

St. Lawrence River
(present day waterline)

St. Lawrence River
(approximate 1775 waterline)

Lower Town

Château
St. Louis

Wall

Récollet

Intendant's
Palace

Wall

Hôtel
Dieu

Palace Gate

CHARLETON

Upper Town

Quebec City

CHARLETON

St. John
Gate

St. Louis
Gate

Wall

CHARLETON
CHARLETON
(~1,800 troops)

Wall

MONTGOMERY

ARNOLD

ARNOLD &
MONTGOMERY
(~1,200 troops)

Plains of Abraham

REVOLUTIONARY WAR BATTLE

QUEBEC, CANADA
DECEMBER 31, 1775

Presented by the American Battlefield Trust

1. Montgomery attacks the Pres de Ville. Montgomery is killed in the attack.

2. Arnold is wounded while attacking the first barricade.

3. Continental troops now under Morgan attack the second barricade. During the attack, British forces reoccupy the first barricade trapping the Americans.

LEGEND

TROOP MOVEMENTS
British   American

LAND FEATURES & PRESERVATION
18th-Century Woodline
18th-Century Structures
18th-Century Roads
18th-Century Roads no longer in existence
18th-Century Fences
52 Modern Roads

AMERICAN BATTLEFIELD TRUST ★★★

—UPDATED OCTOBER 2021—

FEET   1,250
0
MILES   0.30
0

BATTLE *of* SULLIVAN'S ISLAND

JUNE 28, 1776

WHILE 1775 WAS A SETBACK FOR THE BRITISH, THE YEARS 1776 AND 1777 would shake the revolution to its core. In 1776, the British government set the wheels in motion to stamp out the rebellion in their North American colonies. News took weeks to crisscross the Atlantic, and it also took time for the British to consolidate their land and sea forces to bring them to bear on the American rebels. However, the British high command set forth a number of initiatives to bring the rebels to their knees. One such initiative involved the capture of Charleston, South Carolina, by targeting Sullivan's Island, which cradles the coast at the northern mouth of Charleston Harbor.

Along with being the richest port in North America, Charleston was also the fourth-largest city in the colonies. Bolstered by promises of loyalist uprisings by the royal governors of the Carolinas and Virginia, the new commander-in-chief of British land forces, Gen. William Howe, sent his second in command, Gen. Henry Clinton, with a detachment of troops to secure Charleston and pacify the southern colonies. (Both Clinton and Howe would be knighted later that year.)

Standing in the way of the British was the unfinished fort on Sullivan's Island and its commander, Col. William Moultrie. The Americans realized the importance of the island's location as it related to the sandbars and the harbor channel and began the work of erecting the fort in February 1776. Using palmetto trees, earth, and sand, the Americans constructed an unusually sturdy fortress—completing the seaward-facing walls before the June action.

A British flotilla arrived outside the harbor on June 1, 1776. Clinton envisioned a combined army-navy operation to subdue the fort and its defenders. Unfortunately for the British, they were having trouble getting their frigates over the shallow Charles Town Bar because they were too heavy. Thwarted by Mother Nature and the pesky rebels, who refused to surrender the city, Clinton landed his forces on a nearby island and prepared for battle.

Meantime, Gen. Charles Lee arrived in Charleston. Lee was one of the highest-ranking officers in the Continental Army and had been an officer in the British army during the Seven Years' War. The churlish Lee ordered Moultrie out of the fort as he felt the militiamen defending it would be slaughtered. Moultrie refused and was backed by local politicians. While Lee doted over the rest of Charleston's defenses, writing off Moultrie and his 400 troops as lost, Moultrie prepared for action.

On June 28, Clinton personally led his infantry into the waters—said to be shallow—as they attempted to force their way onto Sullivan's Island. The King's men were caught in deep water and a rip current. They next tried to cross using flat boats but were turned back by small-arms fire of 800 or so rebels deployed on the northern end of the island in support of Moultrie. The naval support also failed miserably. Ships ran aground and cannonballs bounced harmlessly off the sides of the palmetto logs or buried themselves in the sand. Clinton called of the attack and withdrew his forces from the area. The fort was later completed and dubbed Fort Moultrie, and Charleston was safe—for now.

✳ ✳ PRESERVATION ✳ ✳

To date, the **American Battlefield Trust** has saved **0.23 acres** at Sullivan's Island Battlefield.

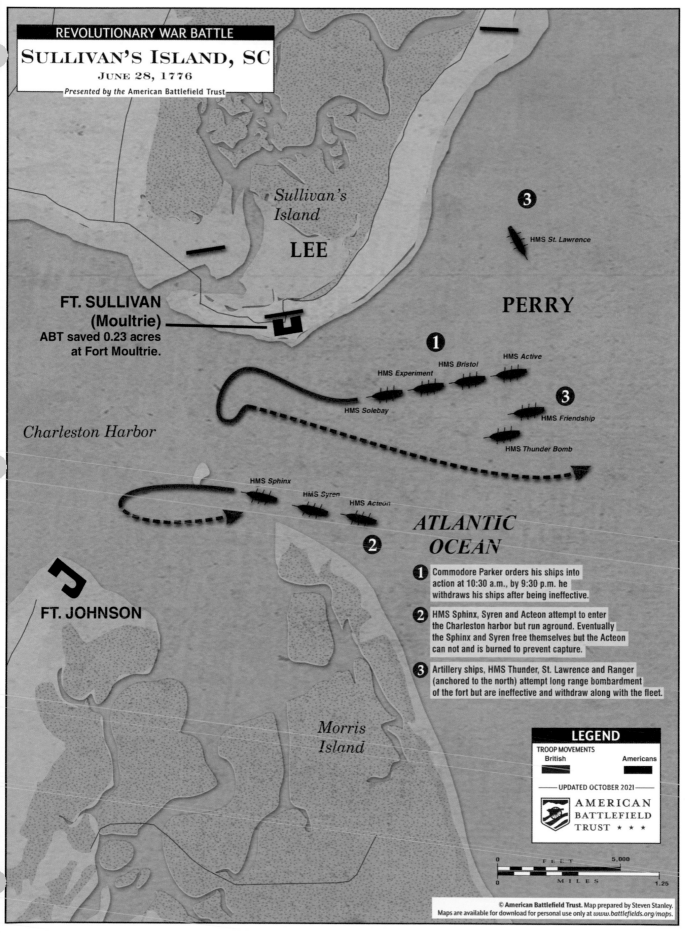

REVOLUTIONARY WAR BATTLE

SULLIVAN'S ISLAND, SC
JUNE 28, 1776
Presented by the American Battlefield Trust

Sullivan's Island

LEE

FT. SULLIVAN (Moultrie)
ABT saved 0.23 acres at Fort Moultrie.

PERRY

HMS *St. Lawrence*

③

①

HMS *Bristol*   HMS *Active*

HMS *Experiment*

HMS *Solebay*

③

HMS *Friendship*

HMS *Thunder Bomb*

Charleston Harbor

HMS *Sphinx*

HMS *Syren*   HMS *Acteon*

FT. JOHNSON

②

ATLANTIC OCEAN

① Commodore Parker orders his ships into action at 10:30 a.m., by 9:30 p.m. he withdraws his ships after being ineffective.

② HMS Sphinx, Syren and Acteon attempt to enter the Charleston harbor but run aground. Eventually the Sphinx and Syren free themselves but the Acteon can not and is burned to prevent capture.

③ Artillery ships, HMS Thunder, St. Lawrence and Ranger (anchored to the north) attempt long range bombardment of the fort but are ineffective and withdraw along with the fleet.

Morris Island

LEGEND

TROOP MOVEMENTS
British   Americans

— UPDATED OCTOBER 2021 —

AMERICAN BATTLEFIELD TRUST ★ ★ ★

0   FEET   5,000
0   MILES   1.25

© **American Battlefield Trust**. Map prepared by Steven Stanley.
Maps are available for download for personal use only at *www.battlefields.org/maps*.

27

THE NORTHERN STRATEGY

1776-1777

FOR ALL INTENT AND PURPOSES, THE OUTBREAK OF THE REVOLUTIONARY WAR was somewhat of a surprise to both sides. Few could have predicted the outright firefight that erupted at Lexington and Concord and that was morphing into an ever-growing conflict. The Continental Congress reconvened in the summer of 1775 and played both sides of the coin. First, they offered peace to King George III in the form of the Olive Branch Petition, in a vain attempt to avert further bloodshed. Should the King and Parliament turn down this overture, Congress also placed the colonies on a war footing by creating the Continental Army and appointing George Washington as its commander-in-chief. Ultimately, George III refused to receive the Olive Branch Petition, and set the British Empire on a war footing.

STAGE 1: Following the humiliating defeat at Boston, the British Empire drew up a plan to sever the rebellious and troublesome New England Colonies from the Mid-Atlantic and Southern Colonies in 1776. It was their hope of cutting the head off of the snake as it were, by seizing New York and its harbor. A position in New York City would allow the powerful Royal Navy to have a base along the American shoreline, from where they could make incursions up the Hudson River, or up and down the Eastern Seaboard— where the Royal Navy could blockade New England. Meantime, British troops could make their way south from Canada and link up with troops landed in New York. Finally, the British could call upon Loyalists to rise up and join their ranks as they sought to land a decisive blow against Washington's army itself.

British troops, ships, and Hessian auxiliaries arrived in Halifax, Nova Scotia, from all over Europe and the empire. Eventually a flotilla of more than 130 ships and 32,000 officers and men arrived at New York. In the following weeks and months, the British out fought and out maneuvered Washington's forces. Yet, they could never land then killing blow

as Washington deftly (and sometimes through sheer luck), escaped time and again; eventually marching his army into Pennsylvania, where Washington seized the initiative from the British and launched a series of actions into New Jersey known collectively as the "ten crucial days."

STAGE 2: The year 1777 witnessed two separate campaigns to subjugate the Northern Colonies undertaken by the British Empire. At first, the two campaigns were to work in unison. But draft after draft of the plans eventually split the forces into two distinct campaigns working at cross purposes, that saw little overall control (or culpability) from William Howe, Prime Minister Lord North, or Secretary of State for the Colonies George Germain. The first campaign was launched by Howe from New York City via a seaward route. The ultimate goal was to decisively defeat Washington's army, the true heart of the rebellion, and to seize the rebel capital o Philadelphia. How accomplished the latter but failed to accomplish the former. While Philadelphia was a worthy enough prize, its ultimate capture and abandonment nine months later came at far too high of a cost.

STAGE 3: That cost was the surrender of the second most principal British army in the colonies, the British Army from Canada commanded by Gen. John Burgoyne. Burgoyne planned to move down from Canada along the traditional invasion route of the Richelieu River, Lake Champaign, and then into the Hudson Valley. While Burgoyne drove south, so too did Howe. With the two principal armies working at cross purposes, Burgoyne became strung out, and although initially victorious, a campaign of exhaustion played out in New York. A new commander, an influx of militia and men from Washington's army, and determined fighting turned the tide in favor of the Continentals and shook the British war effort to its core.

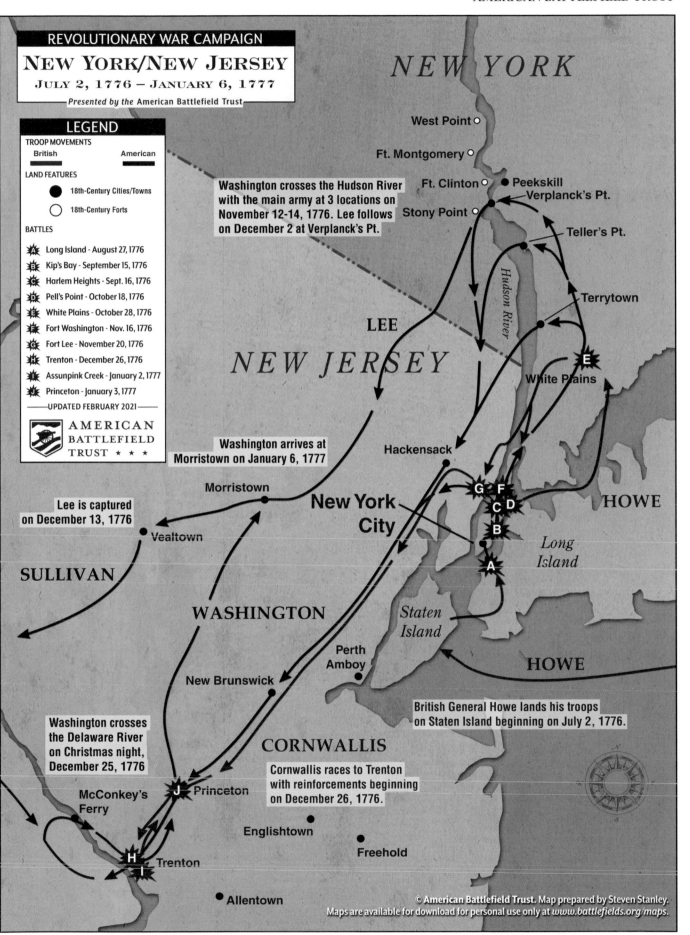

REVOLUTIONARY WAR CAMPAIGN
NEW YORK/NEW JERSEY
JULY 2, 1776 – JANUARY 6, 1777
Presented by the American Battlefield Trust

LEGEND

TROOP MOVEMENTS
British   American

LAND FEATURES
● 18th-Century Cities/Towns
○ 18th-Century Forts

BATTLES
A Long Island - August 27, 1776
B Kip's Bay - September 15, 1776
C Harlem Heights - Sept. 16, 1776
D Pell's Point - October 18, 1776
E White Plains - October 28, 1776
F Fort Washington - Nov. 16, 1776
G Fort Lee - November 20, 1776
H Trenton - December 26, 1776
I Assunpink Creek - January 2, 1777
J Princeton - January 3, 1777

—UPDATED FEBRUARY 2021—

AMERICAN
BATTLEFIELD
TRUST ★ ★ ★

NEW YORK

West Point ○
Ft. Montgomery ○
Ft. Clinton ○ ● Peekskill
Verplanck's Pt.
Stony Point ○

Washington crosses the Hudson River with the main army at 3 locations on November 12-14, 1776. Lee follows on December 2 at Verplanck's Pt.

Teller's Pt.

Terrytown

LEE

NEW JERSEY

Hudson River

E
White Plains

HOWE

Washington arrives at Morristown on January 6, 1777

Hackensack ●

Morristown ●

Lee is captured on December 13, 1776

New York City

G F
C D
B

A

● Vealtown

SULLIVAN

Long Island

WASHINGTON

Staten Island

Perth Amboy ●

HOWE

New Brunswick ●

British General Howe lands his troops on Staten Island beginning on July 2, 1776.

Washington crosses the Delaware River on Christmas night, December 25, 1776

CORNWALLIS

Cornwallis races to Trenton with reinforcements beginning on December 26, 1776.

McConkey's Ferry

J Princeton

Englishtown ●

● Freehold

H
I Trenton

● Allentown

© **American Battlefield Trust. Map prepared by Steven Stanley.**
Maps are available for download for personal use only at *www.battlefields.org/maps.*

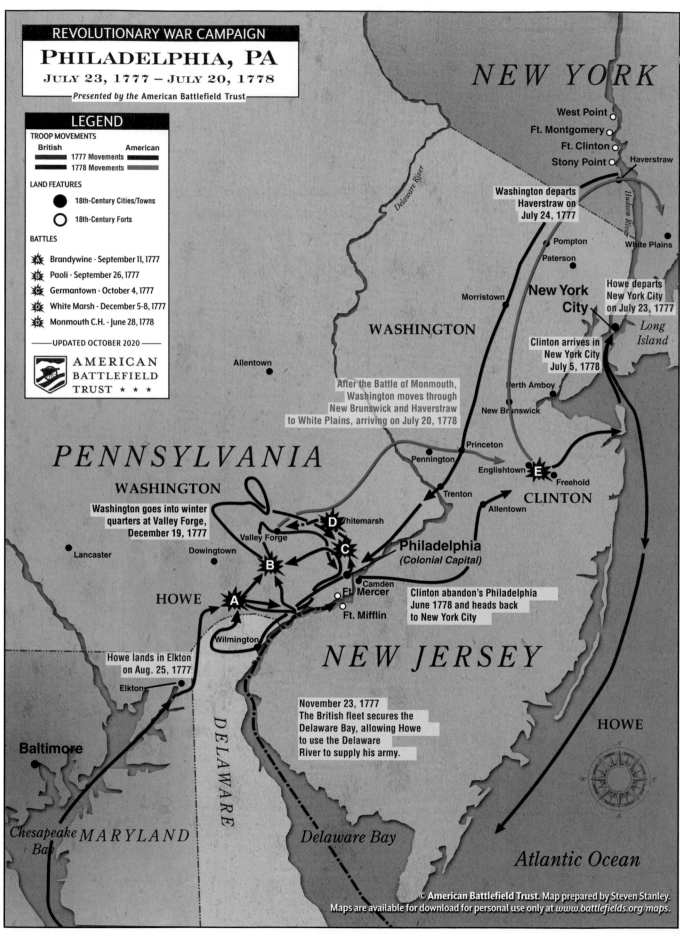

REVOLUTIONARY WAR CAMPAIGN
PHILADELPHIA, PA
JULY 23, 1777 – JULY 20, 1778
Presented by the American Battlefield Trust

LEGEND

TROOP MOVEMENTS

British	American
═══ 1777 Movements	═══
═══ 1778 Movements	═══

LAND FEATURES

● 18th-Century Cities/Towns

○ 18th-Century Forts

BATTLES

✷ Brandywine - September 11, 1777

✷ Paoli - September 26, 1777

✷ Germantown - October 4, 1777

✷ White Marsh - December 5-8, 1777

✷ Monmouth C.H. - June 28, 1778

—UPDATED OCTOBER 2020—

AMERICAN BATTLEFIELD TRUST ★ ★ ★

NEW YORK

West Point

Ft. Montgomery

Ft. Clinton

Stony Point — Haverstraw

Delaware River

Hudson River

Washington departs Haverstraw on July 24, 1777

Pompton

Paterson

White Plains

Morristown

New York City

Howe departs New York City on July 23, 1777

Long Island

Clinton arrives in New York City July 5, 1778

WASHINGTON

Allentown

After the Battle of Monmouth, Washington moves through New Brunswick and Haverstraw to White Plains, arriving on July 20, 1778

Perth Amboy

New Brunswick

Princeton

PENNSYLVANIA

Pennington

Trenton

Englishtown **E** Freehold

CLINTON

WASHINGTON

Washington goes into winter quarters at Valley Forge, December 19, 1777

Lancaster

Dowingtown

Valley Forge

D Whitemarsh

C

Philadelphia *(Colonial Capital)*

Allentown

HOWE

B

A

Camden

Ft. Mercer

Ft. Mifflin

Clinton abandon's Philadelphia June 1778 and heads back to New York City

Wilmington

Howe lands in Elkton on Aug. 25, 1777

Elkton

NEW JERSEY

DELAWARE

November 23, 1777
The British fleet secures the Delaware Bay, allowing Howe to use the Delaware River to supply his army.

HOWE

Baltimore

Chesapeake Bay **MARYLAND**

Delaware Bay

Atlantic Ocean

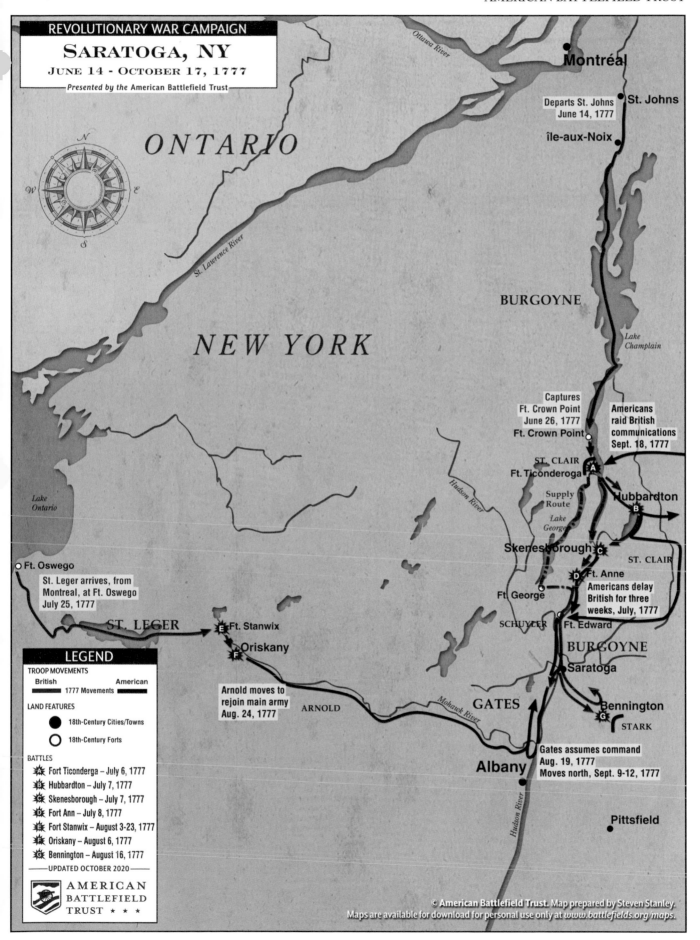

REVOLUTIONARY WAR CAMPAIGN

SARATOGA, NY
JUNE 14 - OCTOBER 17, 1777
Presented by the American Battlefield Trust

ONTARIO

NEW YORK

Ottawa River

Montréal

St. Johns

Departs St. Johns
June 14, 1777

île-aux-Noix

St. Lawrence River

BURGOYNE

Lake
Champlain

Captures
Ft. Crown Point
June 26, 1777

Ft. Crown Point

Americans
raid British
communications
Sept. 18, 1777

ST. CLAIR
Ft. Ticonderoga

A

Supply
Route

Hubbardton

B

Hudson River

Lake
George

Skenesborough

C

ST. CLAIR

Lake
Ontario

Ft. Oswego

St. Leger arrives, from
Montreal, at Ft. Oswego
July 25, 1777

ST. LEGER

Ft. Anne

D

Ft George

Americans delay
British for three
weeks, July, 1777

SCHUYLER
Ft. Edward

Ft. Stanwix

E

Oriskany

F

BURGOYNE

Arnold moves to
rejoin main army
Aug. 24, 1777

ARNOLD

Mohawk River

Saratoga

GATES

Bennington

G

STARK

Gates assumes command
Aug. 19, 1777
Moves north, Sept. 9-12, 1777

Albany

Hudson River

Pittsfield

LEGEND
TROOP MOVEMENTS

British   American
1777 Movements

LAND FEATURES

● 18th-Century Cities/Towns

○ 18th-Century Forts

BATTLES

Fort Ticonderga – July 6, 1777
Hubbardton – July 7, 1777
Skenesborough – July 7, 1777
Fort Ann – July 8, 1777
Fort Stanwix – August 3-23, 1777
Oriskany – August 6, 1777
Bennington – August 16, 1777

—UPDATED OCTOBER 2020—

AMERICAN
BATTLEFIELD
TRUST ★ ★ ★

BATTLE *of* BROOKLYN

AUGUST 27-29, 1776

AFTER COMPELLING THE BRITISH EVACUATION OF BOSTON IN MARCH OF 1776, Gen. George Washington predicted that the next British target would be New York City. Washington transferred his Continental Army to the city in April and May. Should New York fall and the British make their way up the Hudson River Valley, New England would be isolated from the mid-Atlantic and southern colonies, and the tories would hold the strategic initiative in the war.

In early 1776 Washington dispatched Charles Lee to Manhattan. Lee was to assess the tactical situation and make ready the area for a possible British attack. He, too, set about identifying and disarming loyalists. The Continentals fortified the city. Their plan was to make the British army pay for every inch of ground and bleed it white as they had done at Bunker Hill. Doing so would send a message to London and hopefully sate Parliament's will to wage war against their colonists.

On June 12, two Royal Navy frigates sailed into New York Harbor and up the Hudson River unscathed. It was a bad omen. By July 3, some 130 British warships took position off of Long Island. It was the largest expeditionary force launched by Great Britain until 1809. One man remarked that it looked like "all London was afloat." British and Hessian soldiers disembarked, and British warships dominated the river waterways that cut through New York City, rendering the American defense untenable. Nevertheless, Washington sought to fight a battle. His defensive arrangement, however, was fatally flawed. He split his forces between Brooklyn and Manhattan, preventing easy reinforcement or escape across the Hudson and East Rivers.

On August 22, British transports moved 15,000 infantry to Long Island. Wrongly thinking that this was a diversion for a main attack on Manhattan, Washington did not recombine his forces to meet the threat. On August 27, the British launched an attack on the Americans stationed on Long Island.

The Americans were in a poor position. Roughly 3,000 men commanded by Gen. Israel Putnam, who lacked a grasp of the tactical situation, defended key passes through the Heights of Guana—well, they defended most of the passes. Finding the extreme left flank (Jamaica Pass) guarded by only five men, Howe slipped 10,000 men around Putnam's flank as two other British and Hessian columns attacked the other passes, holding the Americans in place. The plan worked to perfection, and Americans streamed back to Brooklyn Heights where they met up with Putnam's remaining 6,500 men— and were trapped.

As the Americans pulled back towards Brooklyn Heights, one contingent of 300-400 Maryland soldiers, now known as the "Maryland 400," counterattacked in order to buy time for their comrades to escape. By nightfall, the Americans were hemmed in on Brooklyn Heights with the East River behind them. However, Howe did not attack, and under the cover of fog, Washington's army escaped to Manhattan.

The Battle of Brooklyn was the largest battle (in terms of soldiers) of the Revolution and the first battle to feature Hessian auxiliaries. It was also the first major battle fought after the Declaration of Independence was announced. It was an action that haunted Washington for the rest of the war.

✳ ✳ PRESERVATION ✳ ✳

The **American Battlefield Trust** has not saved any land at Brooklyn Battlefield.

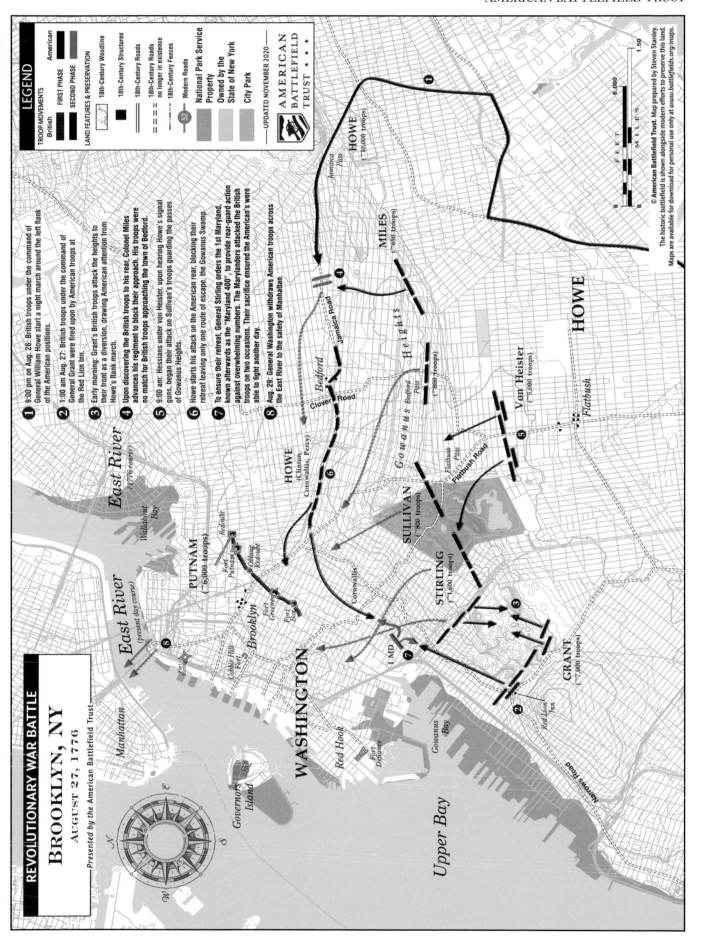

REVOLUTIONARY WAR BATTLE
BROOKLYN, NY
AUGUST 27, 1776
Presented by the American Battlefield Trust

LEGEND

TROOP MOVEMENTS
- British
- American
- FIRST PHASE
- SECOND PHASE

LAND FEATURES & PRESERVATION
- 18th-Century Woodline
- 18th-Century Structures
- 18th-Century Roads
- 18th-Century Roads no longer in existence
- 18th-Century Fences
- 52 Modern Roads
- National Park Service Property
- Owned by the State of New York
- City Park

UPDATED NOVEMBER 2020

AMERICAN BATTLEFIELD TRUST ★ ★ ★

1. 9:00 pm on Aug. 26: British troops under the command of General William Howe start a night march around the left flank of the American positions.

2. 1:00 am Aug. 27: British troops under the command of General Grant were fired upon by American troops at the Red Lion Inn.

3. Early morning: Grant's British troops attack the heights to their front as a diversion, drawing American attention from Howe's flank march.

4. Upon discovering the British troops to his rear, Colonel Miles advances his regiment to block their approach. His troops were no match for British troops approaching the town of Bedford.

5. 9:00 am: Hessians under von Heister, upon hearing Howe's signal guns, began their attack on Sullivan's troops guarding the passes of Gowanus Heights.

6. Howe starts his attack on the American rear, blocking their retreat leaving only one route of escape, the Gowanus Swamp.

7. To ensure their retreat, General Stirling orders the 1st Maryland, known afterwards as the "Maryland 400", to provide rear-guard action against overwhelming numbers. The Marylanders attacked the British troops on two occasions. Their sacrifice ensured the American's were able to fight another day.

8. Aug. 29: General Washington withdraws American troops across the East River to the safety of Manhattan.

© American Battlefield Trust. Map prepared by Steven Stanley. The historic battlefield is shown alongside modern efforts to preserve this land. Maps are available for download for personal use only at www.battlefields.org/maps.

BATTLE *of* WHITE PLAINS

OCTOBER 28, 1776

THE BATTLES AROUND NEW YORK CITY WERE A DISASTROUS CHAPTER in the career of George Washington. The commander-in-chief fielded the largest number of soldiers (~23,000) that he commanded at any one battle of campaign, but taking on the combined might of the Royal Navy and British Army meant taking on 130 ships and some 32,000 of the King's soldiers and Hessian auxiliaries. Washington's forces were saved by the inaction of William Howe at Brooklyn Heights when he failed to land the killing blow on roughly 9,500 Continental soldiers cornered on Long Island. Colonel John Glover and his "Marbleheaders" ferried the Continentals to safety.

On September 11, 1776, the failed Staten Island Peace conference ushered in fighting at Kip's Bay, where the British forced a landing on Manhattan Island. Washington's men made a stand at Harlem Heights, earning a small victory, but William Howe, utilizing the Royal Navy and his tactical sense for maneuver, forced Washington to abandon the island and retreat north.

A slow British pursuit allowed the Continental Army to take up a position at White Plains, New York, along the banks of the Bronx River. The Americans fortified their southward-facing position with the left resting on Hatfield Hill and Horton's Mill Pond, and their center resting on Purdy Hill, and across the 14 foot wide Bronx River sat Washington's right atop Chatterton's Hill. The initial defense of the hill fell to militiamen, who did a poor job of fortifying the wooded ridgeline; rather, they utilized the stone walls of the local farms for their defensive works.

The British Army approached the town and pushed back the Patriot skirmish line. General Howe then marched his 13,000-man army into a wheatfield and deployed it for battle in an impressive display of martial gallantry. Howe seemed to be bluffing Washington into retreat, which he refused to do. Thus, Howe prepared his army for an attack, but rather than marching into the teeth of the American fortifications on Hatfield and Purdy Hills, the British commander spied the weak point in the Rebel line: Chatterton's Hill.

Sending a detachment of infantry and some 20 cannon to bombard and then capture Chatterton's Hill, Howe hoped to uncover the isolated American right flank. The British and Hessians soldiers were met, though, by determined musketry of a Connecticut regiment sent to slow their advance while Washington shifted Continentals to the hill commanded by Gen. Alexander McDougall, Col. John Haslet, and other capable officers. The bombardment by the British unnerved the militia, but the timely American reinforcements slowed the British and Hessians. However, a Hessian force commanded by Col. Johann Rahl was able to dislodge the militia that protected the American right flank. The line began to unravel as more Imperial soldiers rushed in to exploit the breakthrough. Soon, Washington's army was conducting a fighting withdrawal. Once again Howe was slow to pursue the rebels, and Washington and his men slipped farther north as he employed a Fabian strategy to keep his army intact.

Rather than pursue the Americans deeper into New York, Howe turned back toward New York City where he planned to take advantage of another of Washington's mistakes.

✳ ✳ PRESERVATION ✳ ✳

The **American Battlefield Trust** has not saved any land at White Plains Battlefield.

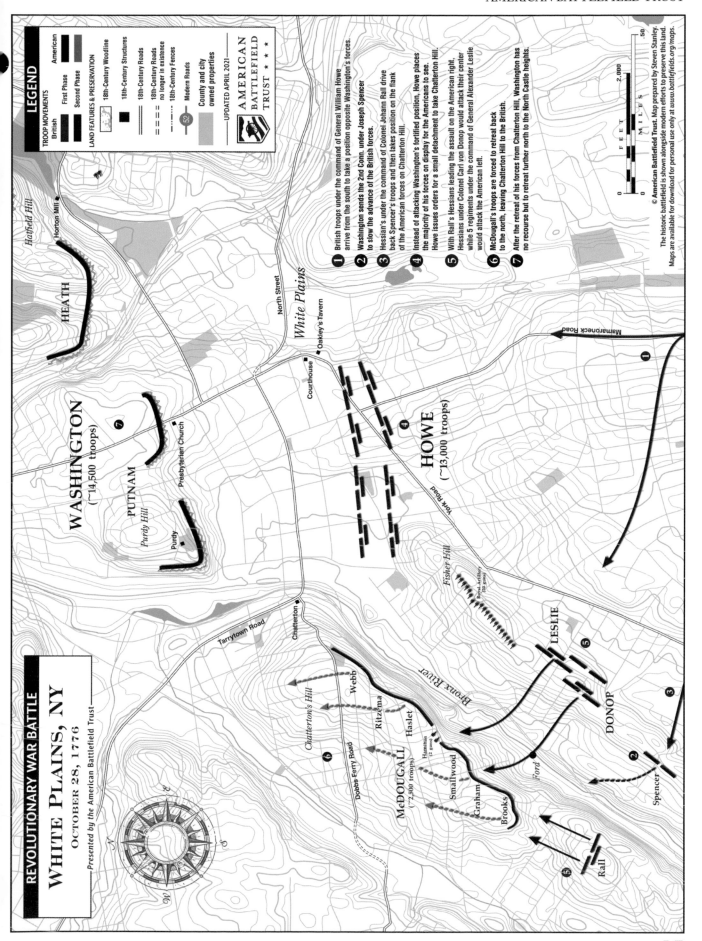

REVOLUTIONARY WAR BATTLE
WHITE PLAINS, NY
OCTOBER 28, 1776
Presented by the American Battlefield Trust

LEGEND

TROOP MOVEMENTS
British   American
First Phase
Second Phase

LAND FEATURES & PRESERVATION
18th-Century Woodline
18th-Century Structures
18th-Century Roads
18th-Century Roads no longer in existence
18th-Century Fences
Modern Roads
County and city owned properties

—UPDATED APRIL 2021—

AMERICAN BATTLEFIELD TRUST ★ ★ ★

1. British troops under the command of General William Howe arrive from the south to take a position opposite Washington's forces.

2. Washington sends the 2nd Conn. under Joseph Spencer to slow the advance of the British forces.

3. Hessian's under the command of Colonel Johann Rall drive back Spencer's troops and then takes position on the flank of the American forces on Chatterton Hill.

4. Instead of attacking Washington's fortified position, Howe places the majority of his forces on display for the Americans to see. Howe issues orders for a small detachment to take Chatterton Hill.

5. With Rall's Hessians leading the assault on the American right, Hessians under Colonel Carl von Donop would attack their center while 5 regiments under the command of General Alexander Leslie would attack the American left.

6. McDougall's troops are forced to retreat back to the north, leaving Chatterton Hill to the British.

7. After the retreat of his forces from Chatterton Hill, Washington has no recourse but to retreat further north to the North Castle heights.

Hatfield Hill

HEATH

Horton Mill

North Street

White Plains

Oakley's Tavern

Courthouse

WASHINGTON (~14,500 troops)

PUTNAM

Purdy Hill

Purdy

Presbyterian Church

HOWE (~13,000 troops)

Fisher Hill

York Road

Royal Artillery (28 guns)

Mamaroneck Road

LESLIE

DONOP

Chatterton

Tarrytown Road

Webb

Ritzema

Haslet

Chatterton's Hill

Dobbs Ferry Road

McDOUGALL (~2,500 troops)

Hamilton (2 guns)

Smallwood

Graham

Brooks

Ford

Bronx River

Rall

Spencer

© American Battlefield Trust. Map prepared by Steven Stanley. The historic battlefield is shown alongside modern efforts to preserve this land. Maps are available for download for personal use only at *www.battlefields.org/maps.*

FEET   MILES

BATTLE *of* FORTS WASHINGTON *and* LEE

NOVEMBER 16 & 20, 1776

SITUATED HIGH ABOVE THE HUDSON RIVER APPROXIMATELY 11 MILES FROM THE SOUTHERN TIP OF MANHATTAN ISLAND, Forts Washington and Lee were among the last remining holdouts of Washington's army in the New York area. Since the defeat at White Plains, Washington and his generals decided to break his army into four pieces. General Charles Lee was assigned 7,000 soldiers and the task of blocking Howe's route north at North Castle. General William Heath with 4,000 men was to fortify the highlands north of Manhattan. Washington with 2,000 men moved into New Jersey to counter any British moves there, while 5,000 men commanded by Gen. Nathanael Greene defended Forts Lee and Washington.

Fort Washington (named for George Washington) was positioned on the highest point of Manhattan Island, 300 feet above the Hudson River on a rock outcropping. If properly constructed, the fort would be impregnable, but unfortunately, it had been hastily built. It nonetheless wreaked havoc on British warships attempting to sail past the position overlooking the Hudson.

With Washington once again splitting his army in the face of a superior foe, William Howe looked to make him pay for this mistake. With the Fort Washington garrison isolated, Howe moved a frigate into the Hudson to bombard the Continental line. Meantime, four British attack columns (with one column acting as a feint) were formed to hit the fort from the three landward sides. Before dawn, General Lord Hugh Percy attacked from the south, driving up the island; another force crossed the Harlem River and attacked from the east; and a force of Hessians struck from the north. The combined British-Hessian assault grossly outnumbered the forts defenders, with Howe brining at least 13,000 men to bear against Greene's 3,000. Nonetheless, the Continentals held out for a brief time against the overwhelming numbers.

George Washington crossed the Hudson from New Jersey to witness the action. After realizing the plight of the defenders, he urged the garrison's commander, Col. Robert Magaw, to hold out until nightfall as Washington, Greene, and other general officers fled across the Hudson River to Safety. Magaw surrendered the fort and its remaining 2,870 men near 3 p.m.

Fort Lee (named for Charles Lee) was the next target of Howe's army. Rather than order the fort abandoned and its stores of supplies, weapons, and ammunition removed as Fort Washington fell, Washington dragged his feet. While Howe was normally slow to respond to a situation, he quickly followed up on his Fort Washington victory. On the rainy evening of November 19, British General Charles Lord Cornwallis landed 5,000 troops at the base of the New Jersey Palisades. After scaling the rain-soaked cliffs, the British-Hessian force found the fort abandoned of troops—yet filled with most of its stores. Washington had waited too long to order the retreat, so most of the supplies and equipment had to be abandoned.

The loss of Forts Washington and Lee, coupled with the loss of New York City, marked a new low point in the war for the Americans. With the Continental Army marching ahead of the enemy through New Jersey, they crossed the Delaware River and into Pennsylvania. As Christmas of 1776 approached, essayist Thomas Paine declared in The American Crisis, "These are the times that try men's souls."

✳ ✳ PRESERVATION ✳ ✳

The **American Battlefield Trust** has not saved any land at Forts Washington and Lee Battlefield.

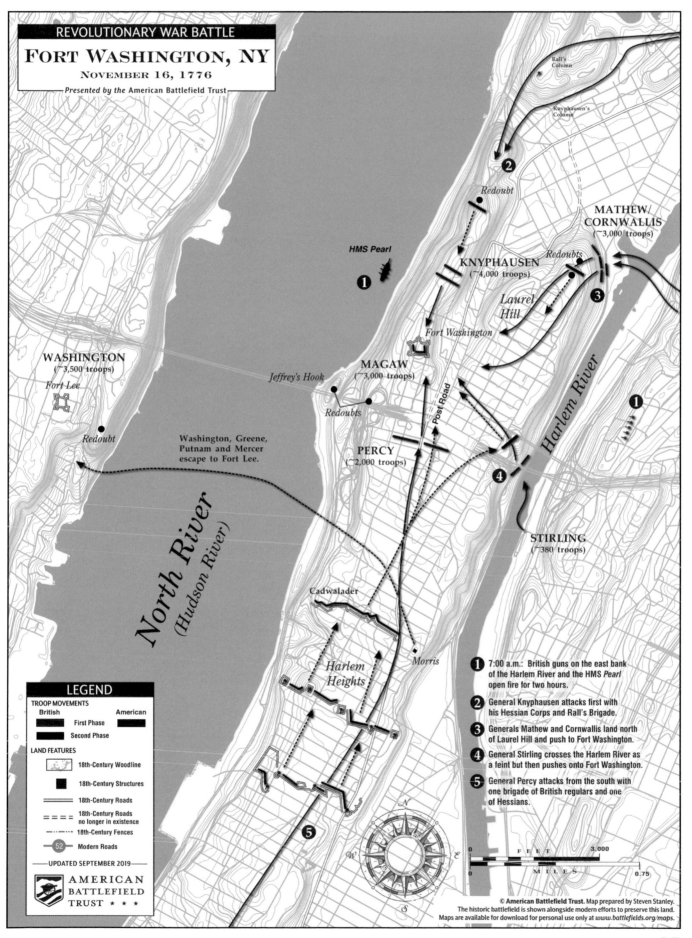

REVOLUTIONARY WAR BATTLE
FORT WASHINGTON, NY
NOVEMBER 16, 1776
Presented by the American Battlefield Trust

Rall's Column

Knyphausen's Column

2

Redoubt

MATHEW/ CORNWALLIS
(~3,000 troops)

HMS Pearl

1

KNYPHAUSEN
(~4,000 troops)

Redoubts

3

Laurel Hill

Fort Washington

WASHINGTON
(~3,500 troops)

Fort Lee

Jeffrey's Hook

MAGAW
(~3,000 troops)

Redoubts

1

Harlem River

Redoubt

Washington, Greene, Putnam and Mercer escape to Fort Lee.

PERCY
(~2,000 troops)

Post Road

4

STIRLING
(~380 troops)

North River
(Hudson River)

Cadwalader

Harlem Heights

Morris

5

1 7:00 a.m.: British guns on the east bank of the Harlem River and the HMS *Pearl* open fire for two hours.

2 General Knyphausen attacks first with his Hessian Corps and Rall's Brigade.

3 Generals Mathew and Cornwallis land north of Laurel Hill and push to Fort Washington.

4 General Stirling crosses the Harlem River as a feint but then pushes onto Fort Washington.

5 General Percy attacks from the south with one brigade of British regulars and one of Hessians.

LEGEND
TROOP MOVEMENTS

British · American

First Phase

Second Phase

LAND FEATURES

18th-Century Woodline

18th-Century Structures

18th-Century Roads

18th-Century Roads no longer in existence

18th-Century Fences

52 · Modern Roads

— UPDATED SEPTEMBER 2019 —

AMERICAN BATTLEFIELD TRUST ★ ★ ★

FEET 3,000

MILES 0.75

FIRST BATTLE *of* TRENTON

DECEMBER 26, 1776

THE AMERICAN WAR FOR INDEPENDENCE WAS AT A NEAR BREAKING POINT following the disaster of the New York Campaign. Patriot victories at Boston, Sullivan's Island, and Harlem Heights proved to be only the eye of the hurricane that was 1776. The Continental Army now found itself in eastern Pennsylvania, with the Delaware River acting as its Rubicon.

In December, newly knighted Sir William Howe called off the "fox chase." Rather than pursuing Washington across the Delaware, Howe called a stop to the campaigning season of 1776, and his army established seventeen outposts near or along the river to guard against a surprise American foray. The King's men were ready for an extended and quiet winter encampment.

General George Washington had other plans. Chaffing at what happened to him and his army since August, the "Old Fox" knew something had to be done to right the proverbial ship or all would be lost. With enlistments running out, Washington and the Continental Congress enacted bold initiatives. Enlistments for the Continental soldiers were extended to three years or the duration of the war. Washington was granted sweeping dictatorial powers for six months. And the financier of the Revolution, Robert Morris, worked diligently to scrape together every last coin he could muster to pay the flagging army.

Washington sought to take the initiative from Howe and take the fight to the enemy. The plan was to cross the Delaware and strike an outpost of Hessian soldiers in Trenton, New Jersey. A Christmas-night crossing of the Delaware and a December 26 morning attack on the Hessian garrison were the orders of the day. In the light of a full moon, Washington moved his 2,400-man force and eighteen cannon across river.

On the outskirts of Trenton, Washington divided his army into three columns. The right column approached Trenton along the River Road while the center and the left columns entered the town by its two principal roads. Continentals quickly overran the Hessian outposts on the edge of town, and on cue, the main body of troops from all sides rushed pell-mell into Trenton.

Continental artillery sprang into action, too, covering the length of the streets and permitting no avenue of escape for the stunned Hessians, who poured out of their barracks to repel the rebels. Close-quarter, hand-to-hand fighting raged in the narrow streets of a town now fully awake.

For two hours the battle raged, with the Americans never relenting. The Hessians pulled back in as orderly a fashion as they could through the streets of Trenton only to be surrounded by the Americans on the outskirts. Hessian Col. Johann Rall attempted to rally his men, but an American soldier felled Rall, mortally wounding him. The Hessians lost 22 men killed 86 wounded, and close to 900 were taken prisoner. The Americans suffered only five men wounded, including eighteen-year-old James Monroe, future president of the United States.

Washington tasted the fruits of victory, and he yearned for more.

✳ ✳ PRESERVATION ✳ ✳

The **American Battlefield Trust** has not saved any land at Trenton Battlefield.

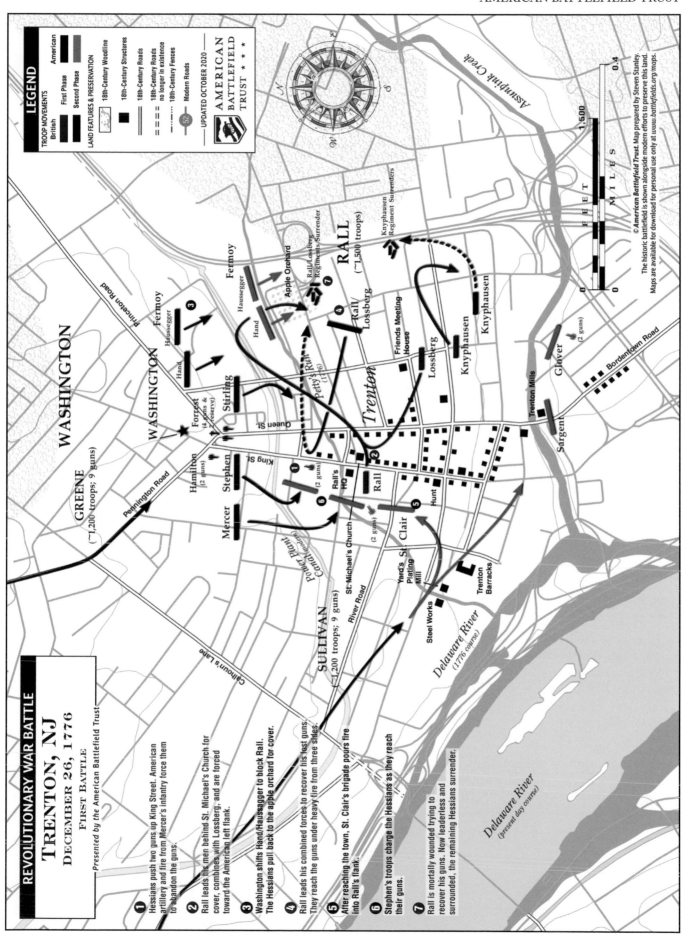

SECOND BATTLE *of* TRENTON

JANUARY 2, 1777

AFTER THE STUNNING VICTORY AT TRENTON ON DECEMBER 26, 1776, Washington expected a British counterattack in force and withdrew back to the Pennsylvania side of the Delaware River. With no immediate British or Hessian pursuit, the Patriot high commanded decided to cross the Delaware once more and take the fight to the enemy in New Jersey. From December 29-31, the Continental Army crossed the Delaware for the third time in a week. With hopes buoyed by Trenton, a modicum of faith was restored within the American cause, but not enough to keep the entire army together. With many of the state militia enlistments set to expire, Washington pleaded with his men to stand with him for just a little while longer. The call largely fell on deaf ears until the money that Robert Morris was able to scrape together reached the fighting men. This kept at least a portion of those ready to leave the army within its ranks for a little while longer. What remained of Washington's army took up a position along Assunpink Creek in Trenton.

General Charles, Second Earl Cornwallis was about to board a ship to travel back to England and his ailing wife when news of the disaster at Trenton reached him. He mustered some 8,000 men and marched south to attack the Americans at Trenton. Upon arriving in Princeton on January 1, Cornwallis consolidated his command and issued his orders. On January 2, he departed with 5,500 men and 28 cannon toward Trenton, eleven miles away, leaving a reserve brigade at Princeton.

Washington, knowing the British must use the main highway as their route of advance, placed a delaying force halfway between Trenton and Princeton under the command of General Matthias Alexis Roche de Fermoy. De Fermoy, however, returned to Trenton drunk, and his command devolved to the veteran

rifleman Col. Edward Hand. Hand's riflemen opened fire on the British-Hessian force, initiating a running battle along the Trenton-Princeton Road. The British advance was slowed to a crawl.

By 3 p.m., with only two hours of daylight remaining, Cornwallis had pushed the Continentals back to the outskirts of Trenton. A pitched fight erupted, with Hand's men firing from the houses in the area. Hand's men slowly gave way, falling back through Trenton towards the Assunpink Creek Bridge. Washington, to bolster his troop's morale, stood his horse beside the southern approach to the bridge. As his men fell back across the bridge, and with muskets and cannon thundering to cover the retreat, Washington did not flinch, sitting calmly until his men were safely across.

As the light faded on January 2, Cornwallis had a critical decision to make: either attempt to storm the bridge or wait until the next day to attack the Americans. Cornwallis attacked the bridge at least three times and was repulsed with heavy losses.

With darkness now washing over the battlefield, Washington had again stunned the British, winning another unlikely victory. Still, the Continental Army was trapped between the Delaware River and the British army. Confident he would finish the "Old Fox" the next day, Cornwallis spent the night in a restful slumber, while Washington rolled the dice once more and slipped away in the night right under nose of the King's men.

✳ ✳ **PRESERVATION** ✳ ✳

The **American Battlefield Trust** has not saved any land at Trenton Battlefield.

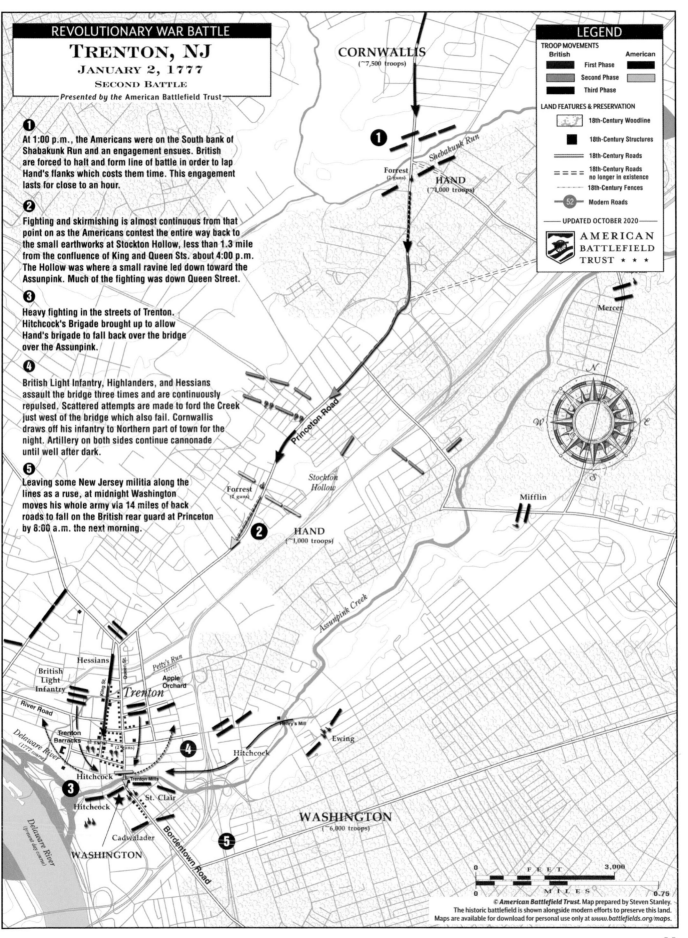

REVOLUTIONARY WAR BATTLE
TRENTON, NJ
JANUARY 2, 1777
SECOND BATTLE
Presented by the American Battlefield Trust

LEGEND

TROOP MOVEMENTS

British	American
First Phase	
Second Phase	
Third Phase	

LAND FEATURES & PRESERVATION

- 18th-Century Woodline
- 18th-Century Structures
- 18th-Century Roads
- 18th-Century Roads no longer in existence
- 18th-Century Fences
- 52 Modern Roads

— UPDATED OCTOBER 2020 —

AMERICAN BATTLEFIELD TRUST ★ ★ ★

❶ At 1:00 p.m., the Americans were on the South bank of Shabakunk Run and an engagement ensues. British are forced to halt and form line of battle in order to lap Hand's flanks which costs them time. This engagement lasts for close to an hour.

❷ Fighting and skirmishing is almost continuous from that point on as the Americans contest the entire way back to the small earthworks at Stockton Hollow, less than 1.3 mile from the confluence of King and Queen Sts. about 4:00 p.m. The Hollow was where a small ravine led down toward the Assunpink. Much of the fighting was down Queen Street.

❸ Heavy fighting in the streets of Trenton. Hitchcock's Brigade brought up to allow Hand's brigade to fall back over the bridge over the Assunpink.

❹ British Light Infantry, Highlanders, and Hessians assault the bridge three times and are continuously repulsed. Scattered attempts are made to ford the Creek just west of the bridge which also fail. Cornwallis draws off his infantry to Northern part of town for the night. Artillery on both sides continue cannonade until well after dark.

❺ Leaving some New Jersey militia along the lines as a ruse, at midnight Washington moves his whole army via 14 miles of back roads to fall on the British rear guard at Princeton by 8:00 a.m. the next morning.

CORNWALLIS
(~7,500 troops)

Shebakunk Run

Forrest
(2 guns)

HAND
(~1,000 troops)

Mercer

Princeton Road

Stockton Hollow

Forrest
(2 guns)

HAND
(~1,000 troops)

Mifflin

Assunpink Creek

Hessians

Petty's Run

Apple Orchard

British Light Infantry

Queen St.

King St.

Trenton

River Road

Delaware River
(1777 course)

Trenton Barracks (2 guns)
(2 guns)

Henry's Mill

Ewing

Hitchcock

Hitchcock

Trenton Mills

St. Clair

Hitchcock

Delaware River
(present day course)

Cadwalader

Bordentown Road

WASHINGTON

WASHINGTON
(~6,000 troops)

FEET 3,000

MILES 0.75

BATTLE *of* PRINCETON

JANUARY 3, 1777

AS THE FIRST RAYS OF SUN STREAKED ACROSS THE COLD MORNING SKY of January 3, 1777, Cornwallis rose and gazed across Assunpink Creek at the enemy lines. To his amazement, the rebels were gone. While Cornwallis slept, Washington had put his own plan into action. Leaving only 400 of his men to maintain a semblance of nocturnal activity in his camp, he had withdrawn his baggage wagons and artillery—with their wheels wrapped in rags to muffle the sound—south to Burlington. At 1 a.m., the bulk of his army had departed on an audacious march around Cornwallis's force to strike at the detachment the Briton had left behind at Princeton, New Jersey. To cut Princeton off from reinforcements, Washington detached 350 troops under Gen. Hugh Mercer to destroy the Stony Brook Bridge.

Cornwallis had left 1,400 troops at Princeton under Lt. Col. Charles Mawhood and 1,200 at Maidenhead (now Lawrenceville) under Gen. Alexander Leslie. In total, he had some 6,000 Redcoats in the vicinity to deal with the amateur army of Americans.

After leaving one regiment to garrison Princeton, Mawhood had set out with 800 soldiers to join Cornwallis at Trenton. Mawhood encountered Mercer's men on the march and ordered his men to seize the high ground on the Thomas Clarke farm. Mercer, too, realized the hill's importance and led his men there. The race turned into a confused melee as the two forces confronted one another at Clarke's orchard.

After several volleys, the British soldiers fixed bayonets and advanced. Few of Mercer's men carried bayonets; in consequence, they fell back before the intimidating British rush. "No," Mercer ordered. "Forward! Forward!" A bayonet pierced his chest, then another and another. After a dozen blows or more, the general slumped down near the hill that would later bear his name.

American reinforcements arrived on the field, but the more experienced British pushed them back, too. A rout of the Americans seemed to be in the offing, but then Washington appeared on the scene. The Virginian advanced to within 30 yards of the British line. A round was fired, and suddenly the Redcoats loosed a full volley of musket balls. When the smoke cleared, however, still atop his fine horse was the tall, lean figure of General Washington. "Charge!" he ordered, "Charge them! Pull up! Pull up!"

The patriots regrouped, and soon it was the Redcoats who fell back. Washington pressed forward, crying out, "It's a fine fox hunt, boys!" American forces pushed the Redcoats back toward Princeton, where they took cover in and around Nassau Hall, part of the College of New Jersey (now Princeton University). Artillerist Capt. Alexander Hamilton bombarded the building, forcing the occupants to surrender.

Although Mawhood broke away from the Americans with part of his force, and Cornwallis pursued, the victories of Trenton, Second Trenton, and Princeton set the American cause on a better footing for the winter of 1777. Washington settled his troops in Morristown for a harsh winter. Although 1777 started off well for Washington, it closed in a far different fashion.

✳ ✳ **PRESERVATION** ✳ ✳

To date, the **American Battlefield Trust** has saved **23.68 acres** at Princeton Battlefield.

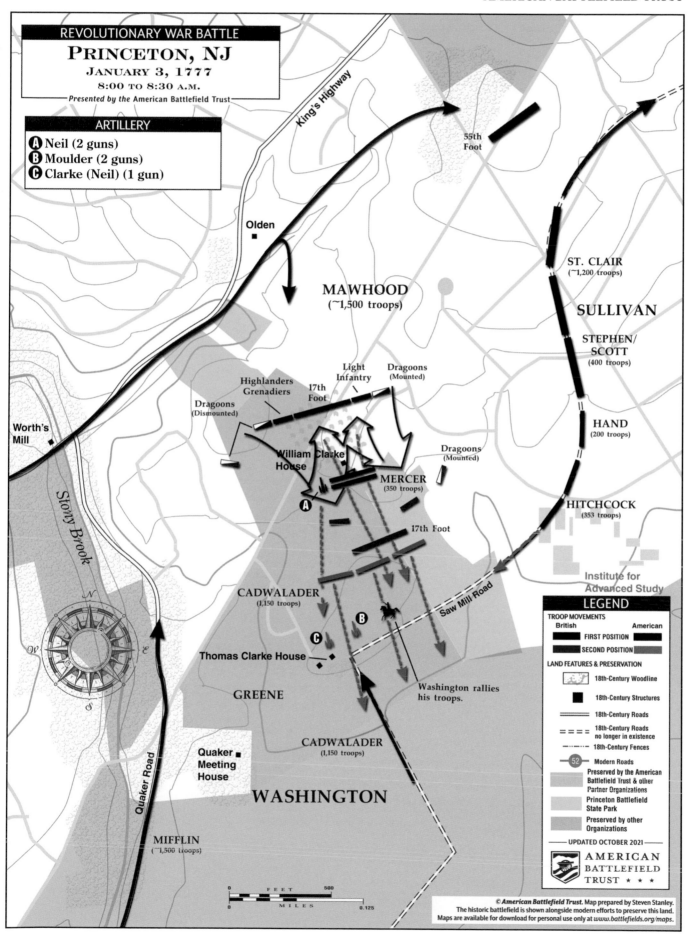

REVOLUTIONARY WAR BATTLE
PRINCETON, NJ
JANUARY 3, 1777
8:00 TO 8:30 A.M.
Presented by the American Battlefield Trust

ARTILLERY
A Neil (2 guns)
B Moulder (2 guns)
C Clarke (Neil) (1 gun)

King's Highway

55th Foot

Olden

ST. CLAIR (~1,200 troops)

MAWHOOD (~1,500 troops)

SULLIVAN

STEPHEN/ SCOTT (400 troops)

Light Infantry

Dragoons (Mounted)

Highlanders Grenadiers

17th Foot

Dragoons (Dismounted)

HAND (200 troops)

Worth's Mill

Dragoons (Mounted)

William Clarke House

MERCER (350 troops)

HITCHCOCK (353 troops)

A

17th Foot

Stony Brook

CADWALADER (1,150 troops)

Saw Mill Road

Institute for Advanced Study

B

C

Thomas Clarke House

Washington rallies his troops.

GREENE

CADWALADER (1,150 troops)

Quaker Meeting House

WASHINGTON

Quaker Road

MIFFLIN (~1,500 troops)

LEGEND
TROOP MOVEMENTS
British · American
FIRST POSITION
SECOND POSITION

LAND FEATURES & PRESERVATION
18th-Century Woodline
18th-Century Structures
18th-Century Roads
18th-Century Roads no longer in existence
18th-Century Fences
52 Modern Roads
Preserved by the American Battlefield Trust & other Partner Organizations
Princeton Battlefield State Park
Preserved by other Organizations

— UPDATED OCTOBER 2021 —

AMERICAN BATTLEFIELD TRUST ★ ★ ★

FEET 500
0
MILES 0.125

43

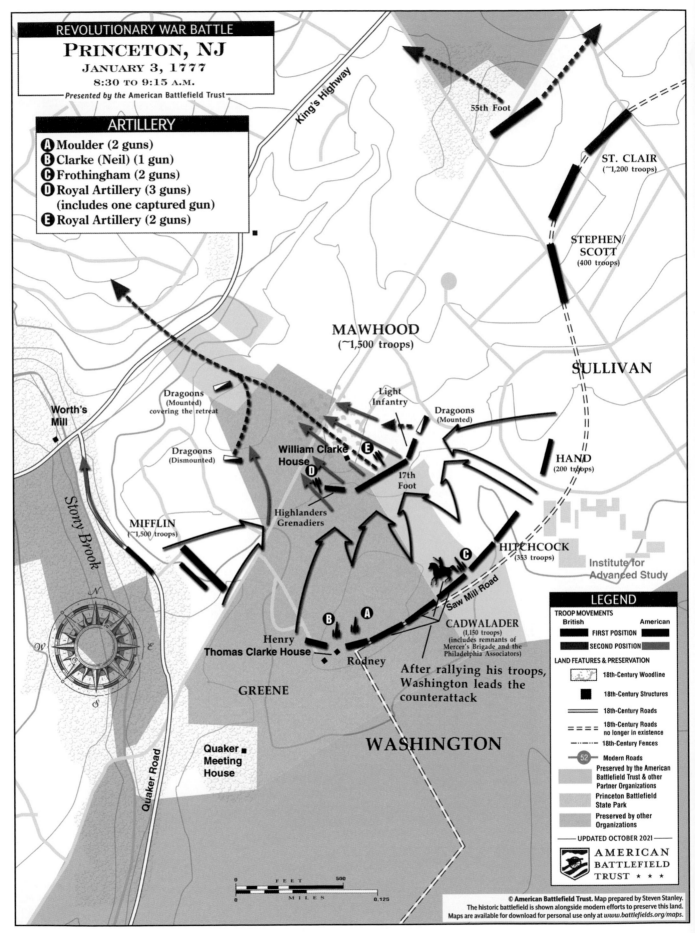

REVOLUTIONARY WAR BATTLE
PRINCETON, NJ
JANUARY 3, 1777
8:30 TO 9:15 A.M.
Presented by the American Battlefield Trust

ARTILLERY
Ⓐ Moulder (2 guns)
Ⓑ Clarke (Neil) (1 gun)
Ⓒ Frothingham (2 guns)
Ⓓ Royal Artillery (3 guns)
   (includes one captured gun)
Ⓔ Royal Artillery (2 guns)

King's Highway

55th Foot

ST. CLAIR
(~1,200 troops)

STEPHEN/
SCOTT
(400 troops)

MAWHOOD
(~1,500 troops)

SULLIVAN

Worth's
Mill

Dragoons
(Mounted)
covering the retreat

Light
Infantry

Dragoons
(Mounted)

Dragoons
(Dismounted)

William Clarke
House
Ⓔ

Ⓓ

17th
Foot

HAND
(200 troops)

Highlanders
Grenadiers

MIFFLIN
(~1,500 troops)

HITCHCOCK
(353 troops)

Ⓒ

Institute for
Advanced Study

Stony Brook

Saw Mill Road

CADWALADER
(1,150 troops)
(includes remnants of
Mercer's Brigade and the
Philadelphia Associators)

Ⓑ Ⓐ

Henry
Thomas Clarke House

Rodney

**After rallying his troops,
Washington leads the
counterattack**

GREENE

WASHINGTON

Quaker
Meeting
House

Quaker Road

LEGEND
TROOP MOVEMENTS
British   American
   FIRST POSITION
   SECOND POSITION

LAND FEATURES & PRESERVATION

▨ 18th-Century Woodline

■ 18th-Century Structures

— 18th-Century Roads

= = = 18th-Century Roads
   no longer in existence

—·—· 18th-Century Fences

52 Modern Roads

Preserved by the American
Battlefield Trust & other
Partner Organizations

Princeton Battlefield
State Park

Preserved by other
Organizations

UPDATED OCTOBER 2021

AMERICAN
BATTLEFIELD
TRUST ★ ★ ★

N

FEET   500
0
MILES   0.125

44

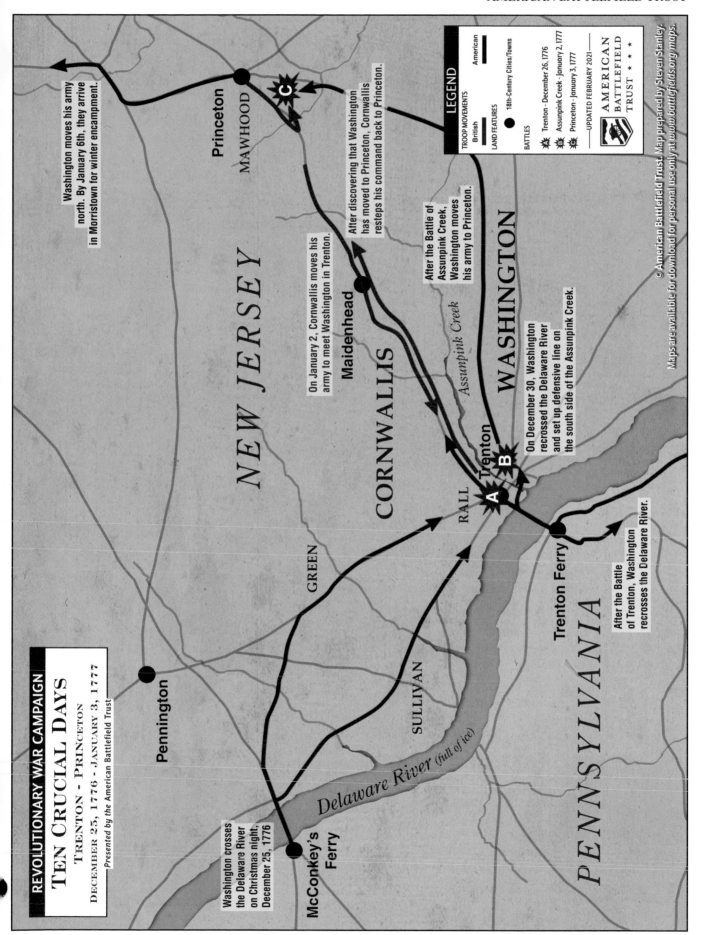

REVOLUTIONARY WAR CAMPAIGN
TEN CRUCIAL DAYS
TRENTON - PRINCETON
DECEMBER 25, 1776 - JANUARY 3, 1777
Presented by the American Battlefield Trust

NEW JERSEY

PENNSYLVANIA

Delaware River (full of ice)

Pennington

Princeton

MAWHOOD

Maidenhead

CORNWALLIS

RALL

Trenton

Assunpink Creek

WASHINGTON

GREEN

SULLIVAN

Trenton Ferry

McConkey's Ferry

Washington moves his army north. By January 6th, they arrive in Morristown for winter encampment.

On January 2, Cornwallis moves his army to meet Washington in Trenton.

After discovering that Washington has moved to Princeton, Cornwallis resteps his command back to Princeton.

After the Battle of Assunpink Creek, Washington moves his army to Princeton.

On December 30, Washington recrossed the Delaware River and set up defensive line on the south side of the Assunpink Creek.

After the Battle of Trenton, Washington recrosses the Delaware River.

Washington crosses the Delaware River on Christmas night, December 25, 1776

LEGEND
TROOP MOVEMENTS
British — American

LAND FEATURES
● 18th-Century Cities/Towns

BATTLES
✳ Trenton - December 26, 1776
✳ Assunpink Creek - January 2, 1777
✳ Princeton - January 3, 1777

— UPDATED FEBRUARY 2021 —

AMERICAN BATTLEFIELD TRUST ★ ★ ★

© American Battlefield Trust. Map prepared by Steven Stanley.
Maps are available for download for personal use only at *www.battlefields.org/maps*.

BATTLE *of* BRANDYWINE

SEPTEMBER 11, 1777

THE BRITISH CAUSE THROUGHOUT THE REVOLUTIONARY WAR LACKED A COHESIVE STRATEGY. The King's Army worked at cross purposes with itself akin to a two-horse team that would not pull together and get the job done. This was worsened by problems that manifested themselves in London, and rivalries there crossed the Atlantic into the new world. General Sir William Howe could not decide on a plan for 1777, having presented four different plans to the ministry in London. Meanwhile, Gen. John Burgoyne wooed King George III and Lord George Germain, Secretary of State for the American Department, with the idea of replacing Guy Carleton and allowing Burgoyne to lead an army out of Canada and into New York, while undermining Howe's plans for the campaign season. Burgoyne eventually got his way— and army and campaign in northern New York—while Howe would drive on the Rebel capital of Philadelphia via a seaborn landing in Maryland. Neither British force was in mutually supporting distance of one another (some 400 miles separated the forces), and the timetables for each operation were woefully misunderstood by the powers in London.

In the summer of 1777, Howe's fleet of 265 ships and 17,000 soldiers sailed out of New York, bound for the Head of Elk, Maryland (modern day Elkton). Howe's men moved through Delaware and into Pennsylvania as Washington rushed his army from outside of New York, marching through the American capital and south of the city to meet the British before they could fall on Philadelphia.

On September 11, 1777, Howe's 15,500-man British and Hessian army clashed with Washington's force of 14,600 along the banks of Brandywine Creek.

Going on the offensive, Howe launched a flank attack. The British commander directed Hessian Gen. Wilhelm von Knyphausen to demonstrate with his division against the American center while Cornwallis marched around Washington's right.

Cornwallis's movement got underway early in the morning and lasted into the afternoon. Plagued by conflicting intelligence reports and harried by Knyphausen, Washington was slow to react to the threat.

Shortly before 4 p.m., three Continental divisions engaged Cornwallis near the Birmingham Meeting House. There, Americans met some of the finest troops in the British army. Outnumbered, the American line broke beneath the weight of Cornwallis's onslaught. As the battle raged for Washington's right flank, von Knyphausen attacked at Chadd's Ford. The Americans gave way, but a stubborn rear guard action kept the Hessians at bay. General Nathanael Greene made a stand south of Dilworth that helped secure Washington's line of retreat.

Darkness brought an end to the fighting with Howe's army in command of the field. Despite the defeat, Washington was able to keep his army intact. Fifteen days later, Philadelphia fell to the British. Although disaster once again befell Washington's Army, the tide of war was changing in the north.

✳ ✳ PRESERVATION ✳ ✳

To date, the **American Battlefield Trust** has saved **187.22 acres** at Brandywine Battlefield.

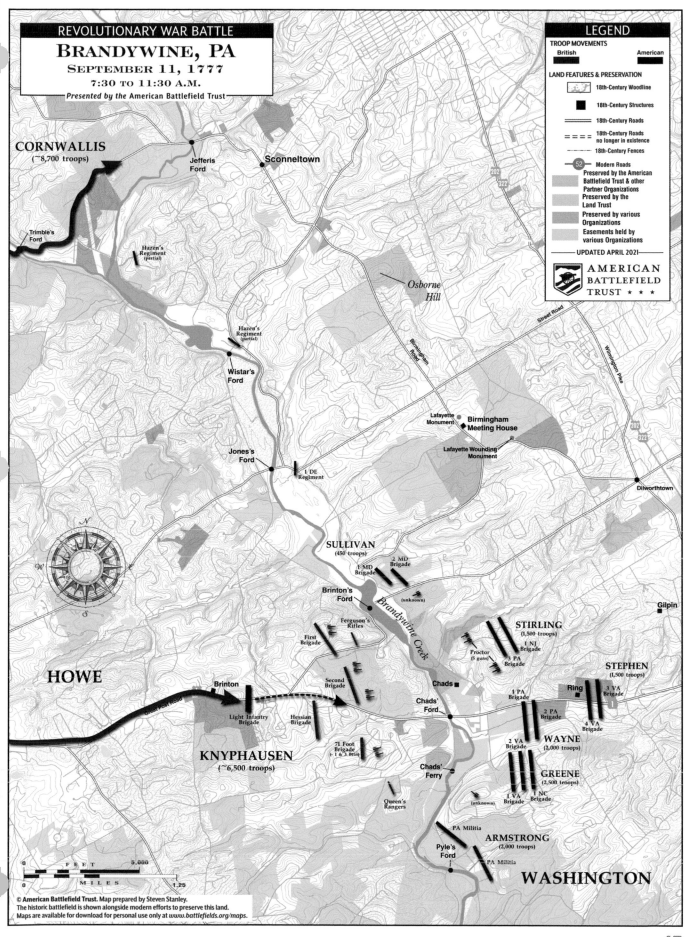

REVOLUTIONARY WAR BATTLE
BRANDYWINE, PA
SEPTEMBER 11, 1777
7:30 TO 11:30 A.M.
Presented by the American Battlefield Trust

LEGEND

TROOP MOVEMENTS
British   American

LAND FEATURES & PRESERVATION
- 18th-Century Woodline
- 18th-Century Structures
- 18th-Century Roads
- 18th-Century Roads no longer in existence
- 18th-Century Fences
- 52 Modern Roads
- Preserved by the American Battlefield Trust & other Partner Organizations
- Preserved by the Land Trust
- Preserved by various Organizations
- Easements held by various Organizations

UPDATED APRIL 2021

AMERICAN BATTLEFIELD TRUST ★ ★ ★

CORNWALLIS (~8,700 troops)

Jefferis Ford

Sconneltown

Trimble's Ford

Hazen's Regiment (partial)

Osborne Hill

Street Road

Wilmington Pike

Hazen's Regiment (partial)

Wistar's Ford

Birmingham Road

Lafayette Monument
Birmingham Meeting House
Lafayette Wounding Monument

Jones's Ford

I DE Regiment

Dilworthtown

SULLIVAN (450 troops)

2 MD Brigade
1 MD Brigade

Brinton's Ford

(unknown)

Gilpin

Brandywine Creek

Ferguson's Rifles

First Brigade

STIRLING (1,500 troops)
1 NJ Brigade
Proctor (5 guns)
3 PA Brigade

STEPHEN (1,500 troops)

HOWE

Brinton

Second Brigade

Chads

Ring
3 VA Brigade

Chads' Ford

1 PA Brigade
2 PA Brigade
4 VA Brigade

Light Infantry Brigade
Hessian Brigade

2 VA Brigade

WAYNE (2,000 troops)

Great Post Road

71 Foot Brigade (+ 1 & 3 Bttn)

KNYPHAUSEN (~6,500 troops)

Chads' Ferry

GREENE (2,500 troops)

1 VA Brigade
NC Brigade

(unknown)

Queen's Rangers

PA Militia

ARMSTRONG (2,000 troops)

Pyle's Ford

PA Militia

WASHINGTON

FEET 5,000
MILES 1.25

© American Battlefield Trust. Map prepared by Steven Stanley.
The historic battlefield is shown alongside modern efforts to preserve this land.
Maps are available for download for personal use only at *www.battlefields.org/maps.*

47

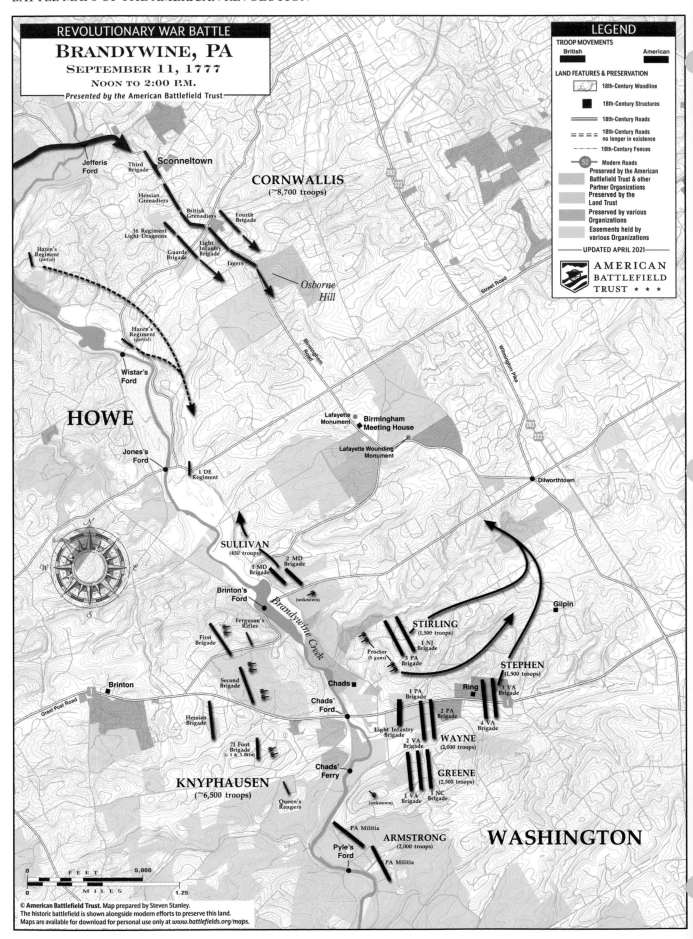

REVOLUTIONARY WAR BATTLE

BRANDYWINE, PA
SEPTEMBER 11, 1777
NOON TO 2:00 P.M.
Presented by the American Battlefield Trust

LEGEND

TROOP MOVEMENTS
British   American

LAND FEATURES & PRESERVATION
18th-Century Woodline
18th-Century Structures
18th-Century Roads
18th-Century Roads no longer in existence
18th-Century Fences
52 Modern Roads
Preserved by the American Battlefield Trust & other Partner Organizations
Preserved by the Land Trust
Preserved by various Organizations
Easements held by various Organizations

— UPDATED APRIL 2021 —

AMERICAN BATTLEFIELD TRUST ★★★

Jefferis Ford
Third Brigade
Sconneltown
Hessian Grenadiers
British Grenadiers
16 Regiment Light Dragoons
Fourth Brigade
Guards Brigade
Light Infantry Brigade
Jagers

CORNWALLIS
(~8,700 troops)

Osborne Hill

Hazen's Regiment (partial)

Hazen's Regiment (partial)

Wistar's Ford

HOWE

Lafayette Monument
Birmingham Meeting House
Lafayette Wounding Monument

Jones's Ford
1 DE Regiment

Dilworthtown

SULLIVAN
(450 troops)
2 MD Brigade
1 MD Brigade
(unknown)

Brinton's Ford

Ferguson's Rifles

First Brigade

STIRLING
(1,500 troops)
1 NJ Brigade
Proctor (5 guns)
3 PA Brigade

Gilpin

STEPHEN
(1,500 troops)

Brinton

Second Brigade

Chads

Chads' Ford

Ring
3 VA Brigade

1 PA Brigade
2 PA Brigade
4 VA Brigade

Great Post Road

Hessian Brigade

Light Infantry Brigade
2 VA Brigade

WAYNE
(2,000 troops)

71 Foot Brigade
(- 1 & 3 Bttn)

Chads' Ferry

GREENE
(2,500 troops)

KNYPHAUSEN
(~6,500 troops)

Queen's Rangers

(unknown)
1 VA Brigade
1 NC Brigade

WASHINGTON

Pyle's Ford

PA Militia

ARMSTRONG
(2,000 troops)

PA Militia

FEET 5,000
MILES 1.25

© **American Battlefield Trust.** Map prepared by Steven Stanley.
The historic battlefield is shown alongside modern efforts to preserve this land.
Maps are available for download for personal use only at *www.battlefields.org/maps*.

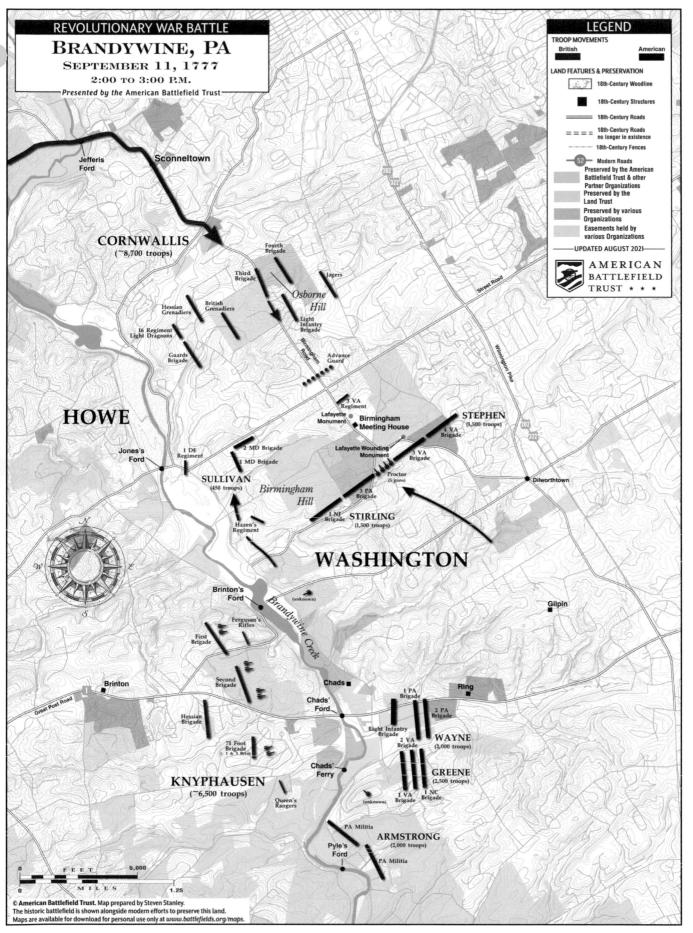

REVOLUTIONARY WAR BATTLE
BRANDYWINE, PA
SEPTEMBER 11, 1777
2:00 TO 3:00 P.M.
Presented by the American Battlefield Trust

LEGEND

TROOP MOVEMENTS
British   American

LAND FEATURES & PRESERVATION
18th-Century Woodline
18th-Century Structures
18th-Century Roads
18th-Century Roads no longer in existence
18th-Century Fences
52 Modern Roads
Preserved by the American Battlefield Trust & other Partner Organizations
Preserved by the Land Trust
Preserved by various Organizations
Easements held by various Organizations

UPDATED AUGUST 2021

AMERICAN BATTLEFIELD TRUST ★★★

Jefferis Ford
Sconneltown

CORNWALLIS (~8,700 troops)

Fourth Brigade
Third Brigade
Jagers
Osborne Hill
Hessian Grenadiers
British Grenadiers
Light Infantry Brigade
16 Regiment Light Dragoons
Guards Brigade
Advance Guard
Birmingham Road

HOWE

3 VA Regiment
Lafayette Monument
Birmingham Meeting House
STEPHEN (1,500 troops)
4 VA Brigade

Jones's Ford
1 DE Regiment
2 MD Brigade
1 MD Brigade
Lafayette Wounding Monument
3 VA Brigade
Proctor (5 guns)
Dilworthtown

SULLIVAN (450 troops)
Birmingham Hill
3 PA Brigade

Hazen's Regiment
LNI Brigade
STIRLING (1,500 troops)

WASHINGTON

Brinton's Ford
Brandywine Creek
(unknown)
Gilpin

Ferguson's Rifles
First Brigade

Second Brigade
Chads
Ring
1 PA Brigade
2 PA Brigade

Brinton
Chads' Ford
Light Infantry Brigade
WAYNE (2,000 troops)
Great Post Road
Hessian Brigade
2 VA Brigade
71 Foot Brigade (- 1 & 3 Britt)
GREENE (2,500 troops)
Chads' Ferry
1 VA Brigade
1 NC Brigade
KNYPHAUSEN (~6,500 troops)
(unknown)
Queen's Rangers

ARMSTRONG (2,000 troops)
PA Militia
Pyle's Ford
PA Militia

FEET 5,000
MILES 1.25

© American Battlefield Trust. Map prepared by Steven Stanley.
The historic battlefield is shown alongside modern efforts to preserve this land.
Maps are available for download for personal use only at www.battlefields.org/maps.

49

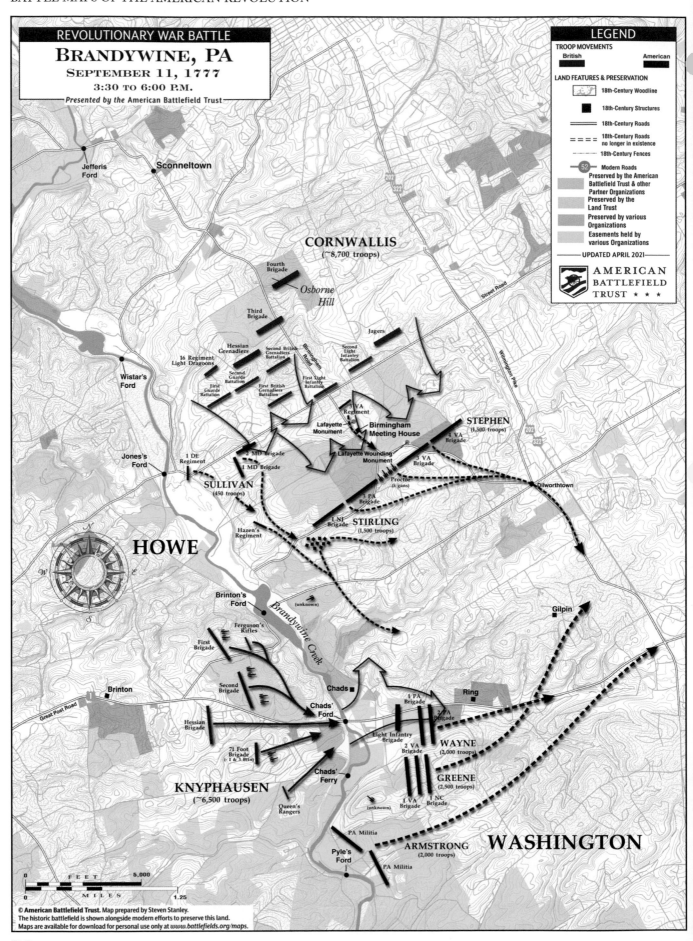

REVOLUTIONARY WAR BATTLE

BRANDYWINE, PA

SEPTEMBER 11, 1777

3:30 TO 6:00 P.M.

Presented by the American Battlefield Trust

LEGEND

TROOP MOVEMENTS
British   American

LAND FEATURES & PRESERVATION
18th-Century Woodline
18th-Century Structures
18th-Century Roads
18th-Century Roads no longer in existence
18th-Century Fences
52 Modern Roads
Preserved by the American Battlefield Trust & other Partner Organizations
Preserved by the Land Trust
Preserved by various Organizations
Easements held by various Organizations

UPDATED APRIL 2021

AMERICAN BATTLEFIELD TRUST ★★★

Jefferis Ford

Sconneltown

CORNWALLIS
(~8,700 troops)

Fourth Brigade

Osborne Hill

Third Brigade

Hessian Grenadiers

16 Regiment Light Dragoons

Second Guards Battalion

First Guards Battalion

Second British Grenadiers Battalion

Birmingham Ridge

First British Grenadiers Battalion

First Light Infantry Battalion

Second Light Infantry Battalion

Jagers

3 VA Regiment

STEPHEN
(1,500 troops)

4 VA Brigade

Lafayette Monument

Birmingham Meeting House

Wistar's Ford

Jones's Ford

1 DE Regiment

2 MD Brigade

1 MD Brigade

SULLIVAN
(450 troops)

Lafayette Wounding Monument

2 VA Brigade

Proctor (5 guns)

Dilworthtown

Hazen's Regiment

1 NJ Brigade

3 PA Brigade

STIRLING
(1,500 troops)

HOWE

Brinton's Ford

Brandywine Creek

(unknown)

Gilpin

Ferguson's Rifles

First Brigade

Second Brigade

Chads

Chads' Ford

1 PA Brigade

Ring

Brinton

Great Post Road

Hessian Brigade

Chads' Ford

2 PA Brigade

Light Infantry Brigade

2 VA Brigade

WAYNE
(2,000 troops)

71 Foot Brigade (- 1 & 3 Bttn)

Chads' Ferry

GREENE
(2,500 troops)

KNYPHAUSEN
(~6,500 troops)

Queen's Rangers

(unknown)

1 VA Brigade

1 NC Brigade

WASHINGTON

PA Militia

Pyle's Ford

ARMSTRONG
(2,000 troops)

PA Militia

FEET   5,000

MILES   1.25

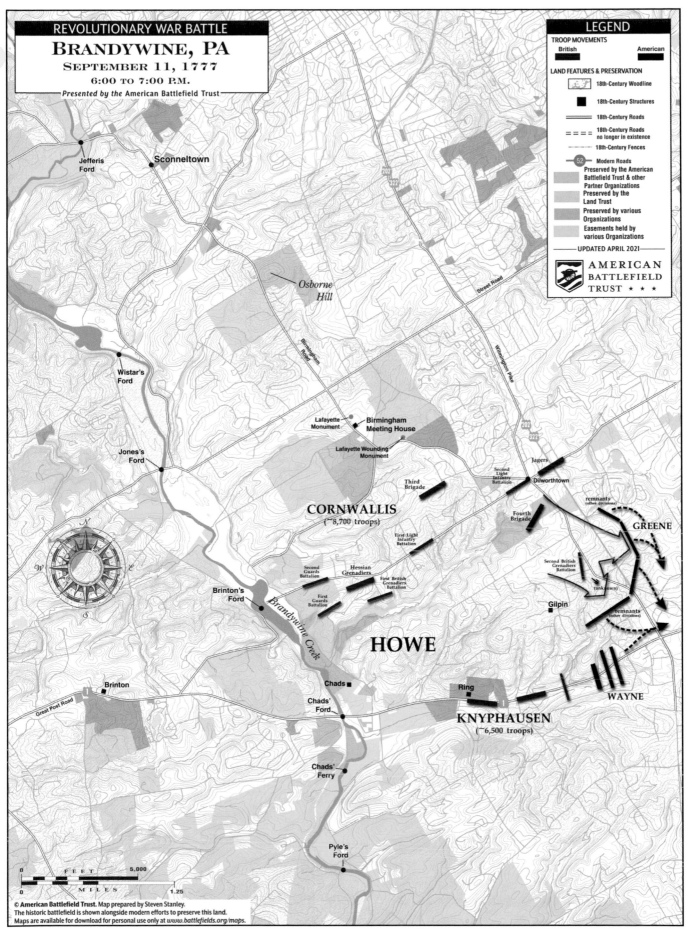

REVOLUTIONARY WAR BATTLE

BRANDYWINE, PA

SEPTEMBER 11, 1777

6:00 TO 7:00 P.M.

Presented by the American Battlefield Trust

LEGEND

TROOP MOVEMENTS

British

American

LAND FEATURES & PRESERVATION

18th-Century Woodline

18th-Century Structures

18th-Century Roads

18th-Century Roads no longer in existence

18th-Century Fences

52 Modern Roads

Preserved by the American Battlefield Trust & other Partner Organizations

Preserved by the Land Trust

Preserved by various Organizations

Easements held by various Organizations

— UPDATED APRIL 2021 —

AMERICAN BATTLEFIELD TRUST ★★★

Jefferis Ford

Sconneltown

Osborne Hill

Wistar's Ford

Jones's Ford

Brinton's Ford

Brinton

Great Post Road

Chads' Ferry

Pyle's Ford

Chads' Ford

Chads

Birmingham Road

Lafayette Monument

Birmingham Meeting House

Lafayette Wounding Monument

Brandywine Creek

CORNWALLIS (~8,700 troops)

Third Brigade

First Light Infantry Battalion

Second Guards Battalion

Hessian Grenadiers

First British Grenadiers Battalion

First Guards Battalion

HOWE

Street Road

Wilmington Pike

Jagers

Second Light Infantry Battalion

Dilworthtown

Fourth Brigade

Second British Grenadiers Battalion

Gilpin

remnants (other divisions)

GREENE

(unknown)

remnants (other divisions)

WAYNE

Ring

KNYPHAUSEN (~6,500 troops)

N

FEET 5,000

MILES 1.25

© **American Battlefield Trust.** Map prepared by Steven Stanley.
The historic battlefield is shown alongside modern efforts to preserve this land.
Maps are available for download for personal use only at *www.battlefields.org/maps.*

BATTLE *of* HUBBARDTON

JULY 7, 1777

AS HOWE'S FORCE GEARED UP FOR ITS STRIKE **AGAINST THE REBEL CAPITAL** at Philadelphia, the wheels were in motion for the second part of the Crown's 1777 campaign. General John Burgoyne envisioned a three-pronged strike to divide New England from the rest of the rebellious American colonies. One force would move down the St. Lawrence River onto Lake Ontario and proceed down the Mohawk River Valley to draw American forces in that direction while also rallying Native American allies. Another force would move up the Hudson River from New York and threaten the American rear, while Burgoyne's main army moved south from Canada via the Richelieu River and Lake Champlain. Coordinating three forces so widely dispersed in the 18th century was an impossible task, and the two other British forces were eventually thwarted by the rebels. Burgoyne did find initial success at Fort Ticonderoga, though, and the "Gibraltar of North America" fell into British hands with relative ease (July 2-6, 1777).

As the American forces retreated from Fort Ticonderoga toward Fort Edward, Burgoyne's army gave chase. General Simon Fraser marched early on the morning of July 6, 1777, with a force of some 850 men. Burgoyne later dispatched a contingent of Hessians commanded by Gen. Friedrich Adolf Riedesel to follow and support Fraser. The next day, Fraser's command made contact with the American rearguard near Hubbardton (in present-day Vermont), where Cantankerous American Col. Seth Warner had assumed command. Warner, who was experienced in rearguard tactics, was a good candidate for the job. Warner's force was exhausted from the evacuation and forced march from Fort Ticonderoga. In a council

of war, Warner decided to allow his men to rest, a decision counter to the orders received from Gen. Arthur St. Clair.

Fraser's men were in hot pursuit of the rebels, and they made contact with the enemy on the morning of July 7 just as the patriots were preparing to continue their march. Initial confusion on the American side gave way to a more determined stand. Colonel Ebenezer Francis and his 11th Massachusetts shook out into a battle line, and the men of Col. Nathan Hale's regiment supported the Bay State men as best as they could following the initial shock of battle.

Each side tried to find a weakness in their opponent's lines. While the Americans manned strong positions behind stone walls bolstered by felled trees, the superior training of the British got the best of them. Taking a risk, Fraser dispatched a contingent of men in an assault on the American right flank. The Scotsman gambled that his slow-to-arrive Hessian support would even the odds when they did finally arrive on the field. Soon, and the combined Crown forces worked their way around the Rebel flanks. Although St. Clair tried to reinforce Warner's force at Hubbardton, there was little he could do. The Americans broke for the rear and, amid the retreat, Francis fell dead and Nathan Hale was captured by the British.

Fraser wanted to pursue his prey, but Riedesel was not up for the challenge and fell back to Burgoyne's main army. A few days later, Fraser did the same. Some of the rebels scattered to the wind while others rejoined St. Clair's force at Fort Edward.

✳ ✳ **PRESERVATION** ✳ ✳

The **American Battlefield Trust** has not saved any land at Hubbardton Battlefield.

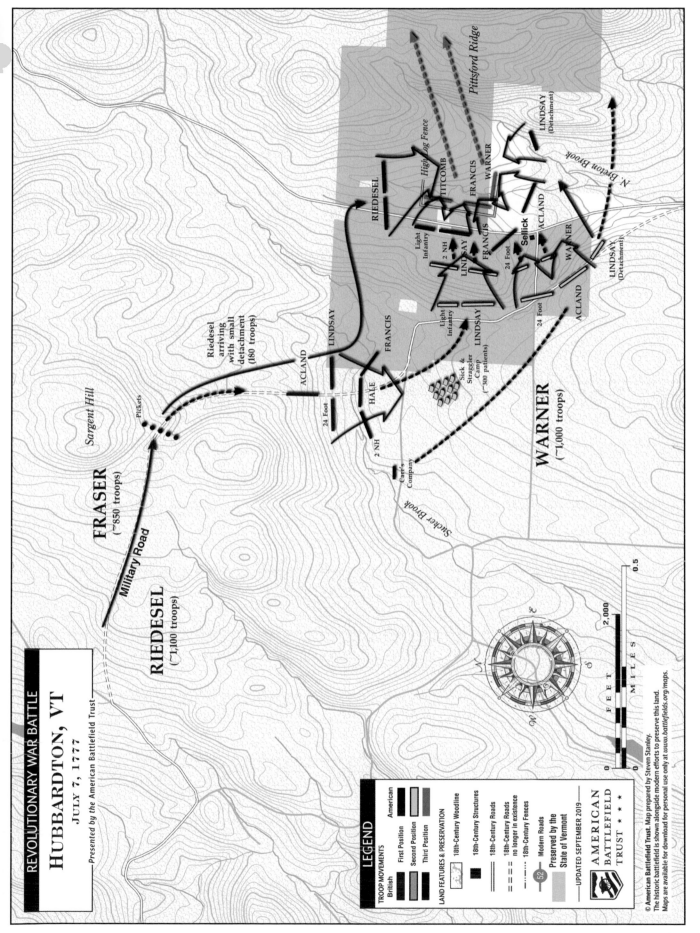

REVOLUTIONARY WAR BATTLE

HUBBARDTON, VT

JULY 7, 1777

Presented by the American Battlefield Trust

LEGEND

TROOP MOVEMENTS

British		American
	First Position	
	Second Position	
	Third Position	

LAND FEATURES & PRESERVATION

18th-Century Woodline

18th-Century Structures

18th-Century Roads

18th-Century Roads no longer in existence

18th-Century Fences

Modern Roads

Preserved by the State of Vermont

—UPDATED SEPTEMBER 2019—

AMERICAN BATTLEFIELD TRUST ★ ★ ★

Pittsford Ridge

High Log Fence

LINDSAY (Detachment)

WARNER

RIEDESEL

TITCOMB

FRANCIS

N. Breton Brook

Light Infantry

2 NH

LINDSAY

FRANCIS

ACLAND

Sellick

WARNER

24 Foot

LINDSAY (Detachment)

Riedesel arriving with small detachment (180 troops)

LINDSAY

ACLAND

FRANCIS

Light Infantry

LINDSAY

24 Foot

ACLAND

24 Foot

HALE

WARNER (~1,000 troops)

Sick & Straggler Camp (~300 patients)

2 NH

Carr's Company

Sucker Brook

Pickets

Sargent Hill

FRASER (~850 troops)

Military Road

RIEDESEL (~1,100 troops)

FEET 0   2,000

MILES 0   0.5

© American Battlefield Trust. Map prepared by Steven Stanley.
The historic battlefield is shown alongside modern efforts to preserve this land.
Maps are available for download for personal use only at *www.battlefields.org/maps.*

BATTLE *of* FORT ANN

JULY 8, 1777

IN THE WAKE OF THE FALL OF FORT TICONDEROGA, GEN. ARTHUR ST. CLAIR split his force into two pieces. The main portion of his army retreated through Hubbardton and then onto Fort Edward, while Col. Pierse Long's New Hampshire Regiment retreated south to Skenesborough via bateau. Burgoyne was in pursuit of the fleeing American flotilla which was comprised mostly of women and sick and wounded soldiers from Fort Ticonderoga. Crown forces dogged Long's motley crew of dissidents. British cannon barked from Burgoyne's fleet, and three redcoat regiments gave chase on land. British naval gunners bombarded and destroyed the American ships Enterprise, Gates, and Liberty, while the Trumbull and Revenge were forced to surrender in the Battle of Skenesborough on Lake Champlain. Morale among the Continental ranks was dangerously low. The abled bodied soldiers among Long's ranks marched along a military road, as the women and the wounded traversed the waters of Wood Creek—the modest Fort Ann their destination.

Pressing on toward Fort Ann (also spelled Fort Anne), Long's force grew in strength and size. Joined by Massachusetts and New Hampshire militiamen, the Patriot confidence also grew. It also became apparent that the British pursuers, namely Col. John Hill and his 9th Regiment of Foot, would not give up the scent.

Having arrived at Fort Ann, the Americans decided now was the time for battle. Colonel Hill's force occupied a hill north of the fort. If given time, the British could swoop down and lay siege to the haggard garrison. On July 7, taking matters into their own hands, some 170 Patriots sallied out of the fort, and observed Hill's men. Skirmishing broke out along the lines, but neither side could gain an advantage. The Americans pulled back into the safety of the fort, while Hill's men remained ensconced upon Battle Hill.

Overnight, reinforcements in the form of the 6th Regiment of Albany Militia arrived at the fort. What had begun as a race for their lives, now morphed into a delaying action. General Philip Schuyler ordered the force at Fort Ann to buy him time to organize the troops and the defense of the area. Meantime, Hill called on Burgoyne for reinforcements. Due to logistics and rain, British reinforcements would not arrive in time for battle on July 8. Hill consolidated his position, and then received intelligence from a captured deserter about the strength of the Rebel force. Unfortunately, this "deserter" disappeared from the British camps, most likely he was a spy sent to ascertain the British strength and disposition. Hill deployed his men along the banks of Wood Creek, with the backs to the creek. To their front was the Skenesborough Road. And to their front and on their flanks were heavy woods.

The Americans decided upon a two-pronged attack, that would strike the British flanks. The New Hampshire militia aimed for the British left flank, while the Albany Militia crossed Wood Creek twice, and positioned themselves on the British right flank. The combined American attack was too much for the British and they retreated up Battle Hill in a running fight. Once back atop the hill, the battle, for a second day in a row, battle devolved into a sustained and static firefight. Neither side could gain an advantage.

Sensing the futility, the Americans broke off the assault, burned most of Fort Ann and fell back to Fort Edward. Burgoyne slowly moved into the area, and by July 28th established a supply base as he prepared to engage and defeat the growing Rebel force at Fort Edward.

❋ ❋ PRESERVATION ❋ ❋

To date, the **American Battlefield Trust** has saved **160 acres** at Fort Ann Battlefield.

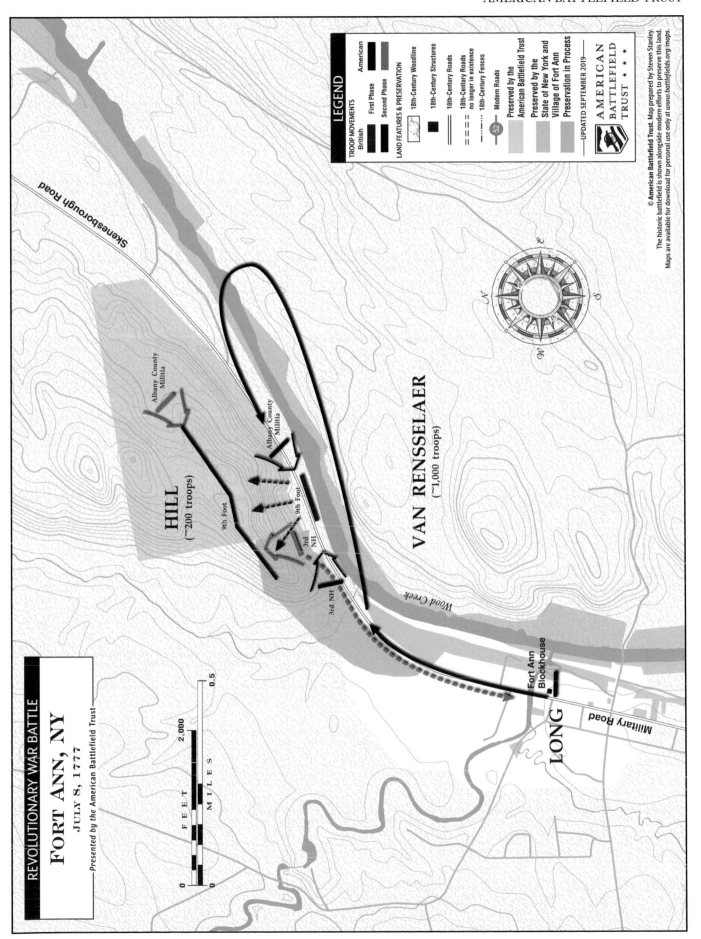

REVOLUTIONARY WAR BATTLE

FORT ANN, NY

JULY 8, 1777

Presented by the American Battlefield Trust

Skenesborough Road

HILL
(~200 troops)

Albany County Militia

Albany County Militia

9th Foot

9th Foot

3rd NH

3rd NH

VAN RENSSELAER
(~1,000 troops)

Wood Creek

Fort Ann Blockhouse

LONG

Military Road

LEGEND

TROOP MOVEMENTS

British   American

First Phase

Second Phase

LAND FEATURES & PRESERVATION

18th-Century Woodline

18th-Century Structures

18th-Century Roads

18th-Century Roads no longer in existence

18th-Century Fences

52   Modern Roads

Preserved by the American Battlefield Trust

Preserved by the State of New York and Village of Fort Ann

Preservation in Process

—— UPDATED SEPTEMBER 2019 ——

AMERICAN BATTLEFIELD TRUST ★ ★ ★

© **American Battlefield Trust.** Map prepared by Steven Stanley.
The historic battlefield is shown alongside modern efforts to preserve this land.
Maps are available for download for personal use only at *www.battlefields.org/maps.*

FEET   2,000

MILES   0.5

BATTLE *of* ORISKANY

AUGUST 6, 1777

WHILE BURGOYNE ADVANCED DOWN THE RICHELIEU RIVER and Lake Champlain, a second force commanded by Lt. Col. Barry St. Leger applied pressure to the rebels in western New York. St. Leger proceeded by water via Lake Ontario to the mouth of the Oswego River, eventually moving up the river to Lake Oneida and Wood Creek. His force of 1,600 men encountered their first point of heavy resistance in the Mohawk River Valley at Fort Stanwix. Fort Stanwix stood in the path of a portage between Wood Creek and the Mohawk River known as the Oneida Carrying Place.

St. Ledger's mixed force of regulars, loyalists, Hessians, and Native Americans arrived at Fort Stanwix after a six-week trek. To intimidate the rebels, St. Ledger paraded his men in front of the garrison and called for its surrender. Colonel Peter Gansevoort, commanding the fort, refused. Word quickly spread of the British incursion. Oneida warriors sympathetic to the American cause notified local militia leader Gen. Nicholas Herkimer, who called out the Tryon County (N.Y.) militia to help bolster the defense of Fort Stanwix.

Herkimer's column was detected as it moved toward the besieged garrison. St. Ledger, who wanted to avoid a prolonged siege, could not allow reinforcements to reach Fort Stanwix. Loyalist from New York, bolstered by Native allies, moved to intercept the approaching militia column. The mixed force laid a trap for the rebels roughly six miles to the southeast of Fort Stanwix along road to the fort.

As Herkimer approached Fort Stanwix, he became apprehensive. He was to receive a signal from Gansevoort to bring his men to the fort, but no such signal had been provided. Some of the militia officers had their fighting blood up, and they accused Herkimer of being a loyalist Tory (one of Herkimer's brothers was, in fact, a Tory in St. Ledger's army). Angered and insulted, Herkimer indignantly ordered his column of four regiments, totaling 800 men, to march to the fort.

As the column entered a narrow ravine, Sir John Johnson planned to surround the Whig militia and destroy the force. When the head of the column halted in the ravine, Native warriors impatiently attacked early, falling upon the patriots, who were caught unawares. Herkimer was struck in the leg by a ball and ordered his men to prop him up using his saddle against a tree, where he directed the battle. His officers begged him to allow them to remove him from his makeshift command post. Perhaps from a sense of duty or perhaps prove he was a loyal Patriot, Herkimer refused and stuck to the field. Much of the American rearguard was wounded or sent to flight, though some of Herkimer's 3rd Regiment did fight their way forward to support their fellow whigs.

The fighting was brutal and, at times, hand-to-hand, but the Americans somehow managed to piece together a defensive perimeter. A lull came over the field as a violent thunderstorm soaked the men and the countryside. Following the storm, loyalists tried turning their coats inside out to trick the patriots into thinking that they were a relief column from the fort. The ruse failed. A column was sent from Fort Stanwix and attacked the nearby Native American camp but did not assist Herkimer in his desperate struggle. The Native Americans broke off the engagement, and the battle came to a merciful end. Herkimer's column retreated to Fort Dayton, and Herkimer died ten days after the battle. Another Patriot relief force was sent to Fort Stanwix commanded by Gen. Benedict Arnold. Hearing of Arnold's approach, St. Ledger lifted the siege and retreated. Burgoyne's western prong had failed to make headway in the Mohawk River Valley.

✸ ✳ PRESERVATION ✳ ✸

The **American Battlefield Trust** has not saved any land at Oriskany Battlefield.

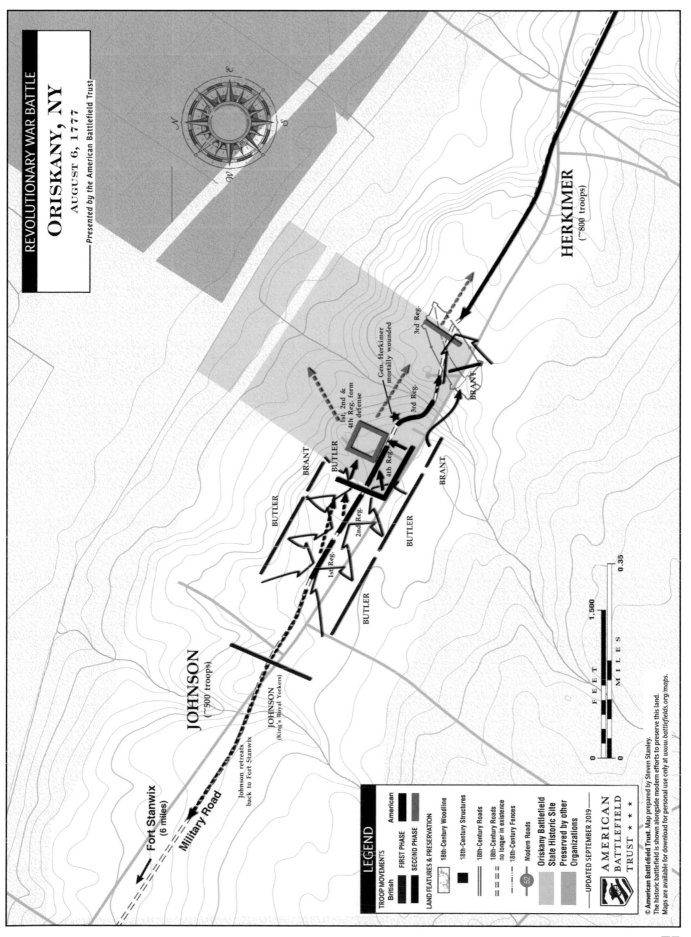

REVOLUTIONARY WAR BATTLE

ORISKANY, NY
AUGUST 6, 1777

Presented by the American Battlefield Trust

HERKIMER
(~800 troops)

JOHNSON
(~500 troops)

JOHNSON
(King's Royal Yorkers)

Johnson retreats
back to Fort Stanwix

Fort Stanwix
(6 miles)

Military Road

BUTLER

BUTLER

BUTLER

BUTLER

BRANT

BRANT

BRANT

BRANT

1st Reg.

2nd Reg.

4th Reg.

3rd Reg.

3rd Reg.

1st, 2nd &
4th Reg. form
defense

Gen. Herkimer
mortally wounded

LEGEND

TROOP MOVEMENTS
British
American

FIRST PHASE
SECOND PHASE

LAND FEATURES & PRESERVATION
18th-Century Woodline
18th-Century Structures
18th-Century Roads
18th-Century Roads
no longer in existence
18th-Century Fences
52 Modern Roads

Oriskany Battlefield
State Historic Site
Preserved by other
Organizations

— UPDATED SEPTEMBER 2019 —

AMERICAN
BATTLEFIELD
TRUST ★ ★ ★

FEET 1,500

MILES 0.35

© American Battlefield Trust. Map prepared by Steven Stanley.
The historic battlefield is shown alongside modern efforts to preserve this land.
Maps are available for download for personal use only at *www.battlefields.org/maps*.

BATTLE *of* BENNINGTON

AUGUST 16, 1777

WHILE THE SIEGE OF FORT STANWIX LINGERED ON, Gen. John Burgoyne planned the next phase of his offensive. The strategic locations of Crown Point, Fort Ticonderoga, and Fort Ann were now under British control. Having made Fort Ann his forward supply base on July 28, the next step south toward Albany would carry Burgoyne and his army to Fort Edward on the Hudson River. Once on the Hudson, Burgoyne had the opportunity to open communications via the waterway with Gen. Henry Clinton's force in New York City. Clinton could move north up the Hudson to support or reinforce Burgoyne—something Burgoyne hoped for. But to get to Fort Edward, the tories were forced to cut a road through the rough country of upstate New York. Precious weeks ticked away as the British made slow progress in their road construction.

Burgoyne's supply line was stretched thin as the British pushed deeper and deeper into enemy territory, forcing the redcoats to engage in a war of outposts. Burgoyne, too, was forced to explore opportunities to replenish his stores by raiding the countryside. Horses and draft animals were a particular need. The Americans seemed to have picked clean the countryside of livestock. Thus, when a subordinate suggested that Burgoyne send out a foraging party, the commanding general authorized the expedition. Burgoyne divided his army and assigned Lt. Col. Friedrich Baum to lead the mission. The inexperienced Baum was a poor selection. As Baum's troops moved southeast, local militia units learned of his activity and prepared for action. Baum, sensing danger, sent couriers to Burgoyne asking for reinforcements.

American forces were led by veteran officer Brig. Gen. John Stark. Stark sent out calls for reinforcements, and soldiers led by Col. Seth Warner was among the forces that responded. On August 16, 1777, after a day of non-stop rain, more than a thousand American militiamen attacked Baum's command in Walloomsac, New York, about 10 miles from Bennington.

Hoping that poor weather might delay an American advance and that reinforcements from Burgoyne would soon arrive, Baum's troops had constructed a small redoubt on a hill. When the weather cleared that afternoon, the Americans made their move. Stark struck Baum's redoubt from two sides. The coordinated assault succeeded in no small part because Baum thought the American militia that were approaching were allies sent from Burgoyne. After heavy fighting, American forces were able to breach the small redoubt. It was a desperate struggle, and former friends who had grown up together in the surrounding area found themselves facing off with each other as patriots and loyalists.

Patriot forces surrounded Baum and his men. Unfortunately for Baum, his reinforcements arrived just after the battle concluded. The defeat placed a major strain on Burgoyne's army, which, in addition to the casualties suffered, never secured the needed provisions. Burgoyne's Native American allies lost confidence in him and left his army. The Battle of Bennington was the precursor of worse things to come for Burgoyne and his army.

✳ ✳ PRESERVATION ✳ ✳

To date, the **American Battlefield Trust** has saved **23.10 acres** at Bennington Battlefield.

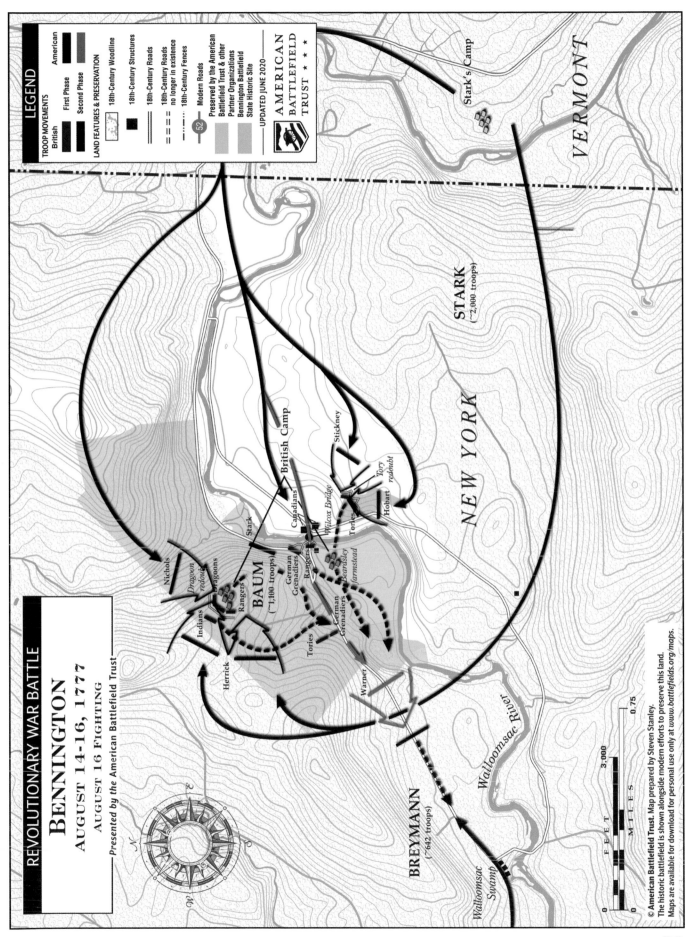

BATTLE *of* SARATOGA

(FREEMAN'S FARM)

SEPTEMBER 19, 1777

IN THE FALL OF 1777, THE WHEELS BEGAN TO COME OFF OF JOHN BURGOYNE'S northern campaign. Early victories at Fort Ticonderoga, Fort Ann, and Hubbardton gave way to defeat at Fort Stanwix and Bennington. The British strategy called for a three-pronged attack coordinated by three separate British armies converging on Albany, New York. The force moving from Lake Ontario and commanded by Lt. Col. Barry St. Leger had besieged Fort Stanwix, but could not crack its defense. A push up the Hudson River by General Sir Henry Clinton fizzled out due to Clinton's lack of aggression. Burgoyne's main force, moving south from Canada, came the closest to reaching its goal, but American resistance and supply problems plagued the 7,500-man force headed by Burgoyne himself. By mid-September, Burgoyne's army reached the northern outskirts of the small village of Saratoga.

The Americans had problems of their own—namely, disfunction at their highest command levels. General Philip Schuyler commanded the Northern Department, but he was disliked by the New England militiamen, and a faction in Congress wanted to replace him. General Horatio Gates, a former British officer turned Patriot, commanded the Northern Department for a time before being replaced by Schuyler, and then Schuyler was once again replaced by Gates. This turnstile command structure hampered early efforts to slow Burgoyne, and it contributed to the loss of Fort Ticonderoga.

On August 4, 1777, Gates assumed command of the Northern Department. He was supported by two capable subordinates, Gen. Benedict Arnold and Col. Daniel Morgan, leader of a storied Virginia rifle regiment. Gates's army numbered some 8,500 men. To disrupt the British advance south, the American commander ordered his men to erect defenses on the crest of Bemis Heights, which was part of a series of bluffs from which both the Hudson River and the paralleling road could be seen. From there, American artillery had the range to hit both the river and the road. In order to attack, the British would have to use the road because the forest and vegetation to the east were too dense to permit effective troop movements.

The Americans erected fortifications that extended about three-quarters of a mile, creating a line shaped like a large "L." Twenty-two cannons were emplaced along the line, providing the Americans with ample artillery cover.

On September 19, 1777, Burgoyne divided his army into three columns. He wanted to use each column to probe American defenses. Morgan's Virginians engaged with the center column on September 19 near the farm of Loyalist John Freeman. It was a hotly contested fight. Gates reinforced Morgan, and a see-saw action occurred throughout the afternoon. Patriots captured British cannon only to have them retaken by the enemy. Morgan and Arnold led counterattacks as American riflemen wreaked havoc on the Tory officer corps. By evening, the British held the field, but the action had blunted their forward motion. Hoping to be reinforced by Clinton from New York City, Burgoyne chose to dig in and wait out the Americans until help arrived.

Help arrived, but for the rebels rather than the British.

✳ ✳ PRESERVATION ✳ ✳

To date, the **American Battlefield Trust** has not saved any land at Freeman's Farm Battlefield.

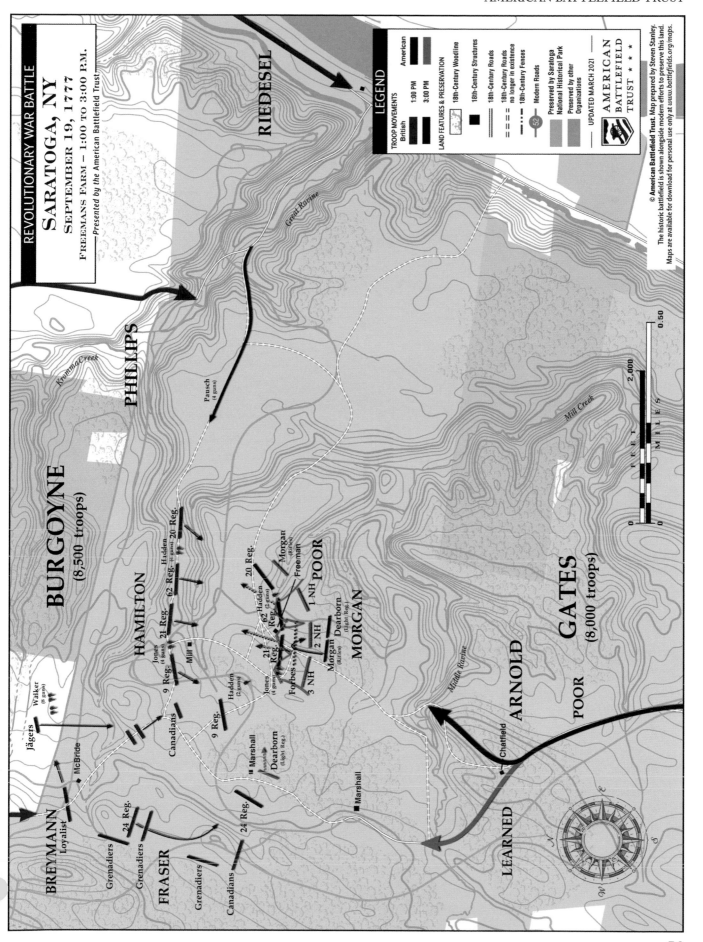

REVOLUTIONARY WAR BATTLE

SARATOGA, NY

SEPTEMBER 19, 1777

FREEMAN'S FARM – 1:00 TO 3:00 P.M.

Presented by the American Battlefield Trust.

LEGEND

TROOP MOVEMENTS
British   American

1:00 PM

3:00 PM

LAND FEATURES & PRESERVATION

18th-Century Woodline

18th-Century Structures

18th-Century Roads

18th-Century Roads
no longer in existence

18th-Century Fences

52   Modern Roads

Preserved by Saratoga
National Historical Park

Preserved by other
Organizations

UPDATED MARCH 2021

AMERICAN
BATTLEFIELD
TRUST ★ ★ ★

© **American Battlefield Trust.** Map prepared by Steven Stanley.
The historic battlefield is shown alongside modern efforts to preserve this land.
Maps are available for download for personal use only at *www.battlefields.org/maps.*

RIEDESEL

Great Ravine

PHILLIPS

Pausch
(4 guns)

KronmaCreek

BURGOYNE

(8,500 troops)

HAMILTON

Walker
(8 guns)

Jägers

McBride

Hadden
20 Reg.

62 Reg. (4 guns)

21 Reg.

Jones
(4 guns)

9 Reg.

Mill

Canadians

9 Reg.

Hadden
(2 guns)

Marshall

Dearborn
(Light Reg.)

20 Reg.

Morgan
(Rifles)

Freeman

62 Hadden
(2 guns)

21
Reg.

Jones
(4 guns)

Forbes

Morgan
(Rifles)

2 NH

Dearborn
(Light Reg.)

1 NH POOR

MORGAN

3 NH

Middle Ravine

Mill Creek

Chatfield

ARNOLD

GATES

(8,000 troops)

POOR

BREYMANN

Loyalist

24 Reg.

Grenadiers

Grenadiers

FRASER

Grenadiers

24 Reg.

Canadians

Marshall

Dearborn
(Light Reg.)

LEARNED

FEET   2,000

0   0.50
MILES

BATTLE *of* GERMANTOWN

OCTOBER 4, 1777

WITH THE AMERICAN CAPITAL IN BRITISH HANDS, WILLIAM HOWE left a contingent of some 3,000 British soldiers in Philadelphia and then moved the remainder of his army north of the city to Germantown, Pennsylvania, on the banks of the Schuylkill River.

Smarting from the defeat at Brandywine, the loss of the capital, and another defeat at Paoli, George Washington sought to take the fight to the enemy before winter descended upon the colonies. After locating Howe's main force, Washington conceived an overly complicated plan that sought to coordinate four columns moving in the night to converge simultaneously on an enemy position. If all went well, Washington's columns would perform a double envelopment and bag Howe's army. Even for a veteran European army of the age, this was a tall order.

Washington set his plan into motion on the night of October 3. Harkening back to Trenton, he divided his army so as to attack the British from multiple directions at dawn. General John Sullivan would attack with the main force while Gen. Nathanael Greene attacked on the British right flank. The militia, under Gen. William Smallwood, would target the British extreme right and rear. Unfortunately for Washington, darkness and a heavy fog delayed the advance and cost him the element of surprise.

Sullivan's column was the first to make contact, driving back the British pickets. The British were so shocked to find a large force of American soldiers that some were cut off from the main body: 120 men under British Col. Thomas Musgrave took shelter in the large stone house of Pennsylvania Supreme Court Chief Justice Benjamin Chew, known as Cliveden. This fortified position proved a thorn in the Americans' side for the remainder of the battle, with numerous assaults being repulsed with heavy casualties. While the fighting around Cliveden raged on, Sullivan pushed his men towards the British center.

On the American left, a division commanded by Gen. Anthony Wayne became separated in the fog. To make matters worse, Sullivan's men began running low on ammunition. The separation, combined with the lack of fire from their comrades and the commotion of the attack on Cliveden behind them, convinced Wayne's men that they were cut off, causing them to withdraw.

Greene's column arrived in time to engage the British before they could rout Wayne. Unfortunately, one of Greene's brigades mistook Wayne's men for the British and opened fire. Wayne's men returned fire. The resulting firefight caused both units to break and flee the field. Eventually, elements of these forces rallied to fight later during the British pursuit from the field.

Washington was thwarted and forced to break off the engagement. Only the steadfastness of Greene's and Wayne's men, with support from the American artillery, prevented the retreat from becoming a disaster. Despite the British victory, many Europeans, especially the French, were impressed by the continued determination of the Continental Army.

✸ ✸ PRESERVATION ✸ ✸

To date, the **American Battlefield Trust** has not saved any land at Germantown Battlefield.

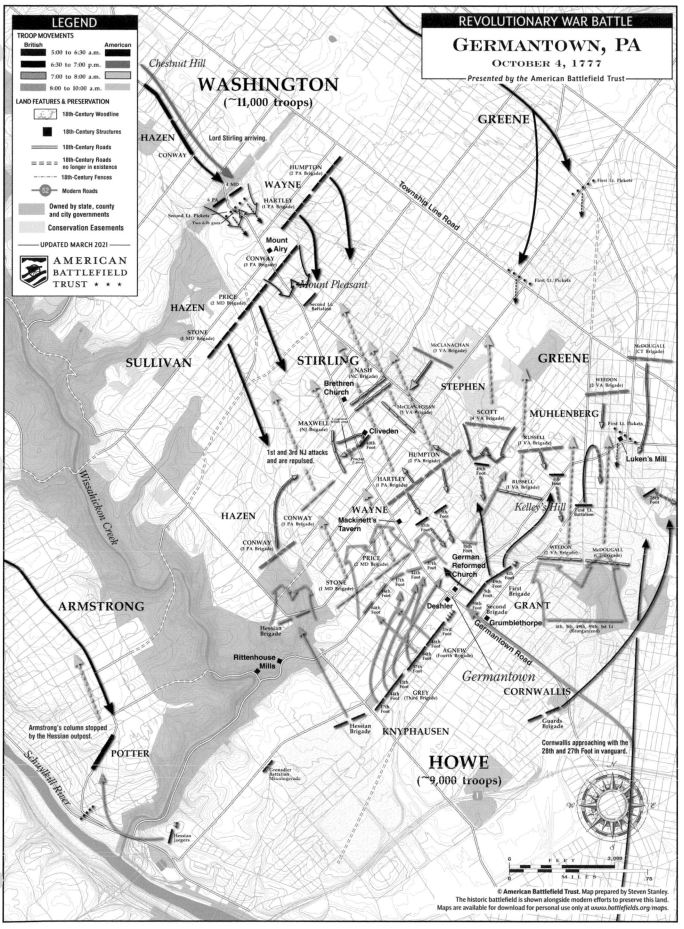

LEGEND

TROOP MOVEMENTS

British	American
5:00 to 6:30 a.m.	
6:30 to 7:00 p.m.	
7:00 to 8:00 a.m.	
8:00 to 10:00 a.m.	

LAND FEATURES & PRESERVATION

18th-Century Woodline

18th-Century Structures

18th-Century Roads

18th-Century Roads no longer in existence

18th-Century Fences

52 Modern Roads

Owned by state, county and city governments

Conservation Easements

— UPDATED MARCH 2021 —

AMERICAN BATTLEFIELD TRUST ★ ★ ★

WASHINGTON
(~11,000 troops)

HOWE
(~9,000 troops)

© **American Battlefield Trust**. Map prepared by Steven Stanley.
The historic battlefield is shown alongside modern efforts to preserve this land.
Maps are available for download for personal use only at *www.battlefields.org/maps*.

BATTLE *of* SARATOGA

(BEMIS HEIGHTS)

OCTOBER 7, 1777

WHILE THE BRITISH OFFENSIVE DOWN THE HUDSON RIVER STALLED, the American army grew to more than 13,000 strong. Prior to the Battle of Freeman's Farm, an incident occurred between Burgoyne's Native American allies and local civilians. In the weeks leading up to the battle of Freeman's Farm, Native American warriors captured a group of women, then killed and scalped one of them. Although Burgoyne and many of the British officers were outraged and condemned the attack, Patriot newspapers turned the story into wartime propaganda. The death of Jane McCrea steeled Patriot resolve against Burgoyne and his army even as the incident undermined Burgoyne's stature with his Native allies because he questioned the word of a warrior and called for a tribunal to investigate the incident.

Now, in October, the grim reality of the situation was setting in on the British officers: Supplies were running low; the army's Native American allies had largely abandoned them; St. Leger's force was to be of no assistance; Clinton's advance stalled 40 miles to the south; and Howe was too far away and too preoccupied with his own campaign to offer anything but a few letters of correspondence.

On the American side, the command situation that should have been remedied when Gates assumed command was instead exacerbated by the senior officer. Gates and his biggest fan—himself—clashed with his egotistical subordinate Benedict Arnold. The clash of egos came to a head when Gates did not acknowledge Arnold's vital role in the victory at Freeman's Farm. Arnold and Gates jabbed at one another through correspondence, but by the second battle of Saratoga, the two men seemed to have buried the hatchet.

On the morning of October 7, 1777, Burgoyne launched a reconnaissance in force led by his most trusted subordinate, Gen. Simon Fraser. Roughly 1,500 British and Hessian officers and men moved south toward the American lines. Gates countered, moving a force overseen by Arnold to meet this threat. In the ensuing fight, Fraser was mortally wounded. The American offensive was too much for the tory forces, and they fell back to two substantial redoubts—Balcarres (Light Infantry) and Breymann's Redoubts—as the rebels pressed their advantage.

Balcarres Redoubt was a formidable and well-defended position. The American forces failed to take the stronghold in a frontal assault, but galloping onto the scene came Arnold, who drove the attack home. Focused on the weaker Breymann Redoubt, rebels surged around the sides of the redoubt, taking the defenders in the rear. The 200 or so defenders were quickly overwhelmed, and Arnold fell wounded.

On the morning of October 8, Burgoyne's army attempted to escape north, but a cold, hard rain forced them to stop and encamp near the town of Saratoga. Burgoyne's army surrendered on October 17, 1777. The Americans proved their worth on the battlefield against the greatest army in the world, lifting flagging American morale, inspiring the cause of independence further, and convincing the French and, later, other European nations to back the new United States. The Continental Congress signed a formal Treaty of Alliance with the French, and the balance of the war tipped in favor of the Americans.

✳ ✳ PRESERVATION ✳ ✳

To date, the **American Battlefield Trust** has not saved any land at Bemis Heights Battlefield.
To date, the **American Battlefield Trust** has saved **25.83 acres** at Saratoga Siege.

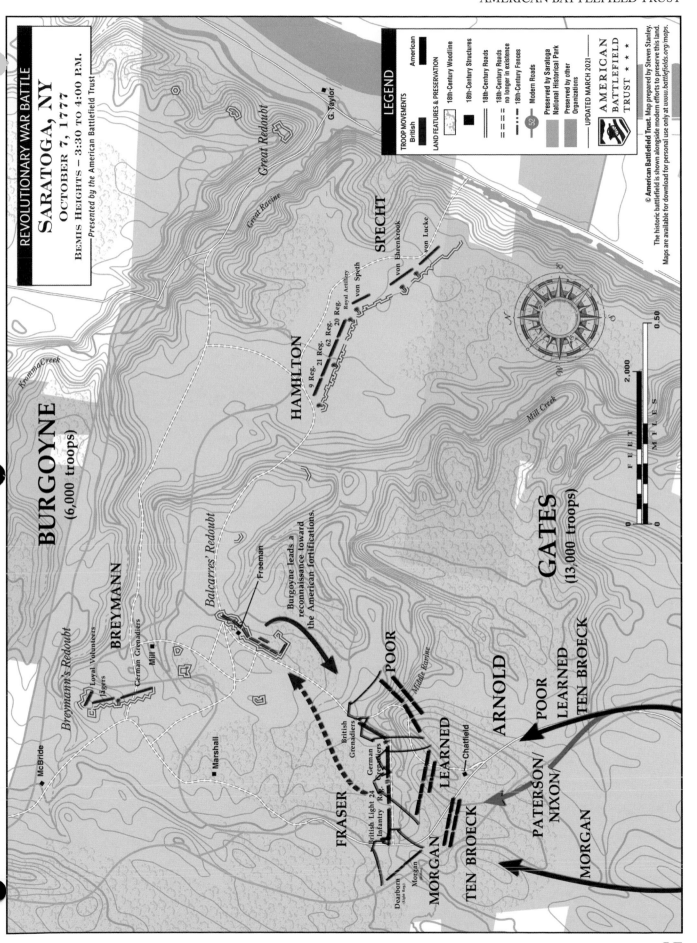

REVOLUTIONARY WAR BATTLE
SARATOGA, NY
OCTOBER 7, 1777
BEMIS HEIGHTS – 3:30 TO 4:00 P.M.
Presented by the American Battlefield Trust

LEGEND

TROOP MOVEMENTS
British   American

LAND FEATURES & PRESERVATION
18th-Century Woodline
18th-Century Structures
18th-Century Roads
18th-Century Roads no longer in existence
18th-Century Fences
Modern Roads

Preserved by Saratoga National Historical Park
Preserved by other Organizations

UPDATED MARCH 2021

AMERICAN BATTLEFIELD TRUST ★ ★ ★

© American Battlefield Trust. Map prepared by Steven Stanley.
The historic battlefield is shown alongside modern efforts to preserve this land.
Maps are available for download for personal use only at *www.battlefields.org/maps.*

BURGOYNE
(6,000 troops)

GATES
(13,000 troops)

Great Redoubt

G. Taylor

Great Ravine

SPECHT

von Lucke
von Ehrenkrook
von Speth
Royal Artillery
20 Reg.
62 Reg.
21 Reg.
9 Reg.

HAMILTON

Krumma Creek

BREYMANN

Breymann's Redoubt

Loyal Volunteers
Jägers
German Grenadiers
Mill
McBride

Balcarres' Redoubt

Freeman

Burgoyne leads a reconnaissance toward the American fortifications.

Marshall

POOR

Middle Ravine

ARNOLD

POOR
LEARNED
TEN BROECK

LEARNED

Chatfield

PATERSON/ NIXON/ MORGAN

FRASER

British Grenadiers
German Grenadiers
British Light Infantry
24 Reg.

MORGAN

TEN BROECK

Morgan guns

Dearborn
(Light Regs.)

Mill Creek

FEET   2,000
MILES   0.50

65

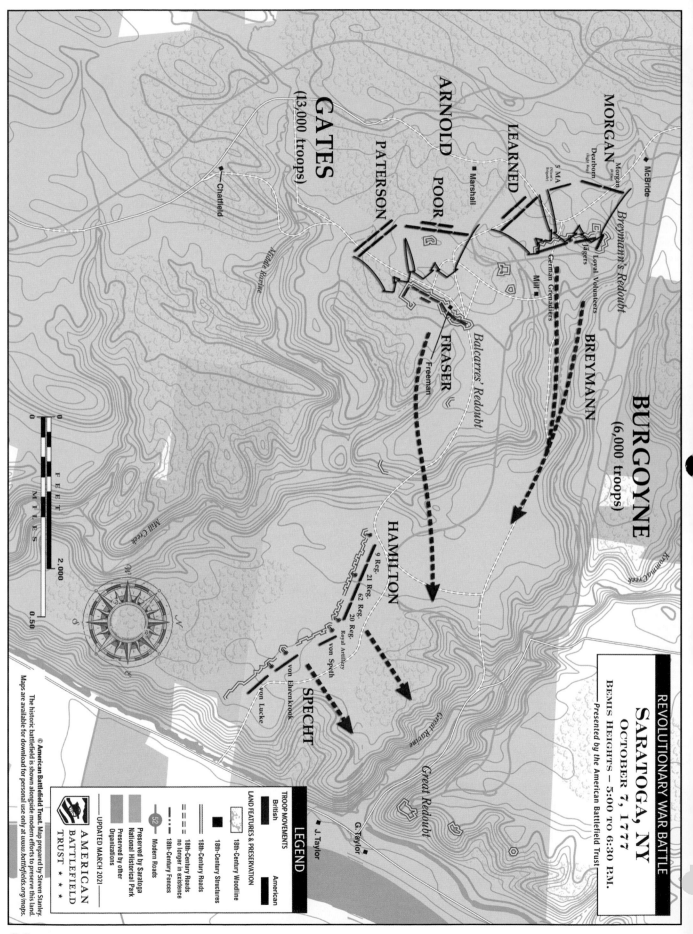

REVOLUTIONARY WAR BATTLE

SARATOGA, NY
OCTOBER 7, 1777 — 5:00 TO 6:30 P.M.
BEMIS HEIGHTS

Presented by the American Battlefield Trust

BURGOYNE
(6,000 troops)

GATES
(13,000 troops)

MORGAN
ARNOLD
LEARNED
PATERSON
POOR
FRASER
BREYMANN
HAMILTON
SPECHT

Dearborn
Morgan
5 MA
Marshall
Jägers
German Grenadiers
Loyal Volunteers
Mill
Freeman
McBride
Chatfield

Breymann's Redoubt
Balcarres' Redoubt

9 Reg.
21 Reg.
62 Reg.
20 Reg.
Royal Artillery
von Speth
von Lucke
von Ehrenkrook

Great Redoubt
Great Ravine

Mill Creek
Middle Ravine

Kromma Creek
Kromma Creek

G. Taylor
J. Taylor

LEGEND

LAND FEATURES & PRESERVATION

18th-Century Woodline

18th-Century Structures

18th-Century Roads

18th-Century Roads
no longer in existence

Modern Roads

18th-Century Fences

52 Preserved by other
Organizations

Preserved by Saratoga
National Historical Park

TROOP MOVEMENTS

British
American

UPDATED MARCH 2021

AMERICAN
BATTLEFIELD
TRUST ★ ★ ★

FEET
MILES
0
2,000
0.50

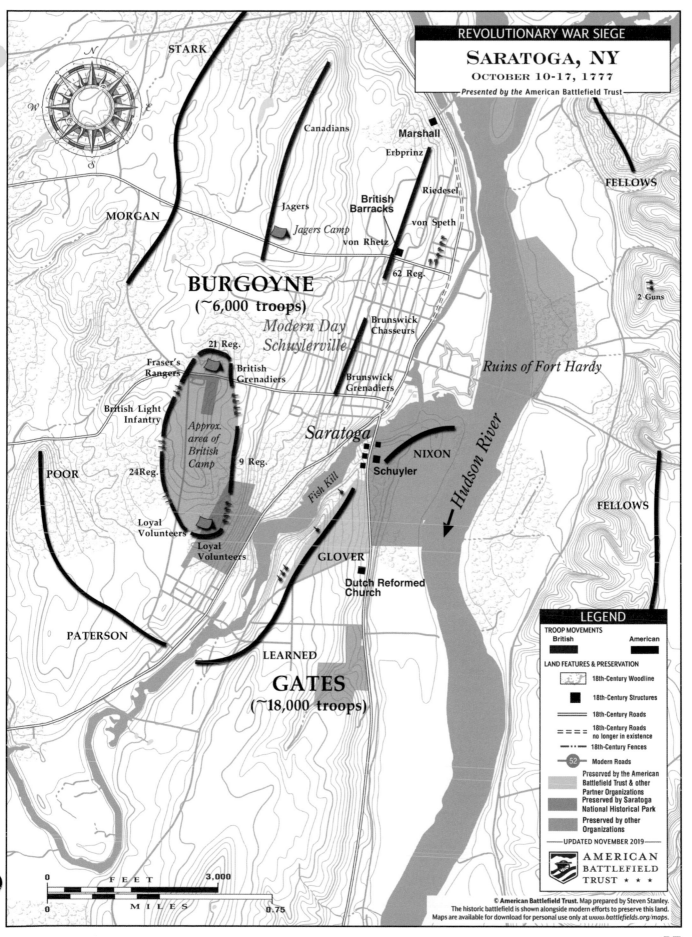

STARK

N

Canadians

Marshall

Erbprinz

FELLOWS

Riedesel

MORGAN

Jagers

British Barracks

von Speth

Jagers Camp

von Rhetz

62 Reg.

2 Guns

BURGOYNE
(~6,000 troops)

Brunswick
Chasseurs

Modern Day
Schuylerville

21 Reg.

Fraser's
Rangers

Ruins of Fort Hardy

British
Grenadiers

Brunswick
Grenadiers

British Light
Infantry

Approx.
area of
British
Camp

Saratoga

NIXON

POOR

24Reg.

9 Reg.

Schuyler

Fish Kill

Hudson River

FELLOWS

Loyal
Volunteers

Loyal
Volunteers

GLOVER

PATERSON

Dutch Reformed
Church

LEARNED

GATES
(~18,000 troops)

REVOLUTIONARY WAR SIEGE
SARATOGA, NY
OCTOBER 10-17, 1777
Presented by the American Battlefield Trust

LEGEND

TROOP MOVEMENTS
British   American

LAND FEATURES & PRESERVATION

18th-Century Woodline

18th-Century Structures

18th-Century Roads

18th-Century Roads
no longer in existence

18th-Century Fences

52 — Modern Roads

Preserved by the American
Battlefield Trust & other
Partner Organizations
Preserved by Saratoga
National Historical Park
Preserved by other
Organizations

— UPDATED NOVEMBER 2019 —

AMERICAN
BATTLEFIELD
TRUST ★ ★ ★

FEET   3,000

MILES   0.75

© **American Battlefield Trust**. Map prepared by Steven Stanley.
The historic battlefield is shown alongside modern efforts to preserve this land.
Maps are available for download for personal use only at *www.battlefields.org/maps*.

BATTLE *of* MONMOUTH

JUNE 28, 1778

THE LONG WINTER OF 1777-1778 AT VALLEY FORGE GAVE A NEW BIRTH to the Continental Army. The harsh Pennsylvania winter steeled the resolve of the patriots who stuck with the army, and that steel was polished into a refined weapon by Prussian drillmaster Friedrich Wilhelm von Steuben. Months of seemingly endless drill worked to professionalize the ragtag army and instill a new confidence in the officers and men.

In the late spring of 1778, William Howe's resignation as commander of the King's forces in North America was accepted, and the apathetic General Sir Henry Clinton assumed the helm of the slowly sinking ship. On June 18, 1778, Clinton began the British evacuation from Philadelphia, falling back toward New York City.

Lying in wait at Valley Forge, Washington quickly moved out in pursuit of Clinton. Washington and his senior subordinate, Gen. Charles Lee, attacked rearguard elements of the British Army in New Jersey on the unbearably hot and humid morning of June 28, 1778.

Like Horatio Gates, Charles Lee was a former British officer turned Patriot who likewise had an overinflated sense of self-worth. Lee, who launched the attack with a 2-1 advantage over his adversary, did not press his advantage because he had little confidence in the ability of the Continental Army. In doing so, he ceded the initiative to his British counterpart, and Clinton's most capable subordinate, Charles Cornwallis.

What had opened as a promising assault by the Americans devolved into a potential rout. Confusion reigned, and the temperature rose to near 100 degrees.

Washington's temper was, too, on the rise. Enraged by Lee's ineptitude, Washington galloped ahead of his wing and, in an angry confrontation on the field of battle, removed Lee from command.

Washington then rallied what troops remained to continue their assault and pursuit of the British. The delaying action led by Washington gave time for the rest of the Continental Army to come up and join the battle. Washington's troops took a position near a ravine on the grounds of the Monmouth Court House. Washington stabilized his lines and bolstered his position with artillery.

Cornwallis attacked but was held at bay by the Continentals. An American counterattack on the British right flank forced them back and forced them to reorganize. The commencement of fighting prompted Cornwallis to move his troops towards the growing fight, which shifted back and forth under the brutal June sun for several hours.

By 6:00 p.m., the British called off the fight. Not wanting to give Washington a chance to renew the battle in the morning, the British slipping away under the cover of darkness and resuming their withdrawal to New York City. Clinton holed up in New York while Washington once again waited and watched from a respectable distance. The British efforts to subjugate or isolate the Northern Colonies had failed. It was time for the British to try their hand at war in another theater and for the patriots to undertake their own offensives.

✳ ✳ PRESERVATION ✳ ✳

To date, the **American Battlefield Trust** has not saved any land at Monmouth Battlefield.

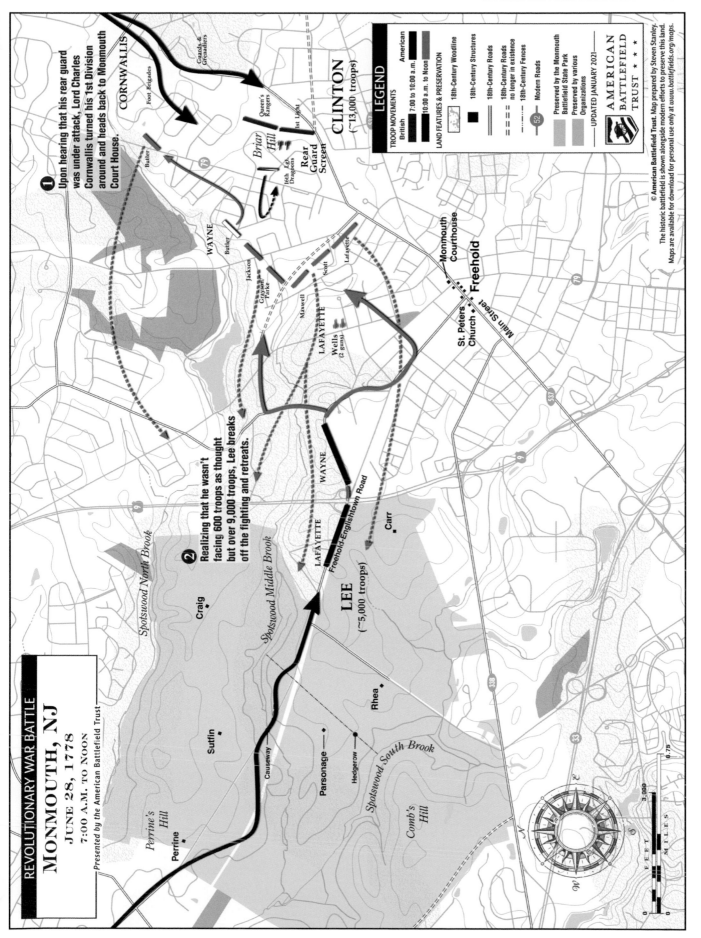

REVOLUTIONARY WAR BATTLE
MONMOUTH, NJ
JUNE 28, 1778
7:00 A.M. TO NOON
Presented by the American Battlefield Trust

1 Upon hearing that his rear guard was under attack, Lord Charles Cornwallis turned his 1st Division around and heads back to Monmouth Court House.

2 Realizing that he wasn't facing 600 troops as thought but over 9,000 troops, Lee breaks off the fighting and retreats.

CORNWALLIS

CLINTON
(~13,000 troops)

LEE
(~5,000 troops)

Guards & Grenadiers
Foot Brigades
Queen's Rangers
Briar Hill
1st Light
Rear Guard Screen
16th Lgt Dragoons
Butler
WAYNE
Butler
Jackson
Crayson's Parke
Scott
Maxwell
Lafayette
LAFAYETTE
Wells (2 guns)

Monmouth Courthouse
St. Peters Church
Freehold
Main Street

WAYNE
LAFAYETTE
Freehold-Englishtown Road
Carr
Rhea

Spotswood North Brook
Craig
Spotswood Middle Brook
Sutfin
Causeway
Parsonage
Hedgerow
Spotswood South Brook
Perrine's Hill
Perrine
Comb's Hill

LEGEND
TROOP MOVEMENTS
British | American
7:00 to 10:00 a.m.
10:00 a.m. to Noon

LAND FEATURES & PRESERVATION
18th-Century Woodline
18th-Century Structures
18th-Century Roads
18th-Century Roads no longer in existence
18th-Century Fences
Modern Roads
52
Preserved by the Monmouth Battlefield State Park
Preserved by various Organizations

UPDATED JANUARY 2021

AMERICAN BATTLEFIELD TRUST ★ ★ ★

© American Battlefield Trust. Map prepared by Steven Stanley. The historic battlefield is shown alongside modern efforts to preserve this land. Maps are available for download for personal use only at www.battlefields.org/maps.

MILES
FEET
3,000
0.75

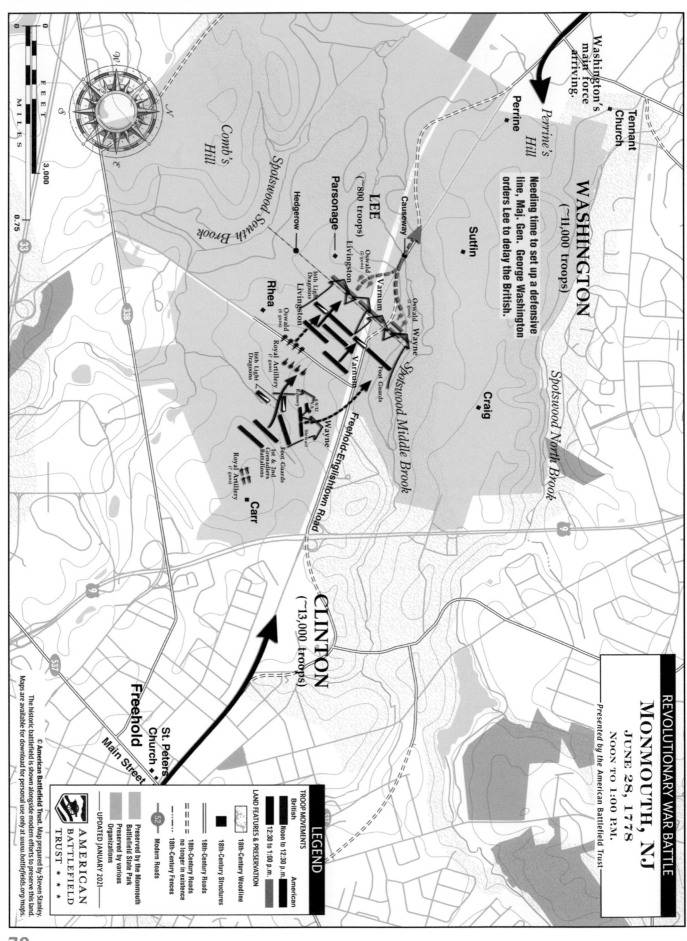

REVOLUTIONARY WAR BATTLE

MONMOUTH, NJ
JUNE 28, 1778
NOON TO 1:00 P.M.

Presented by the American Battlefield Trust

Washington's main force arriving.

Tennant Church

Perrine

WASHINGTON
(~11,000 troops)

Comb's Hill

Perrine's Hill

Spotswood South Brook

Causeway

Hedgerow

Parsonage

LEE
(~800 troops)

Needing time to set up a defensive line, Maj. Gen. George Washington orders Lee to delay the British.

Sutfin

Livingston

Oswald (2 guns)

Varnum

Oswald (2 guns)

Wayne

Foot Guards

Spotswood Middle Brook

Rhea

Livingston

16th Light Dragoons

Oswald (4 guns)

Varnum

Royal Artillery (? guns)

16th Light Dragoons

Ramsey

1st/2d

Stewart

Wayne

Craig

Freehold-Englishtown Road

Foot Guards

1st & 2nd Grenadiers Battalions

Royal Artillery (? guns)

Carr

CLINTON
(~13,000 troops)

Freehold

Main Street

St. Peters Church

Spotswood North Brook

LEGEND

TROOP MOVEMENTS
- British — Noon to 12:30 p.m.
- American — 12:30 to 1:00 p.m.

LAND FEATURES & PRESERVATION
- 18th-Century Woodline
- 18th-Century Structures
- 18th-Century Roads
- 18th-Century Roads no longer in existence
- 18th-Century Fences
- Modern Roads
- Preserved by the Monmouth Battlefield State Park
- Preserved by various Organizations

UPDATED JANUARY 2021

AMERICAN BATTLEFIELD TRUST ★ ★ ★

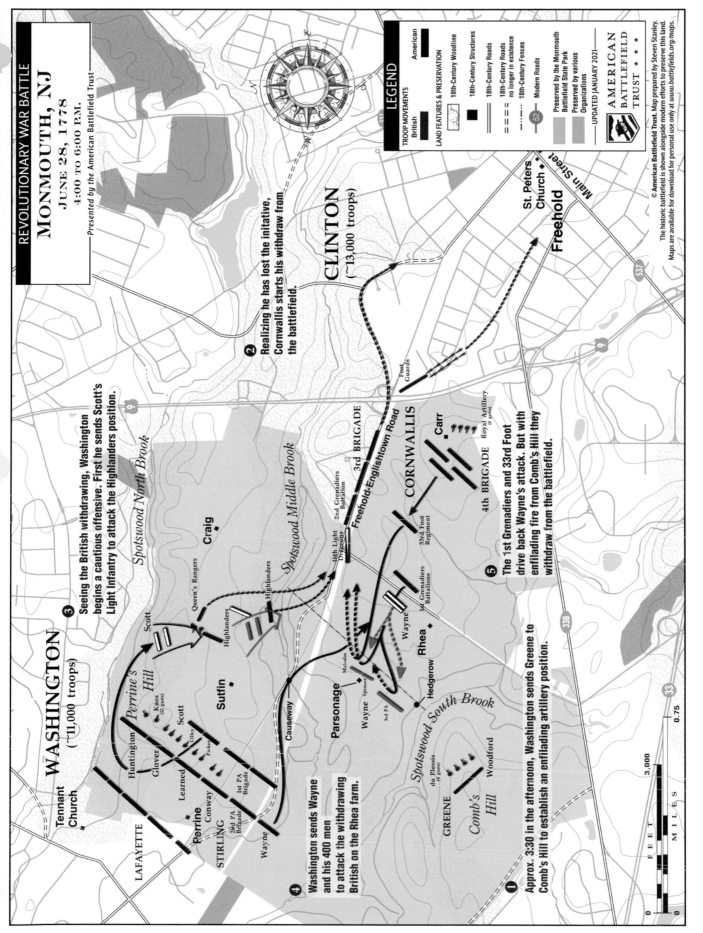

REVOLUTIONARY WAR BATTLE
MONMOUTH, NJ
JUNE 28, 1778
4:00 TO 6:00 P.M.
Presented by the American Battlefield Trust

LEGEND

TROOP MOVEMENTS
British / American

LAND FEATURES & PRESERVATION
18th-Century Woodline / American

18th-Century Structures

18th-Century Roads

18th-Century Roads no longer in existence

18th-Century Fences

52 Modern Roads

Preserved by the Monmouth Battlefield State Park

Preserved by various Organizations

— UPDATED JANUARY 2021 —

AMERICAN BATTLEFIELD TRUST ★ ★ ★

© American Battlefield Trust. Map prepared by Steven Stanley. The historic battlefield is shown alongside modern efforts to preserve this land. Maps are available for download for personal use only at *www.battlefields.org/maps*.

WASHINGTON (~11,000 troops)

CLINTON (~13,000 troops)

③ Seeing the British withdrawing, Washington begins a cautious offensive. First he sends Scott's Light Infantry to attack the Highlanders position.

② Realizing he has lost the initative, Cornwallis starts his withdraw from the battlefield.

④ Washington sends Wayne and his 400 men to attack the withdrawing British on the Rhea farm.

① Approx. 3:30 in the afternoon, Washington sends Greene to Comb's Hill to establish an enfilading artillery position.

⑤ The 1st Grenadiers and 33rd Foot drive back Wayne's attack. But with enfilading fire from Comb's Hill they withdraw from the battlefield.

Tennant Church

LAFAYETTE

Perrine's Hill

STIRLING

Perrine

Conway

2nd PA Brigade

Huntington

Glover

Learned

Scott

Knox (12 guns)

Cilley

Parker

1st PA Brigade

Scott

Suffin

Causeway

Wayne

Parsonage

Wayne

Spencer

3rd PA

Rhea

Hedgerow

Malcolm

GREENE

Comb's Hill

du Plessis (4 guns)

Woodford

Spotswood South Brook

Spotswood Middle Brook

Spotswood North Brook

Craig

Queen's Rangers

Highlanders

Highlanders

16th Light Dragoons

2nd Grenadiers Battalion

Freehold-Englishtown Road

3rd BRIGADE

CORNWALLIS

33rd Foot Regiment

1st Grenadiers Battalions

4th BRIGADE

Carr

Royal Artillery (4 guns)

Foot Guards

St. Peters Church

Freehold

Main Street

33B

33

537

9

0.75

3,000

FEET

MILES

SIEGE *of* FORT VINCENNES

FEBRUARY 23 – 25, 1779

ONE OF THE MOST AUDACIOUS CAMPAIGNS OF THE REVOLUTIONARY WAR centered around the siege of Fort Vincennes, located along the Wabash River near the border of modern-day Indiana and Illinois. The fortification was constructed of timber and served to guard the expanding western frontier. British Lieutenant Governor Edward Abbott began construction in 1777. He was succeeded by Lieutenant Governor Henry Hamilton, who arrived in late 1778 with a force of 90 British Regulars and some 200 Native American allies. Hamilton was upset by the design and state of the fort and immediately began work on strengthening the defenses. The fort was roughly square, with blockhouses on the northeast and southwest corners, a barracks, magazine, and gatehouse. The strongest parts of the fort were the blockhouses, made of thick timbers, rendering them nearly musket-proof, and mounting a three-pounder cannon each. By February of 1779, Hamilton had completed the major construction, but the stockades were still in a poor condition.

Patriot leaders were tipped off to the British exploits in the area. Lieutenant Colonel George Rogers Clark had cleared the Northwest Territory of British threats in 1778, but Hamilton's garrison at Vincennes threatened to tip the balance of power back in the favor of the British.

Clark, the older brother of William Clark of "Lewis and Clark" fame, departed Kaskaskia on February 6, 1779, with 172 American and French-Canadian militiamen. The 180-mile expedition proved to be extremely difficult, even by frontier standards. While the winter was not cold, it was exceedingly wet, forcing the men to endure soggy conditions and wade through standing water in multiple places. By the time Clark arrived at Vincennes on February 23, food had also run dangerously low.

Clark entered the town at sunset. The local population, many of them French, were sympathetic to the American cause and did not alert the fort or oppose Clark's approach. Despite a large commotion, Hamilton did not realize he was under attack until the fort came under fire. Clark ordered a barricade built facing the fort's gate, and both sides traded fire throughout the night. Clark split his men into small groups, spreading them out to give the illusion of greater numbers. On the morning of the 24th, Clark demanded Hamilton's unconditional surrender, which was rejected, but Hamilton agreed to meet Clark to discuss terms.

In the interim, one of the most controversial and brutal episodes of the frontier wars occurred. A war party of Natives Americans and French-Canadians entered the town, unaware of the American occupation. After a short skirmish, Clark captured six and forced the rest to flee. Releasing the two French prisoners, Clark had the four Natives tomahawked to death in view of the fort and then scalped and thrown in the river. Clarke intended this to be both a deterrent and an act of revenge for the raids throughout the frontier. He never denied or apologized for the action.

At 10 a.m. on February 25, Hamilton surrendered the fort, which the Americans renamed Fort Patrick Henry. The war on the frontier continued for years, but played no major role in bringing an end to the conflict.

✳ ✳ **PRESERVATION** ✳ ✳

To date, the **American Battlefield Trust** has not saved any land at Fort Vincennes.

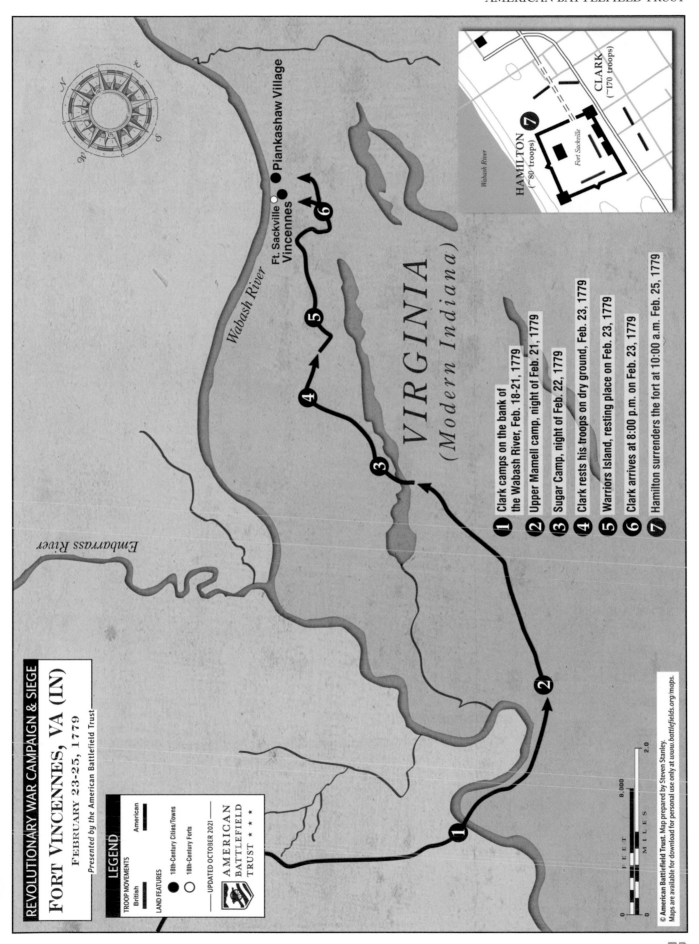

REVOLUTIONARY WAR CAMPAIGN & SIEGE
FORT VINCENNES, VA (IN)
FEBRUARY 23-25, 1779
Presented by the American Battlefield Trust

LEGEND

TROOP MOVEMENTS
British
American

LAND FEATURES
● 18th-Century Cities/Towns
○ 18th-Century Forts
—— UPDATED OCTOBER 2021 ——
★ ★ ★ 18th-Century Forts ★ ★ ★

AMERICAN BATTLEFIELD TRUST

VIRGINIA
(Modern Indiana)

Embarrass River

Wabash River

● Piankashaw Village
○ Ft. Sackville
● Vincennes

① Clark camps on the bank of the Wabash River, Feb. 18-21, 1779
② Upper Mamell camp, night of Feb. 21, 1779
③ Sugar Camp, night of Feb. 22, 1779
④ Clark rests his troops on dry ground, Feb. 23, 1779
⑤ Warriors Island, resting place on Feb. 23, 1779
⑥ Clark arrives at 8:00 p.m. on Feb. 23, 1779
⑦ Hamilton surrenders the fort at 10:00 a.m. Feb. 25, 1779

HAMILTON (~80 troops)
Fort Sackville
CLARK (~170 troops)
Wabash River
⑦

FEET 8,000
MILES 2.0

© American Battlefield Trust. Map prepared by Steven Stanley.
Maps are available for download for personal use only at www.battlefields.org/maps.

73

BATTLE *of* NEWTOWN

AUGUST 29, 1779

FOLLOWING THE AMERICAN VICTORY AT SARATOGA IN 1777, THE BRITISH began to shift their war efforts to the south. This change alleviated some of the pressure on Continental forces in the north, granting George Washington a much-needed reprieve to deal with Native American and Loyalist raids along the frontier, particularly in western Pennsylvania and in New York.

The American Revolution divided the Iroquois Confederacy, prompting the Mohawks, Cayugas, Onondagas, and Senecas to ally themselves with the British, while the Oneidas and Tuscaroras chose to support the rebels. This division transformed the frontier into a war zone, riddled with vicious raids undertaken by both sides. To break the deadlock, Washington ordered Gen. John Sullivan west in the summer of 1779 to subdue the Iroquois.

Sullivan's Expedition was tasked with stopping and ultimately eliminating the Iroquois threat. To achieve this, Sullivan employed a scorched-earth tactic, destroying villages and crops throughout the region. The Iroquois Chiefs, supported by limited numbers of British and Loyalist troops, avoided pitched battles wherever possible. As a result, most of the Expedition's clashes included small skirmishes or ambushes, with one exception at Newtown, New York.

Situated near the New York-Pennsylvania border along a bend in the Chemung River, Newtown's location played a pivotal role in the ensuing battle. The terrain at Newton favored a defensive position and ambush. A hill, flanked by marshy areas and a creek, commanded the road. The landscape prompted the 1,000 Iroquois and 200 Loyalist militiamen to construct an earthwork along the slope of the hill. Sayenqueraghta, the Iroquois leader, hoped to stop the Continental expedition here and protect the towns further along the river.

Sullivan's column left Fort Sullivan on August 26, 1779, and slowly proceeded up the Cayuga River. Around noon, the Patriot troops discovered the hidden breastworks and reported to Gen. Edward Hand, who deployed his light infantry to fire into the earthworks. The defenders tried repeatedly, though unsuccessfully, to lure the Continentals into an ambush before a lull fell over the field.

Sullivan called a council of war, which decided to pursue a complex double envelopment attack on the earthworks. To hold the enemy in place, one unit would feint in the center. Ten artillery pieces would bombard the earthworks and signal the general assault. Once the flanking units engaged, the feint would turn into a full assault.

The plan was complex but skillfully executed by Sullivan's well-trained troops. A brief counterattack by Joseph Brant almost cut off a portion of the American force. By nightfall, the battle was over, and the Patriot forces won the day. Sullivan operated virtually unopposed for the next month, allowing him to complete his expedition and end the Iroquois threat.

✳ ✳ PRESERVATION ✳ ✳

To date, the **American Battlefield Trust** has saved **68.24 acres** at Newtown Battlefield.

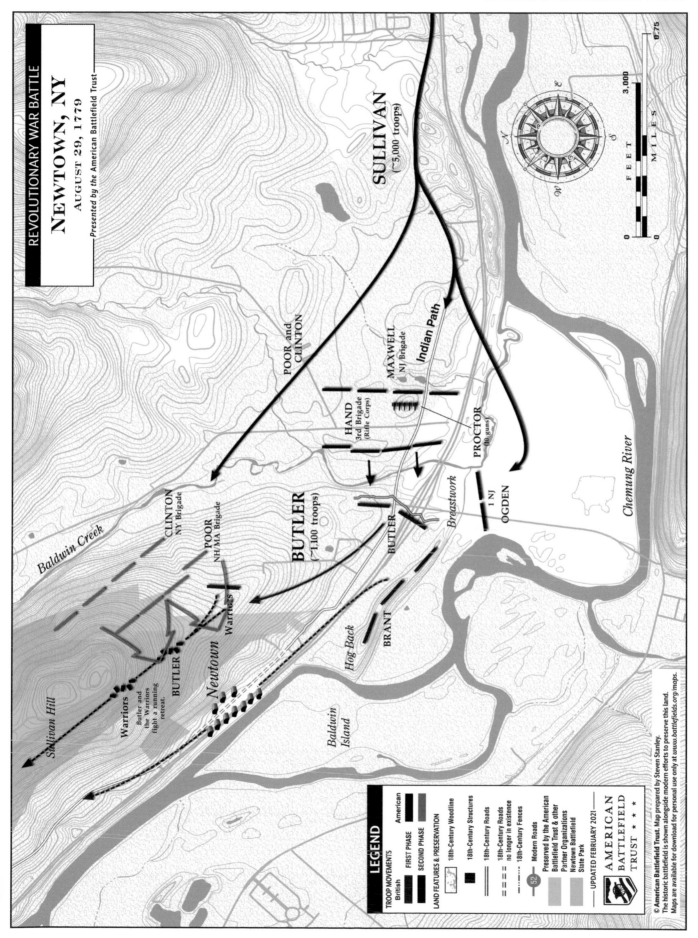

REVOLUTIONARY WAR BATTLE

NEWTOWN, NY

AUGUST 29, 1779

Presented by the American Battlefield Trust

SULLIVAN
(~5,000 troops)

POOR and CLINTON

MAXWELL
NJ Brigade

Indian Path

HAND
3rd Brigade
(Rifle Corps)

PROCTOR
(6 guns)

Chemung River

Breastwork

1 NJ
OGDEN

CLINTON
NY Brigade

POOR
NH/MA Brigade

BUTLER
(~1,100 troops)

BUTLER

Baldwin Creek

Warriors

Butler and the Warriors fight a running retreat.

Warriors

BUTLER

Newtown

Sullivan Hill

Hog Back

BRANT

Baldwin Island

LEGEND

TROOP MOVEMENTS
British   American

FIRST PHASE

SECOND PHASE

LAND FEATURES & PRESERVATION

18th-Century Woodline

18th-Century Structures

18th-Century Roads

18th-Century Roads no longer in existence

18th-Century Fences

52 Modern Roads

Preserved by the American Battlefield Trust & other Partner Organizations

Newtown Battlefield State Park

AMERICAN
BATTLEFIELD
TRUST ★ ★ ★ ★

UPDATED FEBRUARY 2021

FEET   3,000

MILES   0.75

THE SOUTHERN STRATEGY

1778-1781

IN THE WAKE OF THE SARATOGA CAMPAIGN, THE BRITISH HIGH COMMAND in London began to reassess how they prosecuted the war in North America. To many members of the Cabinet, New England was the problem child they could not discipline. It seemed as if this entire rebellion manifested itself in New England—from the Boston Tea Party to the Boston Massacre and the Battles of Lexington & Concord, New England was the hotbed of hotheads. Militarily, Crown forces attempted to suppress and then cut off the northern colonies from their sister colonies in the south—thus far, to no avail. The British needed a new strategy if the Empire in North America was to remain mostly intact.

Enter Charles Jenkinson, an undersecretary in the Treasury. Jenkinson suggested that the war effort be shifted from New England to the south. Why did he propose this new "Southern Strategy?" Simply put: economics. The New England colonies produced many of the same products and goods as the British Isles, but the Southern colonies were a different story. Rice, indigo, tobacco, and other cash crops abounded—crops that could not be produced in other parts of the Empire. The institution of chattel slavery helped to keep the wholesale prices of these products low, and British mercantilism could profit from cornering the market and selling the goods for substantial profits.

The undersecretary and others in London also felt that the Southern people supported Toryism and, by default, were more apt to take up arms as loyalists. These Loyalist forces could be relied upon to bolster the British war effort, lending manpower to an army that had been at war with the Empire's own colonists since 1775 while still having to maintain vast holdings elsewhere. If the Crown's forces could subdue the South and isolate it from their sister colonies, the Empire would have a powerful bargaining chip when it came to peace negotiations. From a coldly economic standpoint, if the New England colonies became independent, that was not as great of a loss to Britain financially as the loss of the Southern colonies.

As usual, the powers-that-be in London were out of touch with the war on the ground in North America. Apparently, they forgot about the Mecklenburg (N.C.) Resolves (1775), the Virginia Declaration of Rights (1776), and the Battles at Moore's Creek Bridge, Great Bridge, and Charleston (Sullivan's Island) earlier in the war. While they may not have been as vocal as their Northern brethren, the Southern colonies were just as prepared to fight for their independence.

In late 1778, the British renewed their dormant efforts to subjugate their Southern colonies by launching a foray into Georgia. As the southernmost rebellious colony, Georgia bordered Florida, which had come into British hands at the end of the Seven Years' War and was divided by the British into East and West Florida. It was believed that the Georgians would welcome Crown assistance and protection from Native Americans. On December 29, 1778, the city of Savannah fell to a tory expedition. As George Washington held the principal British army at bay in New York and nurtured the new Franco-American alliance, the battle for the fate of the British North American colonies now rested on the shoulders of patriots in the South. And these patriots were more than up to the task of throwing off the yolk of King George III.

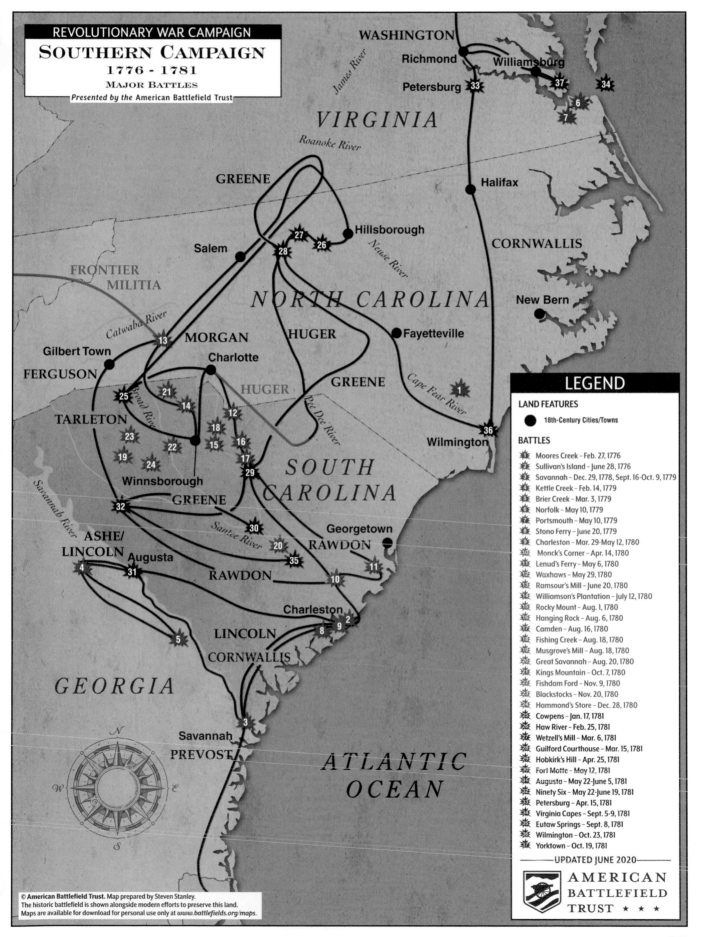

REVOLUTIONARY WAR CAMPAIGN
SOUTHERN CAMPAIGN
1776 - 1781
MAJOR BATTLES
Presented by the American Battlefield Trust

WASHINGTON

Richmond · Williamsburg

James River

Petersburg · 33 · 37 · 34

6
7

VIRGINIA

Roanoke River

GREENE

Halifax

Salem · 27 · 26 · Hillsborough

28 · **CORNWALLIS**

Neuse River

FRONTIER MILITIA

NORTH CAROLINA

New Bern

Catawba River

13 · **MORGAN** · **HUGER**

Gilbert Town · Charlotte · Fayetteville

FERGUSON · *HUGER* · **GREENE**

Cape Fear River

25 · 21 · 1

TARLETON · 14 · 12

23 · 22 · 18 · 16 · Wilmington · 36

19 · 15 · 17

24 · 29

Winnsborough · *SOUTH*

32 · **GREENE** · *CAROLINA*

Santee River · 30 · Georgetown

ASHE/ LINCOLN · Augusta · 20 · **RAWDON**

4 · 31 · 35 · 11

RAWDON · 10

5 · Charleston · 2

GEORGIA · **LINCOLN** · 8 · 9

CORNWALLIS

3

Savannah
PREVOST

ATLANTIC OCEAN

N
W · E
S

LEGEND

LAND FEATURES

● 18th-Century Cities/Towns

BATTLES

- Moores Creek – Feb. 27, 1776
- Sullivan's Island – June 28, 1776
- Savannah – Dec. 29, 1778, Sept. 16-Oct. 9, 1779
- Kettle Creek – Feb. 14, 1779
- Brier Creek – Mar. 3, 1779
- Norfolk – May 10, 1779
- Portsmouth – May 10, 1779
- Stono Ferry – June 20, 1779
- Charleston – Mar. 29-May 12, 1780
- Monck's Corner – Apr. 14, 1780
- Lenud's Ferry – May 6, 1780
- Waxhaws – May 29, 1780
- Ramsour's Mill – June 20, 1780
- Williamson's Plantation – July 12, 1780
- Rocky Mount – Aug. 1, 1780
- Hanging Rock – Aug. 6, 1780
- Camden – Aug. 16, 1780
- Fishing Creek – Aug. 18, 1780
- Musgrove's Mill – Aug. 18, 1780
- Great Savannah – Aug. 20, 1780
- Kings Mountain – Oct. 7, 1780
- Fishdam Ford – Nov. 9, 1780
- Blackstocks – Nov. 20, 1780
- Hammond's Store – Dec. 28, 1780
- Cowpens – Jan. 17, 1781
- Haw River – Feb. 25, 1781
- Wetzell's Mill – Mar. 6, 1781
- Guilford Courthouse – Mar. 15, 1781
- Hobkirk's Hill – Apr. 25, 1781
- Fort Motte – May 12, 1781
- Augusta – May 22-June 5, 1781
- Ninety Six – May 22-June 19, 1781
- Petersburg – Apr. 15, 1781
- Virginia Capes – Sept. 5-9, 1781
- Eutaw Springs – Sept. 8, 1781
- Wilmington – Oct. 23, 1781
- Yorktown – Oct. 19, 1781

—— UPDATED JUNE 2020 ——

AMERICAN BATTLEFIELD TRUST ★ ★ ★

BATTLE *of* KETTLE CREEK

FEBRUARY 14, 1779

THE WAR IN THE NORTH AND THE SOUTH TURNED INTO A WAR OF OUTPOSTS for the British army throughout the American rebellion. As a sea power, Crown forces found it difficult to project their power from the ports into the interior of North America. While successful at winning battles in the interior, the Crown forces were not prepared for the prolonged engagement with insurgents on home territory that drained manpower resources, taxed supply trains, and wore away at British morale.

General Augustine Prevost arrived in the newly captured city of Savannah, Georgia, with aspirations of gaining Loyalist support. Prevost ordered Lt. Col. Archibald Campbell to Augusta, where the recruiting of loyalists began in earnest. Soon, recruiting officers moved through Georgia and into the Carolinas. Colonel John Boyd managed to put together a force of some 800 tory loyalists from the Carolinas. Upon returning to Georgia, his force was shadowed by patriots commanded by Col. Andrew Pickens. Boyd sought to link up with another group of Loyalists commanded by Maj. John Hamilton and then the two newly formed groups would join Campbell's force at Augusta. The loyalists pillaged along their marching route, though, which angered the locals, driving many to take up arms against the Crown.

Pickens, in his pursuit, could expect little help from the commander of the American Southern Department, Gen. Benjamin Lincoln. While Lincoln was an able officer with years of experience in the Continental Army, he lacked the resources to retake Savannah, let alone pursue the growing Loyalist forces in the Deep South. Thus, it was up to Patriot militia to take up the cause.

During their march back into Georgia, Boyd's

men suffered about 100 casualties, inflicted upon them by the pursuing Patriot partisans. After crossing the Savannah River, Boyd ordered his men to rest and make camp on the north side of Kettle Creek in Wilkes County, Georgia. Unbeknownst to Boyd, Pickens and about 350 patriots were close by, preparing to strike.

The American attack plan was straightforward. Pickens divided his force into three parts. Lieutenant Colonel Elijah Clarke commanded the left column, while Col. John Dooly commanded the Patriot Right. Pickens assumed command of the center of the line. Around 10 a.m., Pickens attacked. Lax security around the camp allowed the rebels to catch the tories by surprise. Loyalist pickets fled back into the main British camp as Boyd tried to scrape together a defensive line.

Although the tories enjoyed numerical superiority, the patriots' sudden attack left them with little time to prepare. Boyd ordered his main force to take defensive positions on a hill at the rear of the camp while he advanced with 100 men and took position behind a makeshift breastwork. Boyd's small detachment fought bravely, but patriots outflanked them and drove them back, and Boyd was mortally wounded.

As Pickens attacked in the center, his flanking columns under Dooly and Clarke emerged from swampy ground on the left and right to join the assault on the tories' main line. Despite outnumbering the patriots roughly two-to-one and commanding the higher ground, the Tories began to give way, fleeing across the creek. By the time the fighting ceased, the tory regiment Boyd had raised was all but destroyed, and patriots once again proved that they were ready and willing to fight for their independence.

✹ ✺ PRESERVATION ✺ ✹

To date, the **American Battlefield Trust** has saved **180 acres** at Kettle Creek Battlefield.

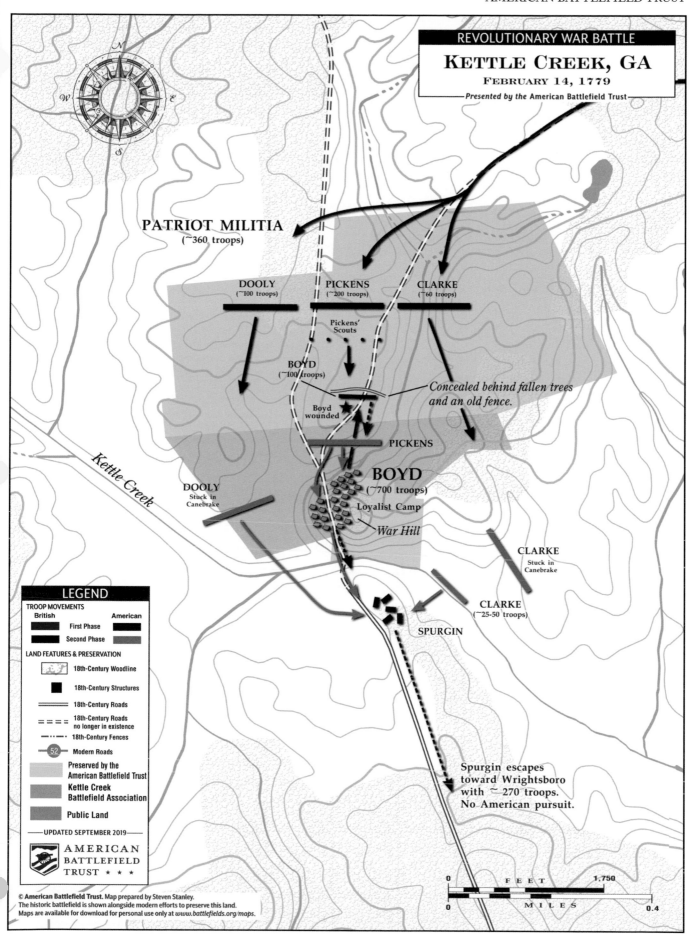

REVOLUTIONARY WAR BATTLE

KETTLE CREEK, GA

FEBRUARY 14, 1779

Presented by the American Battlefield Trust

PATRIOT MILITIA
(~360 troops)

DOOLY
(~100 troops)

PICKENS
(~200 troops)

CLARKE
(~60 troops)

*Pickens'
Scouts*

BOYD
(~100 troops)

*Boyd
wounded*

*Concealed behind fallen trees
and an old fence.*

PICKENS

DOOLY
Stuck in
Canebrake

Kettle Creek

BOYD
(~700 troops)

Loyalist Camp

War Hill

CLARKE
Stuck in
Canebrake

CLARKE
(~25-50 troops)

SPURGIN

LEGEND

TROOP MOVEMENTS

British	American
First Phase	
Second Phase	

LAND FEATURES & PRESERVATION

- 18th-Century Woodline
- 18th-Century Structures
- 18th-Century Roads
- ==== 18th-Century Roads no longer in existence
- —·— 18th-Century Fences
- 52 Modern Roads
- Preserved by the American Battlefield Trust
- Kettle Creek Battlefield Association
- Public Land

—UPDATED SEPTEMBER 2019—

**AMERICAN
BATTLEFIELD
TRUST ★ ★ ★**

*Spurgin escapes
toward Wrightsboro
with ~ 270 troops.
No American pursuit.*

0	FEET	1,750
0	MILES	0.4

© **American Battlefield Trust**. Map prepared by Steven Stanley.
The historic battlefield is shown alongside modern efforts to preserve this land.
Maps are available for download for personal use only at *www.battlefields.org/maps*.

SIEGE *of* SAVANNAH

SEPTEMBER 16 – OCTOBER 20, 1779

GREAT BRITAIN RELIED ON THE ROYAL NAVY TO PROJECT THEIR POWER ABROAD. To even the playing field, the Americans, too, required a navy. That navy came in the form of the French alliance in 1778. In 1779, the first test in the South of the Franco-American alliance took place as the combined allied forces attempted to retake Savannah.

From September 16 to October 18, 1779, the Franco-American forces worked to dislodge the approximately 3,000-man British garrison led by Gen. Augustine Prevost. The British had constructed an extended entrenched defensive position, which included several redoubts to defend the city. By the end of the siege, the British had more than a hundred pieces of artillery placed along their line.

American forces in the south—between 5,000 and 7,000 men—were based in Charleston, S.C., under the command of Gen. Benjamin Lincoln. Lincoln recognized that he would need assistance from the French navy and army to retake Savannah. On September 3, he learned that the French forces led by Admiral Comte d'Estaing were en route to Savannah, bringing with them ships-of-the-line and a force of soldiers. On September 11, Lincoln marched out of Charleston with 2,000 Continentals to link up with d'Estaing. Arriving first, d'Estaing began offensive operations to take the city. As was the European custom, he offered Prevost an opportunity to surrender, but Prevost demurred.

The American and French commanders held a council of war. Lincoln reluctantly ceded de facto command to d'Estaing. The French commander believed that a frontal assault against the British position would be futile and instead proposed to bombard the city. Lincoln concurred. French cannons were removed from their ships, and a five-day cannonade began. While the city itself bore the brunt of the artillery assault, the defensive positions remained relatively untouched, so d'Estaing eventually agreed to a frontal assault in spite of objections by his officers. He worried that a protracted siege would take too long —the hurricane season was moving in and a British fleet was still lurking somewhere off the coast nearby.

On the morning of October 9, the Franco-American assault began. Fog shrouded the battlefield and impeded forward progress as troops got lost in the swamps in front of the redoubt they were attacking. This redoubt, the Spring Hill Redoubt, had been selected by d'Estaing because he erroneously believed it to be only lightly defended by local Loyalist militia. In reality, that militia was backed up by battle-hardened British Regulars.

Once the fog lifted, the French lines were fully exposed and crumbled in the face of a withering and incessant fire from the defenders. Admiral d'Estaing himself received two wounds as he personally led the attack. Mortally wounded in the first assault was the Polish cavalry officer, Casimir Pulaski, who had done much to shape the American cavalry forces of the Continental Army. After an hour, the attack was called off. A week later, d'Estaing sailed away, leaving Lincoln behind and the Franco-American Alliance strained. Lincoln's forces lifted their siege on October 19. Savannah remained in British hands until the end of the war, although Lincoln soon found himself in another siege.

✳ ✳ **PRESERVATION** ✳ ✳

To date, the **American Battlefield Trust** has not saved any land at Savannah Battlefield.

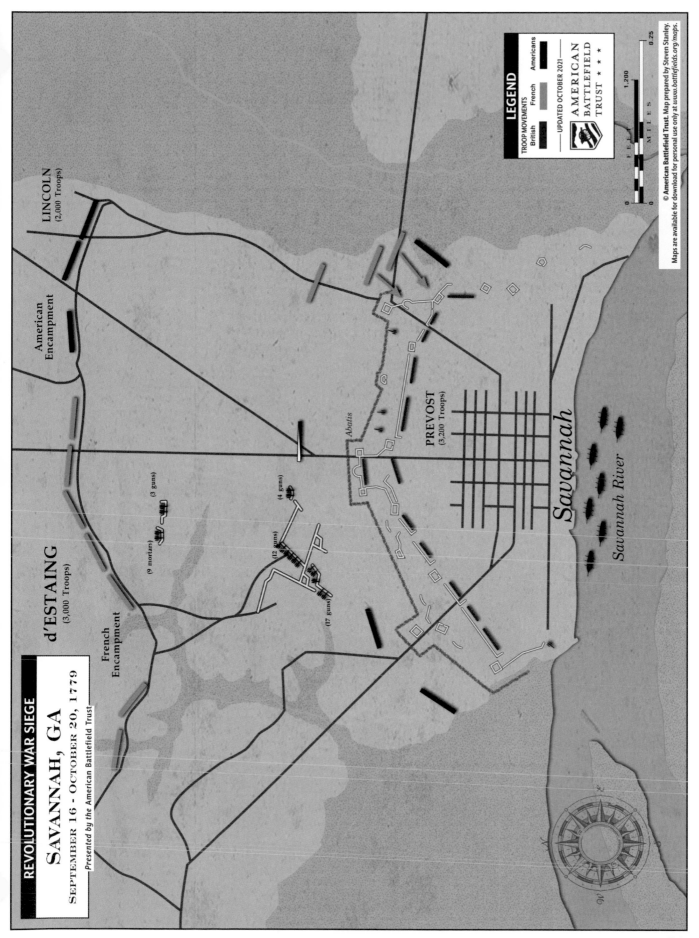

REVOLUTIONARY WAR SIEGE

SAVANNAH, GA

SEPTEMBER 16 - OCTOBER 20, 1779

Presented by the American Battlefield Trust

LINCOLN
(2,000 Troops)

d'ESTAING
(3,000 Troops)

American
Encampment

French
Encampment

PREVOST
(3,200 Troops)

Abatis

(3 guns)

(9 mortars)

(4 guns)

(12 guns)

(17 guns)

Savannah

Savannah River

LEGEND

TROOP MOVEMENTS

British · French · Americans

UPDATED OCTOBER 2021

AMERICAN BATTLEFIELD TRUST ★ ★ ★

0 — 1,200 — FEET
0 — 0.25 — MILES

© American Battlefield Trust. Map prepared by Steven Stanley.
Maps are available for download for personal use only at www.battlefields.org/maps.

SIEGE *of* CHARLESTON

MARCH 29 – MAY 12, 1780

CHARLESTON, S.C., WAS THE WEALTHIEST PORT CITY IN THE SOUTH, and the fourth-most prosperous harbor in the colonies. After the failed tory attempt to take the city in 1776, the war in the Southern colonies had largely quieted down. This was about to change on Christmas Day of 1779. On that holiday, Sir Henry Clinton stepped aboard a ship of the line bound for the Deep South. A British fleet carrying about 9,000 soldiers set off to bolster the "Sothern Strategy." Severe storms hampered the progress of the British fleet, but 40 days later—on February 11, 1780—the first British soldiers of Clinton's force set foot on South Carolina soil.

After the failed siege of Savannah, Gen. Benjamin Lincoln had moved back to Charleston. In the following weeks, Lincoln was able to muster perhaps 5,000 effectives to combat Clinton's expeditionary force. Now standing in defense of Charleston, Lincoln and his men were in an unenviable position. The city of Charleston sits on a peninsula flanked by the Ashley and Cooper Rivers to the south and north and Charleston Harbor to the east. While Lincoln was not under orders to defend the city to the last, this is the course of action he decided upon.

Clinton slowly pushed his land forces north from where they made landfall in February. City fathers became uneasy with the British army's approach. The state employed 600 slaves to build Patriot fortifications. Slowly, ever so slowly, the noose tightened. Clinton, too, undertook siege preparations. A first parallel was prepared, and 12 warships ran the Charleston Bar and the guns of Fort Moultrie. Infantry and cavalry cut off the landward side of the city.

Outnumbered more than 2-to-1 and outmatched on the water, Lincoln's command was doomed.

On April 5, the first parallel was complete, and the British opened with an artillery bombardment. On April 14, a small band of Patriot reinforcements bound for Charleston was defeated at the Battle of Monck's Corner. With civilian authorities pressing for action and with the gravity of the situation weighing upon him, Lincoln called at least three councils of war. On April 21, Lincoln offered to surrender the city to Clinton if his army and navy were allowed to march away free men. Clinton rejected these terms outright.

The bombardment of Charleston continued as Lincoln's situation grew more and more dire. The incessant bombardment made life in the city unbearable for soldiers and civilians alike. In early May, Fort Moultrie fell to the British. Clinton demanded the American garrison surrender. He hoped to avoid a mass frontal assault against a fixed fortified position. Surprisingly, Lincoln refused to capitulate. Clinton upped the ante and fired hot shot into the city. Homes caught fire, and the South Carolinans pleaded with Lincoln to surrender.

On May 11, 1780, Lincoln raised the white flag and agreed to surrender the city and his army to Clinton. The British army took position of Charleston the next day. Lincoln's surrender was the largest surrender of American forces during the war, and the largest surrender of American forces until the Siege of Harpers Ferry in 1862. The Southern Strategy seemed to be paying off.

✳ ✳ PRESERVATION ✳ ✳

To date, the **American Battlefield Trust** has saved **0.23 acres** at Charleston Battlefield.

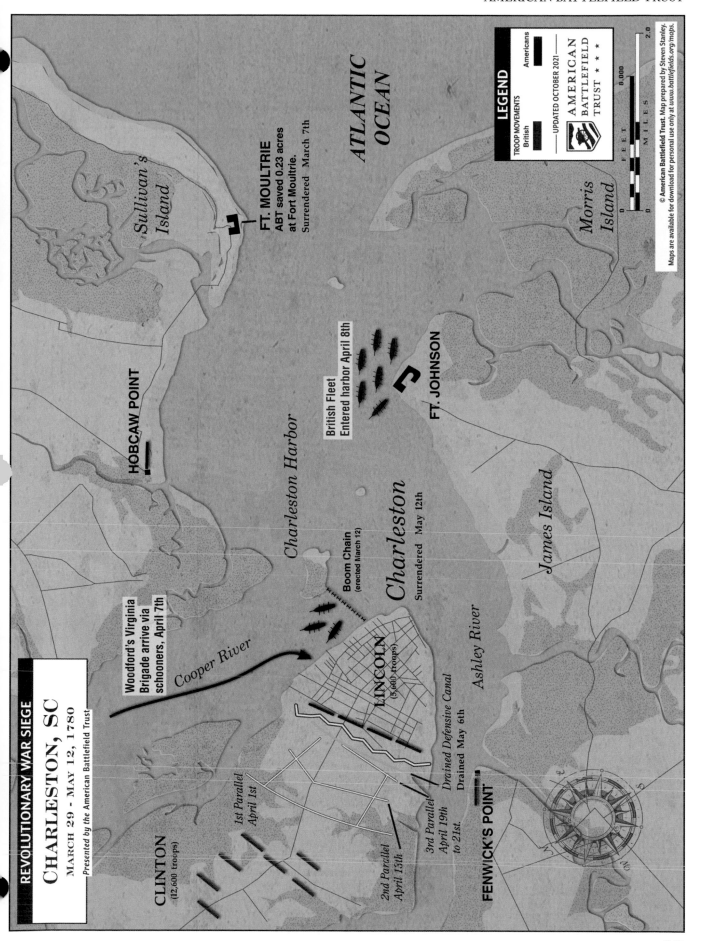

REVOLUTIONARY WAR SIEGE

CHARLESTON, SC
MARCH 29 - MAY 12, 1780
Presented by the American Battlefield Trust

LEGEND

TROOP MOVEMENTS
British
Americans

— UPDATED OCTOBER 2021 —

★ ★ ★   ★ ★ ★

AMERICAN BATTLEFIELD TRUST

FEET   8,000

0

MILES   2.0

0

© American Battlefield Trust. Map prepared by Steven Stanley.
Maps are available for download for personal use only at www.battlefields.org/maps.

Sullivan's Island

FT. MOULTRIE
ABT saved 0.23 acres
at Fort Moultrie.
Surrendered March 7th

*ATLANTIC
OCEAN*

*Morris
Island*

HOBCAW POINT

**British Fleet
Entered harbor April 8th**

FT. JOHNSON

Charleston Harbor

Boom Chain
(erected March 12)

Charleston
Surrendered May 12th

James Island

**Woodford's Virginia
Brigade arrive via
schooners, April 7th**

Cooper River

LINCOLN
(5,600 troops)

Ashley River

Drained Defensive Canal
Drained May 6th

CLINTON
(12,600 troops)

*1st Parallel
April 1st*

*2nd Parallel
April 13th*

*3rd Parallel
April 19th
to 21st.*

FENWICK'S POINT

BATTLE *of* WAXHAWS
(BUFORD'S MASSACRE)

MAY 29, 1780

AFTER THE FALL OF SAVANNAH AND CHARLESTON, THE BRITISH BEGAN MOVING into the backcountry. One of the goals of the Southern Strategy was to draw loyalists out of their homes and into the service of the Crown. The presence of British troops should have steeled the resolve of the loyalists, but the actions of some officers and men steeled the resolve of the patriots instead.

The Battle of Waxhaws (also known as Buford's Massacre) was one of the most controversial actions to take place during the American Revolutionary War in the South.

A relief column of 380 or so Virginia Continentals commanded by Col. Abraham Buford was dispatched south to help Lincoln during the Siege of Charleston. Buford's command failed to reach the city in time and began making its way north toward North Carolina. Along the way, the column was bolstered by some Virginia dragoons and North Carolina Militia.

On the British side, General Charles, Second Earl Cornwallis assumed command of the Southern Theater. Cornwallis learned of Buford's presence and sent a force under Lt. Col. Banastre Tarleton in pursuit.

Even though the Americans were a week ahead of Tarleton, the aggressive British commander moved his men 150 miles at a rapid pace, catching up with Buford on the afternoon of May 29, 1780. The area in which the two forces caught sight of each other lies along the border of North and South Carolina in an area called the Waxhaws.

Tarleton sent a message to Buford, demanding the patriots surrender. Buford refused, and then formed a battle line in an open field across the route of march, his infantry in a single line with orders not to fire until the British approached within 10 yards.

Approaching Buford's position, Tarleton divided his force into three attacking columns, with the intention of having the mounted infantry dismount and pour fire upon the Americans, pinning them down. At the same time, he formed a center column of his elite troops, the regular soldiers of the 17th Light Dragoons, as well as 40 Legion dragoons, to charge straight towards the American center. The left column was led by Tarleton himself and consisted of 30 handpicked men of the Legion, ready to sweep the American right flank.

Tarleton's men fell upon the Americans. Buford's order to hold his men's fire until the last moment marked their demise. The British men overran the Patriot line, causing panic in the ranks. Many American survivors of the battle claimed that their comrades were massacred while trying to surrender. While another account claims that the Americans were allowed to surrender, but a soldier fired at Tarleton after the surrender and this set off the "massacre." Colonel Buford managed to escape from the slaughter. He reported what happened on the field, and the battle was dubbed "Buford's Massacre." Those who surrendered received "Tarleton's Quarter." The battle cry "Remember the Waxhaws!" rallied patriots throughout the South to the American cause.

✸ ✸ PRESERVATION ✸ ✸

To date, the **American Battlefield Trust** has saved **50.84 acres** at Waxhaws Battlefield.

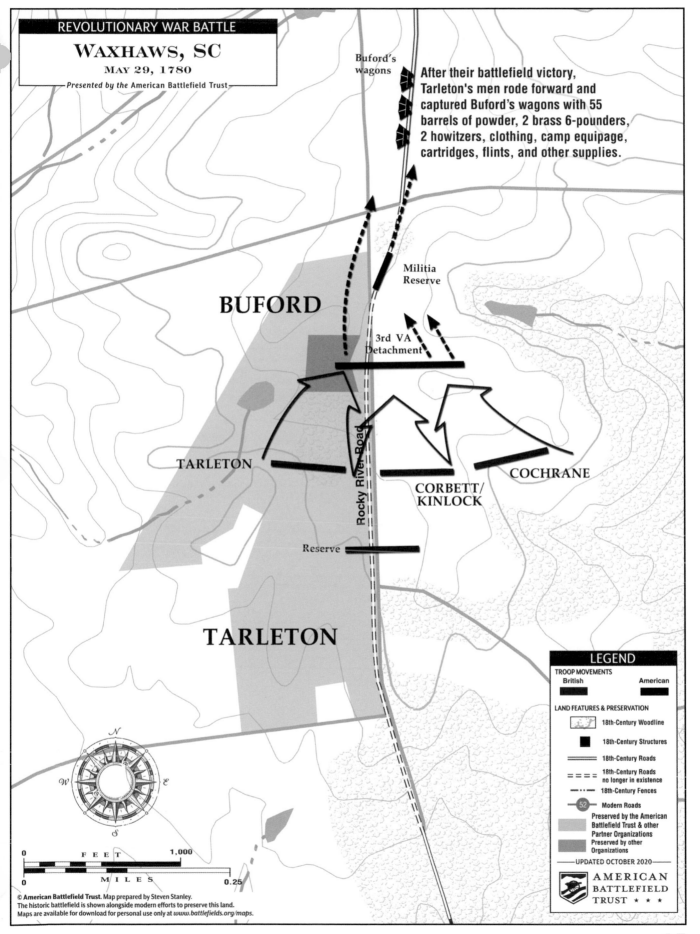

REVOLUTIONARY WAR BATTLE
WAXHAWS, SC
MAY 29, 1780
Presented by the American Battlefield Trust

Buford's wagons

After their battlefield victory, Tarleton's men rode forward and captured Buford's wagons with 55 barrels of powder, 2 brass 6-pounders, 2 howitzers, clothing, camp equipage, cartridges, flints, and other supplies.

Militia Reserve

BUFORD

3rd VA Detachment

TARLETON

Rocky River Road

CORBETT/ KINLOCK

COCHRANE

Reserve

TARLETON

LEGEND
TROOP MOVEMENTS
British   American

LAND FEATURES & PRESERVATION

18th-Century Woodline

18th-Century Structures

18th-Century Roads

18th-Century Roads no longer in existence

18th-Century Fences

52   Modern Roads

Preserved by the American Battlefield Trust & other Partner Organizations

Preserved by other Organizations

— UPDATED OCTOBER 2020 —

AMERICAN
BATTLEFIELD
TRUST ★ ★ ★

N

W   E

S

0   FEET   1,000

MILES   0.25

© **American Battlefield Trust.** Map prepared by Steven Stanley.
The historic battlefield is shown alongside modern efforts to preserve this land.
Maps are available for download for personal use only at *www.battlefields.org/maps.*

BATTLE *of* HANGING ROCK

AUGUST 6, 1780

ENRAGED THAT THE BRITISH BURNED HIS HOME AND BY THE WAXHAWS MASSACRE, General Thomas Sumter and his South Carolina militia embarked on a guerrilla campaign that split the backcountry like never before between Loyalists and Patriots.

Following the May 1780 fall of Charleston, the British moved inland and established several outposts intending to restore Royal authority over South Carolina's population and resources. Confident that the British could not quickly assemble a substantial number of troops to defend any one outpost, Sumter proposed small, calculated attacks on the British strongholds. His ultimate goal: make the remaining locations along the Santee and Wateree Rivers undesirable and unsustainable.

On July 17, 1780, Sumter wrote General Johann de Kalb from his camp on the Catawaba River expressing his desire to, "prevent them [the British] from forcing the Militia to retreat…and also from stripping the country of all its resources." He also gave de Kalb the best intelligence at his disposal. The British had 800 men in Charleston, 12 in Beaufort, 250 at Ninety Six, 200 at Rocky Mount, 700 at Camden; 280 men of foot, and 70 dragoons occupied Hanging Rock. Another 1,100 British lurked in Georgia. All told, Sumter estimated 3,482 British troops were within reasonable striking distance.

Located on the road between Camden, South Carolina—considered the key to controlling the backcountry of the Carolinas—and Charlotte, North Carolina, the outpost at Hanging Rock provided the British with a significant amount of natural cover. The east side of Hanging Rock Creek was heavily wooded with steep banks that led down to a creek full of massive boulders. The British camped on the west side of the stream, where the ground rose sharply from the watercourse and plateaued. The rocks and trees surrounding Hanging Rock were essential factors in the success of the Patriot attacks.

While Sumter staged an attack on the nearby Rocky Mount, Maj. William Richardson Davie and his North Carolina Independent Corps of Light Horse prepared to ambush Col. Samuel Bryan's North Carolina Loyalist Militia at Hanging Rock on July 30, 1780. With 40 dragoons and roughly the same number of mounted riflemen, Davie's force was far too small to take on the Loyalist force of 500. Instead, Davie focused his efforts on a garrisoned house near the fort at Hanging Rock.

Utilizing the similarities in dress, speech, and manner between his men and Bryan's Loyalists to his advantage, Davie's mountain riflemen casually rode into three companies of Loyalist mounted infantry and opened fire.

Thwarted by a thunderstorm at Rocky Mount, Sumter was also determined to strike a blow. On August 5th, Sumter staged his own attack on Hanging Rock. Reinforced by Davie and nearly 800 troops, Sumter marched 16 miles through the night, stopping just short of Hanging Rock. Crossing Hanging Rock Creek at 6:00 a.m., the attack began.

The British charged Sumter's force twice. The Patriots took shelter behind rocks and trees, using the cover while firing into the British lines. Within a few minutes, the majority of the British officers were killed. The Battle of Hanging Rock raged on for roughly three hours in the sweltering South Carolina summer. Exhausted, many of Sumter's men could no longer continue fighting. Each side believed that they were the victor—the British because they did not give up all of their ground and the Patriot's because they captured significant amounts of British stores and were able to withdraw unmolested. Hanging Rock ushered in a brutal phase of fighting in the Southern Theater.

✳ ✳ PRESERVATION ✳ ✳

To date, the **American Battlefield Trust** has saved **171.84 acres** at Hanging Rock Battlefield.

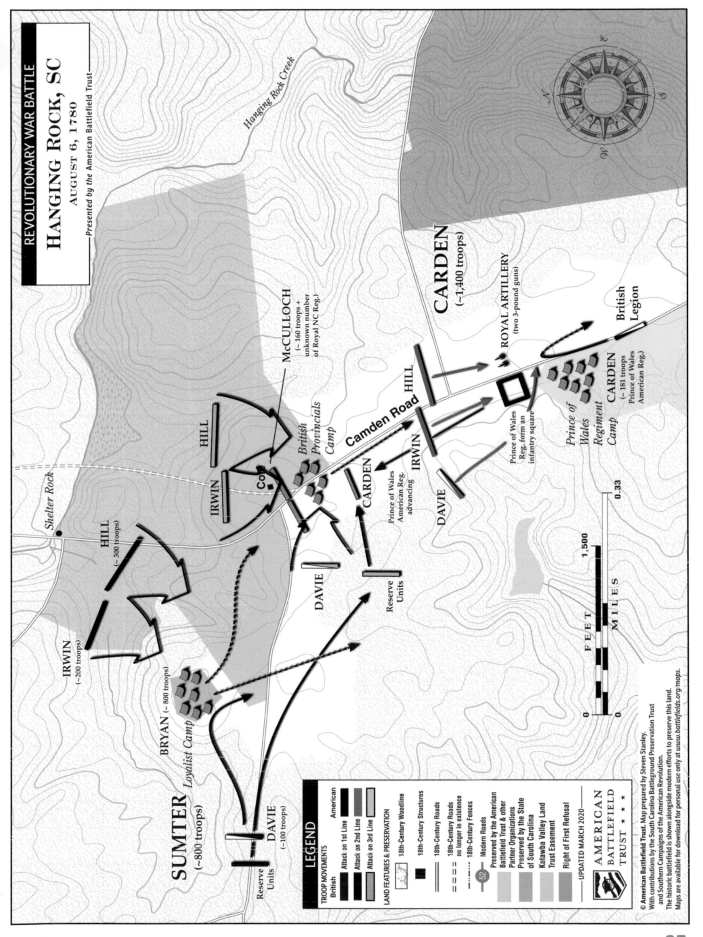

REVOLUTIONARY WAR BATTLE
HANGING ROCK, SC
AUGUST 6, 1780
Presented by the American Battlefield Trust

Hanging Rock Creek

McCULLOCH
(~ 160 troops +
unknown number
of Royal NC Reg.)

CARDEN
(~1,400 troops)

ROYAL ARTILLERY
(two 3-pound guns)

British Legion

British Provincials Camp

HILL

HILL Co.

IRWIN

HILL
(~ 300 troops)

Shelter Rock

CARDEN

IRWIN

Prince of Wales American Reg. advancing

CARDEN
(~ 181 troops
Prince of Wales
American Reg.)

Prince of Wales Regiment Camp

Prince of Wales Reg. form an infantry square

Camden Road

DAVIE

IRWIN
(~ 200 troops)

DAVIE

BRYAN (~ 800 troops)

Loyalist Camp

Reserve Units

SUMTER
(~800 troops)

DAVIE
(~100 troops)

Reserve Units

FEET 1,500
MILES 0.33

LEGEND
TROOP MOVEMENTS
British | American
- Attack on 1st Line
- Attack on 2nd Line
- Attack on 3rd Line

LAND FEATURES & PRESERVATION
- 18th-Century Woodline
- 18th-Century Structures
- 18th-Century Roads
- 18th-Century Roads no longer in existence
- 18th-Century Fences
- Modern Roads
- Preserved by the American Battlefield Trust & other Partner Organizations
- Preserved by the State of South Carolina
- Katawba Valley Land Trust Easement
- Right of First Refusal

UPDATED MARCH 2020

AMERICAN BATTLEFIELD TRUST ★ ★ ★

BATTLE *of* CAMDEN

AUGUST 16, 1780

IN THE WAKE OF CHARLESTON, THE CONTINENTAL CONGRESS SOUGHT A NEW LEADER for the Southern Department of the Continental Army. George Washington wanted to appoint one of his protégés, Nathanael Greene, to this vital command. Instead, Congress tapped Horatio Gates—the victor of the Battles of Saratoga. In late July Gates arrived in the Southern Theater.

Meanwhile, the British Army under Charles Cornwallis pressed deeper into the back country, establishing outposts and supply depots along the way. This outpost war depleted the number of effectives that Cornwallis could bring to battle because his army had to man each of the newly established garrisons. Still, Cornwallis was confident that even an undersized British Army could easily defeat a large Rebel force. He was soon proven correct.

Gates amassed an army of more than 5,000 men and, against the wishes of the majority of his officers, moved south from North Carolina into South Carolina, with Camden as the army's destination. The Patriot force consisted largely of North Carolina and Virginia militia. A core of Continentals from Delaware and Maryland formed the backbone of Gates's army. The march south during the hot summer and through inhospitable territory depleted the ranks of the army with each passing day. By mid-August, Gates could muster perhaps 3,700 effectives.

Alerted to the Rebel movement by the garrison commander, Lord Rawdon, Cornwallis personally led a relief column to Camden. While Gates claimed that he did not wish to attack the garrison, he dangled his army in the open as unsuspecting bait for the aggressive Cornwallis.

After a taxing march to Camden, the two sides made contact with one another in the early morning hours of August 16, 1780. Gates and Cornwallis deployed their troops for battle in traditional European linear formations. This formation called for the best troops of each army to be placed on the right flanks of their respective lines—a formation that doomed the Americans from the start.

Gates deployed his experienced Maryland and Delaware regiments on his right, and militia from North Carolina in the center. On the American left were green militiamen from Virginia. British regulars under Gen. James Webster met Gates's Virginians who, upon seeing the first gleam of British bayonets, ran off the field in a panic. North Carolina militiamen holding the center line similarly fled despite the best efforts of American officers to hold them in line.

With the American left and center running, the British concentrated on the American right flank. These Americans, unlike their counterparts to the left, fought valiantly, but could not stand in the face of overwhelming firepower. In the midst of the action, Gen. Johann DeKalb fell mortally wounded, and Gates's reputation was ruined as rumors of him riding hell for leather back to North Carolina plagued him (and do to this day). For the third time in 20 months, an American Army in the South was no more.

✳ ✳ **PRESERVATION** ✳ ✳

To date, the **American Battlefield Trust** has saved **294.45 acres** at Camden Battlefield.

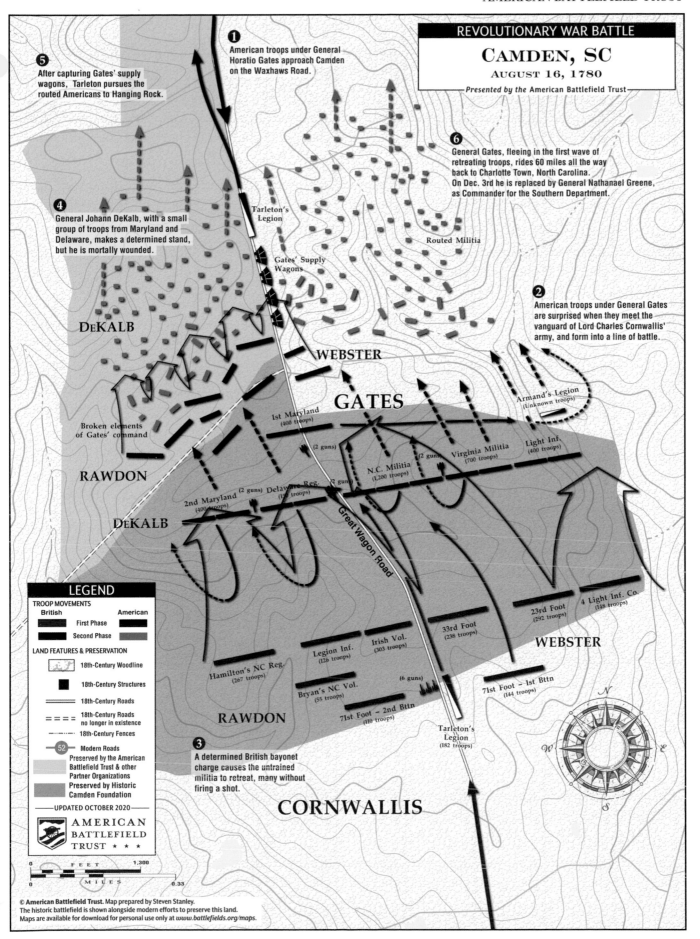

REVOLUTIONARY WAR BATTLE

CAMDEN, SC
AUGUST 16, 1780
Presented by the American Battlefield Trust

1 American troops under General Horatio Gates approach Camden on the Waxhaws Road.

5 After capturing Gates' supply wagons, Tarleton pursues the routed Americans to Hanging Rock.

6 General Gates, fleeing in the first wave of retreating troops, rides 60 miles all the way back to Charlotte Town, North Carolina. On Dec. 3rd he is replaced by General Nathanael Greene, as Commander for the Southern Department.

4 General Johann DeKalb, with a small group of troops from Maryland and Delaware, makes a determined stand, but he is mortally wounded.

Tarleton's Legion

Gates' Supply Wagons

Routed Militia

2 American troops under General Gates are surprised when they meet the vanguard of Lord Charles Cornwallis' army, and form into a line of battle.

DeKALB

WEBSTER

Broken elements of Gates' command

GATES

1st Maryland (400 troops)

(2 guns)

(2 guns)

N.C. Militia (1,200 troops)

Virginia Militia (700 troops)

Light Inf. (400 troops)

Armand's Legion (Unknown troops)

RAWDON

DeKALB

2nd Maryland (400 troops)

(2 guns) Delaware Reg. (150 troops)

(2 guns)

Great Wagon Road

23rd Foot (292 troops)

4 Light Inf. Co. (148 troops)

LEGEND

TROOP MOVEMENTS

British — First Phase — American

Second Phase

LAND FEATURES & PRESERVATION

- 18th-Century Woodline
- 18th-Century Structures
- 18th-Century Roads
- 18th-Century Roads no longer in existence
- 18th-Century Fences
- 52 Modern Roads
- Preserved by the American Battlefield Trust & other Partner Organizations
- Preserved by Historic Camden Foundation

— UPDATED OCTOBER 2020 —

AMERICAN BATTLEFIELD TRUST ★ ★ ★

Hamilton's NC Reg. (267 troops)

Legion Inf. (126 troops)

Irish Vol. (303 troops)

33rd Foot (238 troops)

WEBSTER

Bryan's NC Vol. (55 troops)

(6 guns)

71st Foot – 1st Bttn (144 troops)

RAWDON

71st Foot – 2nd Bttn (110 troops)

3 A determined British bayonet charge causes the untrained militia to retreat, many without firing a shot.

Tarleton's Legion (182 troops)

CORNWALLIS

FEET 1,300

MILES 0.33

N / E / W / S

BATTLE *of* KINGS MOUNTAIN

OCTOBER 7, 1780

THE AMERICAN REVOLUTIONARY WAR IN THE DEEP SOUTH WAS A CIVIL WAR inside of a civil war. Prewar feuds boiled over into bloodshed as colonists stood with the Crown or fought for independence. The British regular officers in the South did little to help the situation or ingratiate themselves with the local populous. Enter Maj. Patrick Ferguson. Ferguson, an officer in the 71st Regiment of Foot, was a skilled marksman. He designed the Ferguson Rifle, and allegedly had the opportunity to fell George Washington at the battle of Brandywine. After a wound in the arm at the aforementioned battle, Ferguson eventually found himself in the Southern Theater of the war with Cornwallis's army.

In the early fall of 1780, Gen. Cornwallis began a three-pronged movement, north, through South Carolina. Ferguson commanded the left (western) prong of this advance. He attempted to rally Loyalist troops, but his threats and proclamations against the local population, drew the ire of a group known as the "Over Mountain Men," residents of the Carolina Backcountry, the Appalachian Mountain range, and from places that would later become the states of Tennessee and Kentucky.

Several bands of Over Mountain Men (900 in all) led by James Johnston, William Campbell, John Sevier, Joseph McDowell, and Isaac Shelby took up arms against Ferguson and the Crown. Learning of the approaching threat, Ferguson chose to retreat from his forward position and pull back closer to the main body of the British Army. Ferguson's command was shadowed by the Over Mountain Men, and he chose to dig in and fortify a hill two miles inside the South Carolina border: Kings Mountain. An American scouting party learned of Ferguson's position, giving the Militia commanders the intelligence that they needed to plan an attack.

Sensing an impending battle, the American commanders told their men, "Don't wait for the word of command. Let each one of you be your own officer and do the very best you can." The American plan was simple: surround the Loyalist position and assault from all sides. To differentiate friend from foe, Patriot militia placed pieces of paper in their hats. One of the enduring myths of the American Revolutionary War is that patriots fought every battle in loose formations, hiding behind rocks and trees for cover. That myth was reality at Kings Mountain.

Early in the afternoon of October 7, the Over Mountain Men crept quietly towards Ferguson's position. Finally, a shot rang out, and then scores more. Ferguson deployed his Loyalist militia in the center of the hilltop. Mounted atop his horse and utilizing a silver whistle to issue commands, Ferguson's men stood in a traditional battle line, blasting ineffectual volleys into the woods. The loyalists tried to employ bayonet charges, but every time they advanced, the rebels melted into the woods only to rematerialize later. Ferguson and his men were surrounded, and additional counterattacks failed to stop the Americans.

With his defensive perimeter shrinking, Ferguson tried to lead his men past the onslaught. Mounted on his horse, he proved the perfect target for the crack-shot contingents he faced. He was shot multiple times, his body hanging from his horse, as his mount dragged his body down the hill, fleeing the battle. Shortly after Ferguson's death, the loyalists surrendered.

Henry Clinton summed up the impact of Kings Mountain, which "proved the first Link of a Chain of Evils that followed each other in regular succession until they at last ended in the total loss of America."

✳ ✳ PRESERVATION ✳ ✳

To date, the **American Battlefield Trust** has not saved any land at Kings Mountain Battlefield.

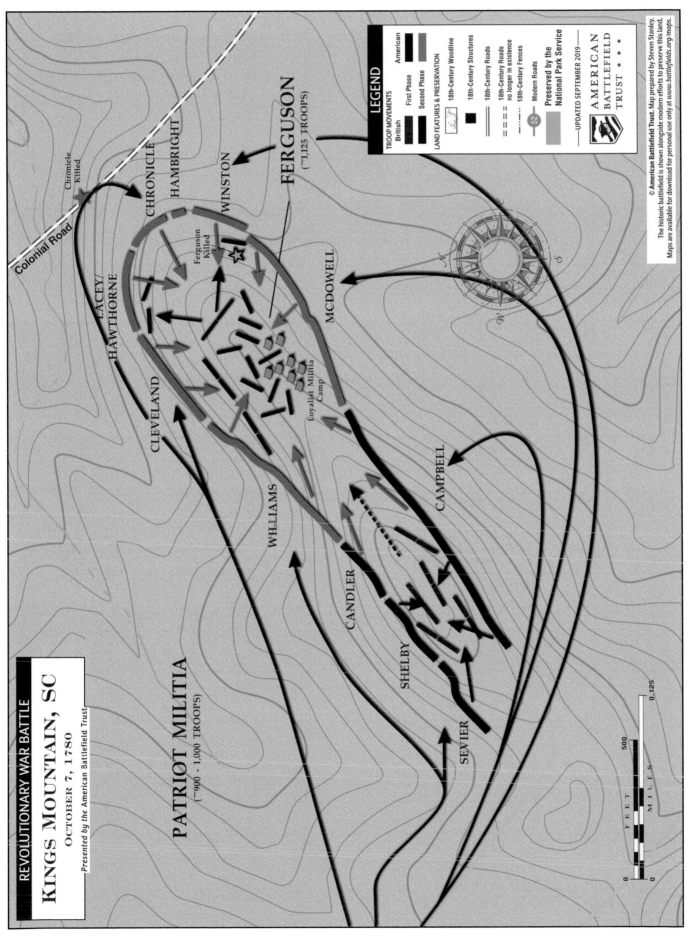

REVOLUTIONARY WAR BATTLE

KINGS MOUNTAIN, SC

OCTOBER 7, 1780

Presented by the American Battlefield Trust

PATRIOT MILITIA
(~900 - 1,000 TROOPS)

FERGUSON
(~1,125 TROOPS)

SEVIER

SHELBY

CANDLER

WILLIAMS

CAMPBELL

MCDOWELL

CLEVELAND

HAWTHORNE

LACEY/

CHRONICLE

HAMBRIGHT

WINSTON

Ferguson Killed

Loyalist Militia Camp

Chronicle Killed

Colonial Road

LEGEND

TROOP MOVEMENTS

British   American

First Phase

Second Phase

LAND FEATURES & PRESERVATION

18th-Century Woodline

18th-Century Structures

18th-Century Roads

18th-Century Roads no longer in existence

18th-Century Fences

52 Modern Roads

Preserved by the National Park Service

— UPDATED SEPTEMBER 2019 —

AMERICAN BATTLEFIELD TRUST ★ ★ ★

© American Battlefield Trust. Map prepared by Steven Stanley.
The historic battlefield is shown alongside modern efforts to preserve this land.
Maps are available for download for personal use only at *www.battlefields.org/maps*.

FEET   500

M I L E S   0.125

BATTLE *of* COWPENS

JANUARY 17, 1781

KINGS MOUNTAIN STAGGERED BUT DID NOT ENTIRELY STOP THE FORWARD movement of Cornwallis's army. With a renewed vigor from their recent victory and thanks to receiving a new overall commander in the South, Nathanael Greene, Patriot fortunes seemed to be on the rise. Greene split his small force, sending one part of his army, commanded by General Daniel Morgan, into the South Carolina backcountry. Dubbed the "Old Wagoneer," Morgan was a veteran, no-nonsense commander.

In an effort to drive a physical wedge between Greene and Morgan, and to potentially destroy the patriot force in detail, Cornwallis dispatched Banastre Tarleton to intercept Morgan's force. Ever the aggressor, Tarleton set with 1,150 men in pursuit of Morgan's force of 1,050 officers and men.

After a cat-and-mouse game, and with mother nature raising the levels of the Broad River, Morgan turned to meet Tarleton at a place locally known as the "Cowpens." The Cowpens was kept clear by cattle grazing for most the year, creating an almost park-like setting that allowed for Morgan's swift military maneuvering. The night before, Morgan had emboldened his men by meeting with them on a personal level. His confidence was infectious, and his men were ready for the task at hand.

Morgan drew up a simply battle plan for the morning of January 17. He deployed his army into three lines—a defense in depth. The first line consisted of skirmishers and marksmen while the second line consisted of militia who were asked to fire two volleys and retreat to the third line, which consisted of veteran Continental soldiers. If all worked out as planned, the first two American lines would slow the British while breaking up their unit cohesion, and the third line would land the coup de grâce.

Tarleton's men drove forward, sustaining losses from the first American line, which, as ordered, melted away into the second line. Parts of Morgan's second line unleashed their promised two volleys, while some fired one shot and fled. Sensing victory, Tarleton sent in mounted dragoons to mop up the fleeing militiamen. Countering this threat was Col. William Washington, who led his Continental dragoons onto the field.

Tarleton next sent in his infantry, which included the 71st Regiment of Foot (Fraser's Highlanders). A stand-up infantry fight ensued. As Col. John Eager Howard attempted to redeploy his line, the Continentals misinterpreted the order, and they began withdrawing from the field. Morgan appeared at the crisis moment, ordering the men to face about and unleashed a point-blank volley into the faces of the British. The militia and William Washington's cavalry stormed back onto the field, hitting the flanks of Tarleton's force simultaneously, performing a rare battlefield double envelopment. Hundreds of British officers and men threw down their arms and surrendered, while "Bloody Tarleton" rallied what few soldiers he could and withdrew from the field. In less than an hour, Morgan had given Tarleton "a devil of a whipping!"

Although Cornwallis doggedly pursued Morgan and Greene over the next two months, Cowpens boosted the morale of patriots across the South while pushing Cornwallis to go for broke.

✳ ✳ **PRESERVATION** ✳ ✳

To date, the **American Battlefield Trust** has not saved any land at Cowpens Battlefield.

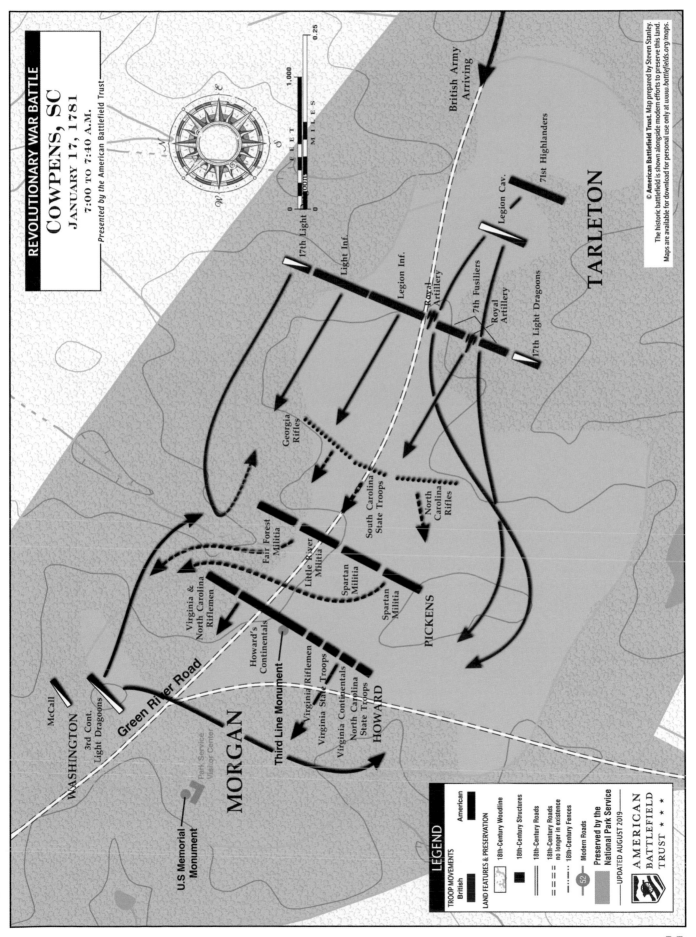

REVOLUTIONARY WAR BATTLE

COWPENS, SC

JANUARY 17, 1781

7:00 TO 7:40 A.M.

Presented by the American Battlefield Trust

FEET
MILES

0.25

1,000

0

© American Battlefield Trust. Map prepared by Steven Stanley.
The historic battlefield is shown alongside modern efforts to preserve this land.
Maps are available for download for personal use only at *www.battlefields.org/maps.*

British Army Arriving

17th Light

Light Inf.

Legion Inf.

Royal Artillery

7th Fusiliers

Royal Artillery

Legion Cav.

71st Highlanders

17th Light Dragoons

TARLETON

Georgia Rifles

South Carolina State Troops

North Carolina Rifles

Fair Forest Militia

Little River Militia

Spartan Militia

Spartan Militia

PICKENS

Virginia & North Carolina Riflemen

McCall

3rd Cont. Light Dragoons

WASHINGTON

Green River Road

MORGAN

U.S Memorial Monument

Park Service Visitor Center

Third Line Monument

Howard's Continentals

Virginia Riflemen

Virginia State Troops

Virginia Continentals

North Carolina State Troops

HOWARD

LEGEND

TROOP MOVEMENTS

British

American

LAND FEATURES & PRESERVATION

18th-Century Woodline

18th-Century Structures

18th-Century Roads

18th-Century Roads no longer in existence

18th-Century Fences

52 Modern Roads

Preserved by the National Park Service

— UPDATED AUGUST 2019 —

AMERICAN BATTLEFIELD TRUST ★ ★ ★

93

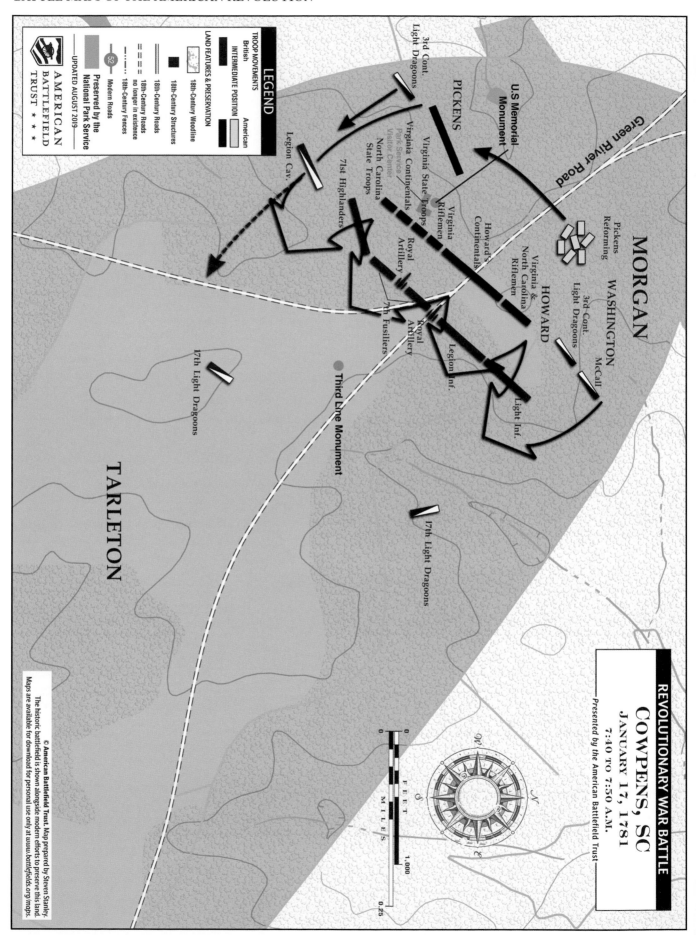

LEGEND

TROOP MOVEMENTS
British
American

INTERMEDIATE POSITION

LAND FEATURES & PRESERVATION
18th-Century Woodline
18th-Century Structures
18th-Century Roads
18th-Century Roads no longer in existence
18th-Century Fences
52 Modern Roads

Preserved by the National Park Service
— UPDATED AUGUST 2019 —

AMERICAN BATTLEFIELD TRUST ★ ★ ★

MORGAN

WASHINGTON

Pickens Reforming

PICKENS

U.S Memorial Monument

3rd Cont. Light Dragoons

McCall

Virginia & North Carolina Riflemen

3rd Cont. Light Dragoons

Virginia Riflemen

Virginia Continentals

Virginia State Troops

North Carolina State Troops

Park Service Visitor Center

Howard's Continentals

HOWARD

71st Highlanders

Royal Artillery

Legion Inf.

Light Inf.

7th Fusiliers

Royal Artillery

Legion Cav.

Third Line Monument

17th Light Dragoons

17th Light Dragoons

TARLETON

TARLETON

Green River Road

REVOLUTIONARY WAR BATTLE

COWPENS, SC
JANUARY 17, 1781
7:40 TO 7:50 A.M.

Presented by the American Battlefield Trust

0   FEET   1,000

0   MILES   0.25

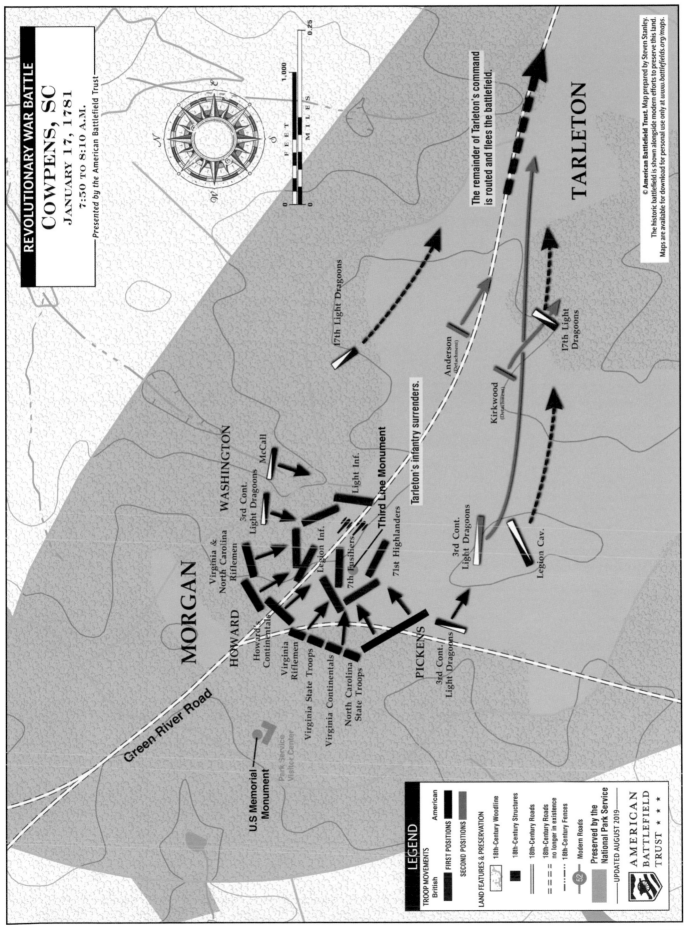

REVOLUTIONARY WAR BATTLE
COWPENS, SC
JANUARY 17, 1781
7:50 TO 8:10 A.M.
Presented by the American Battlefield Trust

The remainder of Tarleton's command is routed and flees the battlefield.

TARLETON

17th Light Dragoons

17th Light Dragoons

Anderson (Detachment)

Kirkwood (Detachment)

3rd Cont. Light Dragoons

Legion Cav.

Tarleton's infantry surrenders.

Third Line Monument

Light Inf.

McCall

3rd Cont. Light Dragoons

WASHINGTON

Legion Inf.

7th Fusiliers

71st Highlanders

Virginia & North Carolina Riflemen

MORGAN

HOWARD

Howard's Continentals

Virginia Riflemen

Virginia State Troops

Virginia Continentals

North Carolina State Troops

PICKENS

3rd Cont. Light Dragoons

Green River Road

Park Service Visitor Center

U.S Memorial Monument

© American Battlefield Trust. Map prepared by Steven Stanley.
The historic battlefield is shown alongside modern efforts to preserve this land.
Maps are available for download for personal use only at *www.battlefields.org/maps.*

FEET
MILES
0   1,000
0   0.25

LEGEND
TROOP MOVEMENTS
British   American
FIRST POSITIONS
SECOND POSITIONS

LAND FEATURES & PRESERVATION
18th-Century Woodline
18th-Century Structures
18th-Century Roads
18th-Century Roads no longer in existence
18th-Century Fences
52   Modern Roads
Preserved by the National Park Service
UPDATED AUGUST 2019

AMERICAN BATTLEFIELD TRUST ★ ★ ★

SIEGE *of* PENSACOLA

MARCH 9 – MAY 10, 1781

OLD-WORD RIVALRIES CARRIED INTO THE AMERICAN REVOLUTIONARY WAR. What started as colonial rebellion quickly morphed into a small world war. France was the first to throw its hat in with the American colonists, and in 1779, the two Bourbon powers, France and Spain, signed the Treaty of Aranjuez, which aligned the two countries against the British Empire. The Dutch Republic took advantage of the economics of the war and supplied American colonists with French arms and munitions. This led to Britain declaring war on the Dutch.

While Spain did not directly support the American cause through a formal treaty, their attempts to regain lost territories from the earlier wars of empire benefited the Americans. At the conclusion of the Seven Years' War, Great Britain claimed Florida from Spain through the Treaty of Paris (1763). Since 1763, British forces improved the defense of Pensacola, a natural harbor on the Gulf Coast panhandle. As a variety of military threats loomed on the horizon, the British built forts, stockades, and redoubts.

The Spanish occupied nearby New Orleans, Natchez, and Baton Rouge. Spanish General Don Bernardo de Gálvez aggressively sought to capture another British holding, leading him to Pensacola.

On his way to Pensacola, Galvez led a force of 40 ships and 3,500 men west along the Gulf of Mexico to Mobile Bay. There Galvez laid siege to British Fort Charlotte, a stronghold in what is today's Mobile, Alabama. After a Spanish victory there, Spanish troops garrisoned the fort, and a second fort—referred to as the "Spanish Fort"—was built across from Mobile Bay. Leaving behind the men who garrisoned the new forts, Gálvez sought out troops and fresh supplies in Havana, Cuba.

Gálvez finally sailed his fleet toward Pensacola and arrived at Santa Rosa Island on March 9, 1781. The first attempt at entering the bay went awry when the Spanish flagship, Galveztown, ran aground. In a second foray, Gálvez sailed the flagship into the bay himself.

While the British main army gathered in Fort George to prepare for a siege, Gálvez deployed his infantry and artillery—until a hurricane struck the area. Undaunted, Gálvez kept the pressure on Pensacola and its defenders. He undertook siege operations and began digging parallels. By early May, the Spanish force reached approximately 7,800 officers and men. They faced a British force of only 2,000 defenders. Gálvez positioned a battery on a hill within range of Fort George and opened fire on May 5, 1781. The British responded in kind.

After four days of ruthless firing, a Spanish shell hit a powder magazine in the Queen's Redoubt on May 8, 1781, destroying the fort and killing approximately 100 British soldiers. With an opportunity in reach, Spanish troops moved to occupy the redoubt. Moving artillery into place, the Spanish opened fire on Fort George at short range. No longer capable of defending the fort, the British surrendered their garrison on May 8. Pensacola officially came under control of the Spanish on May 10 and remained Spanish control for the next 40 years.

✳ ✳ PRESERVATION ✳ ✳

To date, the **American Battlefield Trust** has not saved any land at Pensacola Battlefield.

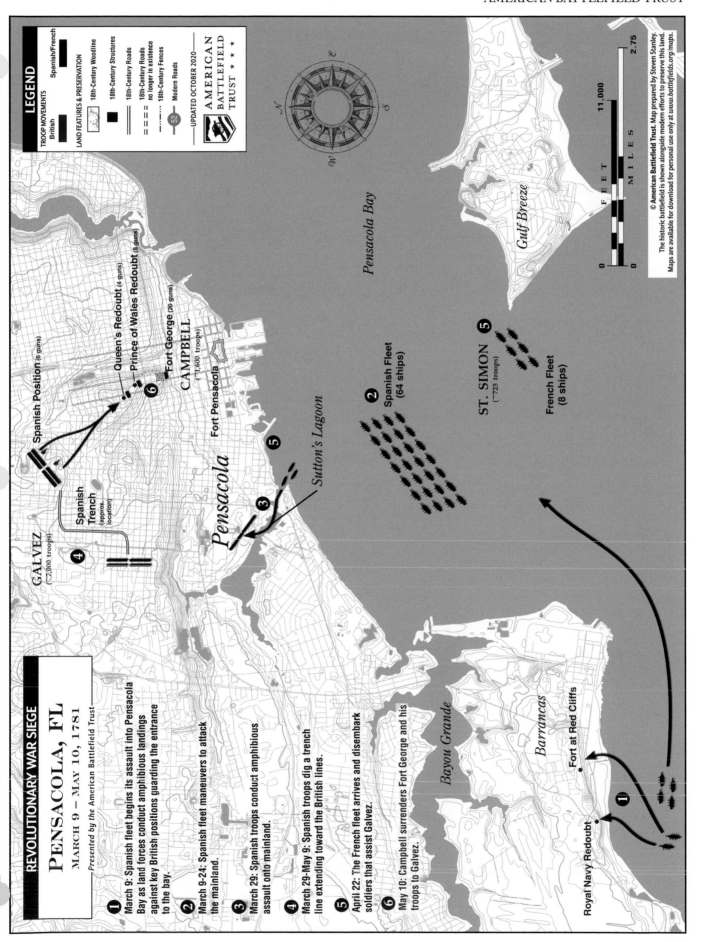

REVOLUTIONARY WAR SIEGE
PENSACOLA, FL
MARCH 9 – MAY 10, 1781

Presented by the American Battlefield Trust

1 March 9: Spanish fleet begins its assault into Pensacola Bay as land forces conduct amphibious landings against key British positions guarding the entrance to the bay.

2 March 9-24: Spanish fleet maneuvers to attack the mainland.

3 March 29: Spanish troops conduct amphibious assault onto mainland.

4 March 29-May 9: Spanish troops dig a trench line extending toward the British lines.

5 April 22: The French fleet arrives and disembark soldiers that assist Galvez.

6 May 10: Campbell surrenders Fort George and his troops to Galvez.

LEGEND

TROOP MOVEMENTS
British   Spanish/French

LAND FEATURES & PRESERVATION
18th-Century Woodline
18th-Century Structures
18th-Century Roads
18th-Century Roads no longer in existence
18th-Century Fences
52 Modern Roads

—— UPDATED OCTOBER 2020 ——

AMERICAN BATTLEFIELD TRUST ★ ★ ★

© American Battlefield Trust. Map prepared by Steven Stanley.
The historic battlefield is shown alongside modern efforts to preserve this land.
Maps are available for download for personal use only at *www.battlefields.org/maps.*

FEET   11,000
MILES   2.75

0

GALVEZ
(~7,000 troops)

Spanish Position (6 guns)

Queen's Redoubt (4 guns)
Prince of Wales Redoubt (8 guns)
Fort George (20 guns)

Spanish Trench (approx. location)

CAMPBELL
(~1,600 troops)

Fort Pensacola

Pensacola

Fort Pensacola

Sutton's Lagoon

Pensacola Bay

Spanish Fleet (64 ships) **2**

ST. SIMON
(~725 troops) **5**

French Fleet (8 ships)

Gulf Breeze

Bayou Grande

Barrancas

Fort at Red Cliffs

Royal Navy Redoubt

1

3

4

5

6

97

BATTLE *of* GUILFORD COURTHOUSE

MARCH 15, 1781

IN THE WEEKS FOLLOWING THE DEFEAT OF TARLETON'S FORCE AT CAMDEN, Greene and Cornwallis initiated a series of marches that carried the two armies out of South Carolina, into North Carolina, and then into a race to the Dan River in southern Virginia. In early March, thousands of militia from Virginia and North Carolina joined Greene's growing army in southern Virginia. In the second week of the month, Greene marched his army of 4,500 back into North Carolina. Meanwhile, Cornwallis had cut away from his own supply line to live off of the land as he pursued Greene through North Carolina. The choice was a poor one, as the Tory forces moved through an area already picked clean by the rebels. Facing supply shortages, and with Greene moving back into North Carolina, Cornwallis sought an immediate battle.

On March 15, 1781, Greene arrayed his arrayed his army for battle near Guilford Courthouse (modern-day Greensboro, North Carolina). Utilizing similar tactics to Morgan at Cowpens, Greene set his men in three lines. The first line consisted of North Carolina militia bolstered by two cannon, riflemen, and dragoons on the respective flanks. The second line consisted of Virginia militia. The third and final line was the backbone of the army: Virginia, Delaware, and Maryland Continentals and eventually four cannon.

Although his army was outnumbered by 2-to-1, Cornwallis went on the offensive. After an early clash between Tarleton's legions and Col. Henry Lee, Cornwallis deployed his army in two lines, with the bulk of his men in the first line, and clashed with Greene's army in the late morning. Roughly 40 yards from the American first line, the North Carolina militia opened fire in one grand volley. The British line staggered but pushed forward. The Tar Heels fled, and the British pursued even as the flanking units sparred with the American riflemen, who opened and disrupted the British lines.

Entering a wood line, the disjointed British line met the second line of Rebel resistance, the Virginia militia. For perhaps thirty minutes, knots of combatants battled it out in the woods. Confusion reigned on parts of the line. Americans mistook Hessians as their own Continentals, allowing the Hessians to closely approach and fire deadly volleys into the Virginians. Patriot forces gave ground reluctantly, but their staggered defense slowed and broke up the British ranks.

Cornwallis and his men finally reached the third American line. In piecemeal fashion, the redcoats thrust their attack uphill into Greene's Continentals. A Maryland Continental regiment broke, and a melee ensued as Continentals and the elite units of Cornwallis's army battled it out. William Washington's Dragoons entered the fray, and vicious hand-to-hand combat ensued.

Greene had seen enough. Wanting to preserve his core of Continentals, he withdrew his army in good order. The redcoats could not pursue. Although victorious, the Pyrrhic victory cost Cornwallis 28% of his army, and the hard campaign overall had taken an even harder toll on them. A few days later, Cornwallis marched his army to the Cape Fear River and Wilmington. After experiencing the obstinate nature of patriots in the Carolinas, Cornwallis set his sights on the richest of the Southern colonies, Virginia.

✳ ✳ PRESERVATION ✳ ✳

To date, the **American Battlefield Trust** has saved **0.40 acres** at Guilford Courthouse Battlefield.

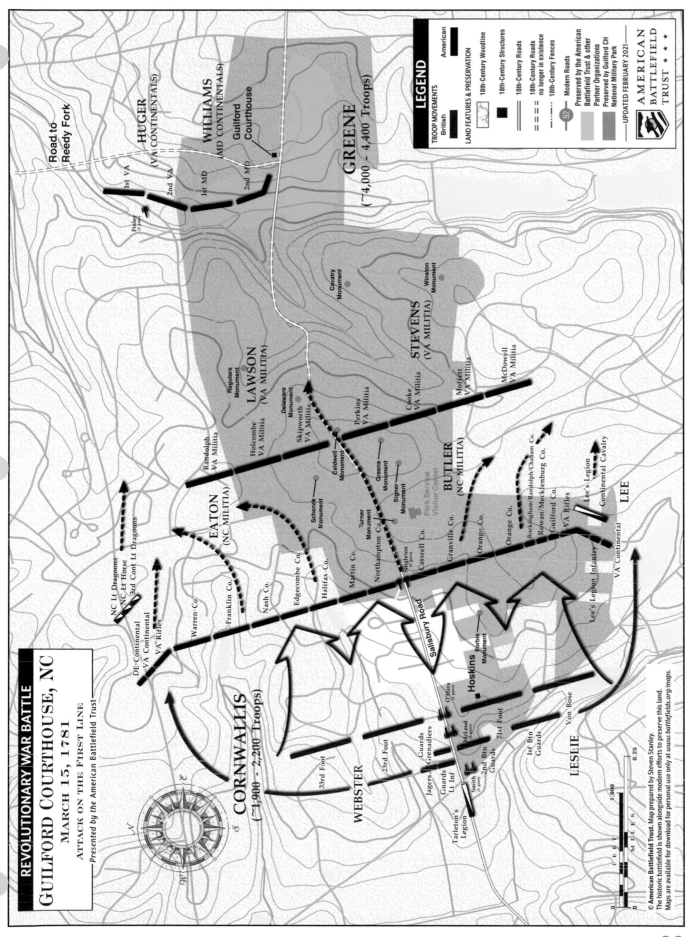

REVOLUTIONARY WAR BATTLE
GUILFORD COURTHOUSE, NC
MARCH 15, 1781
ATTACK ON THE FIRST LINE
Presented by the American Battlefield Trust

LEGEND

TROOP MOVEMENTS
British
American

LAND FEATURES & PRESERVATION
18th-Century Woodline
18th-Century Structures
18th-Century Roads
18th-Century Roads no longer in existence
18th-Century Fences
52 Modern Roads
Preserved by the American Battlefield Trust & other Partner Organizations
Preserved by Guilford CH National Military Park
—UPDATED FEBRUARY 2021—

AMERICAN BATTLEFIELD TRUST ★ ★ ★

Road to Reedy Fork

HUGER
(VA CONTINENTALS)

WILLIAMS
(MD CONTINENTALS)

Guilford Courthouse

1st VA
2nd VA
1st MD
2nd MD
Finley (2 guns)

GREENE
(~4,000 – 4,400 Troops)

Cavalry Monument

Winston Monument

STEVENS
(VA MILITIA)

LAWSON
(VA MILITIA)

Regulars Monument

Delaware Monument

Holcombe VA Militia

Skipworth VA Militia

Caldwell Monument

Perkins VA Militia

Cooke VA Militia

Moffett VA Militia

McDowell VA Militia

Randolph VA Militia

Greene Monument

Signer Monument

Schenck Monument

Turner Monument

Park Service Visitor Center

BUTLER
(NC MILITIA)

Lee's Legion

Continental Cavalry

LEE

EATON
(NC MILITIA)

Edgecombe Co.

Halifax Co.

Martin Co.

Northampton Co.

Singleton (2 guns)

Caswell Co.

Granville Co.

Orange Co.

Orange Co.

Rockingham/Randolph/Chatham Co.

Rowan/Mecklenburg Co.

Guilford Co.

VA Rifles

VA Continental

Lee's Legion Infantry

NC Lt Dragoons
NC Lt Horse
3rd Cont Lt Dragoons

DE Continental
VA Continental
VA Rifles

Warren Co.

Franklin Co.

Nash Co.

Salisbury Road

Forbis Monument

Hoskins

O'Hara (2 guns)

CORNWALLIS
(~1,900 – 2,200 Troops)

WEBSTER

33rd Foot

23rd Foot

Guards Grenadiers

Jägers

Guards Lt Inf

Smith (2 guns)

McLeod (2 guns)

2nd Btn Guards

71st Foot

1st Btn Guards

LESLIE

Von Bose

Tarleton's Legion

MILES
0   0.25
FEET
0   1,000

© American Battlefield Trust. Map prepared by Steven Stanley.
The historic battlefield is shown alongside modern efforts to preserve this land.
Maps are available for download for personal use only at www.battlefields.org/maps.

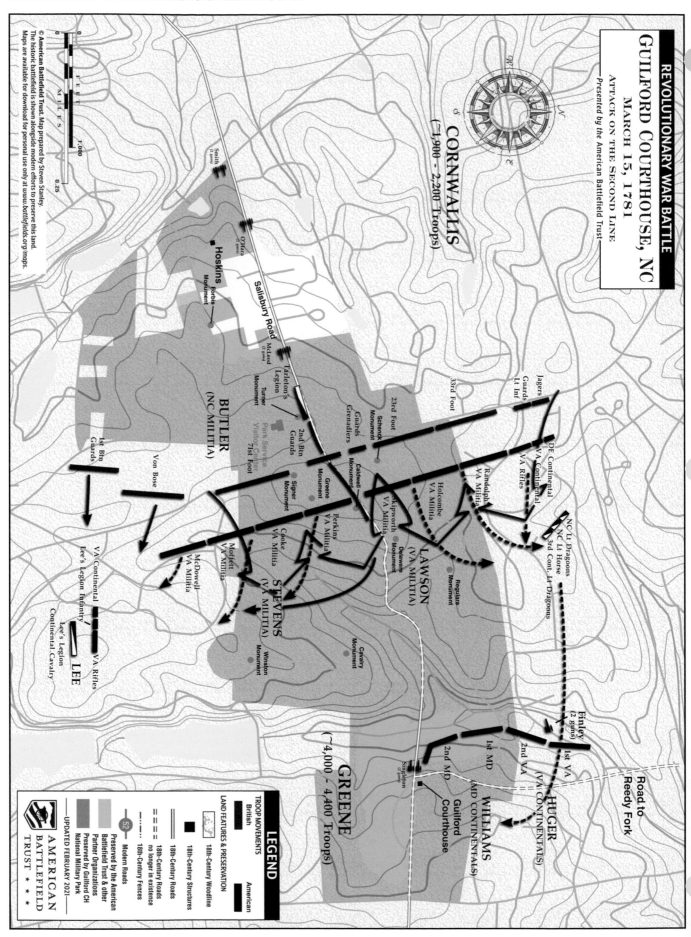

REVOLUTIONARY WAR BATTLE

GUILFORD COURTHOUSE, NC
MARCH 15, 1781
ATTACK ON THE SECOND LINE
Presented by the American Battlefield Trust

CORNWALLIS
(~1,900 - 2,200 Troops)

GREENE
(~4,000 - 4,400 Troops)

LEGEND

TROOP MOVEMENTS
- British
- American

LAND FEATURES & PRESERVATION
- 18th-Century Woodline
- 18th-Century Structures
- 18th-Century Roads
- 18th-Century Roads no longer in existence
- 18th-Century Fences
- Modern Roads
- Preserved by the American Battlefield Trust & other Partner Organizations
- Preserved by Guilford CH National Military Park

UPDATED FEBRUARY 2021

AMERICAN BATTLEFIELD TRUST ★★★

© American Battlefield Trust. Map prepared by Steven Stanley. The historic battlefield is shown alongside modern efforts to preserve this land. Maps are available for download for personal use only at www.battlefields.org/maps.

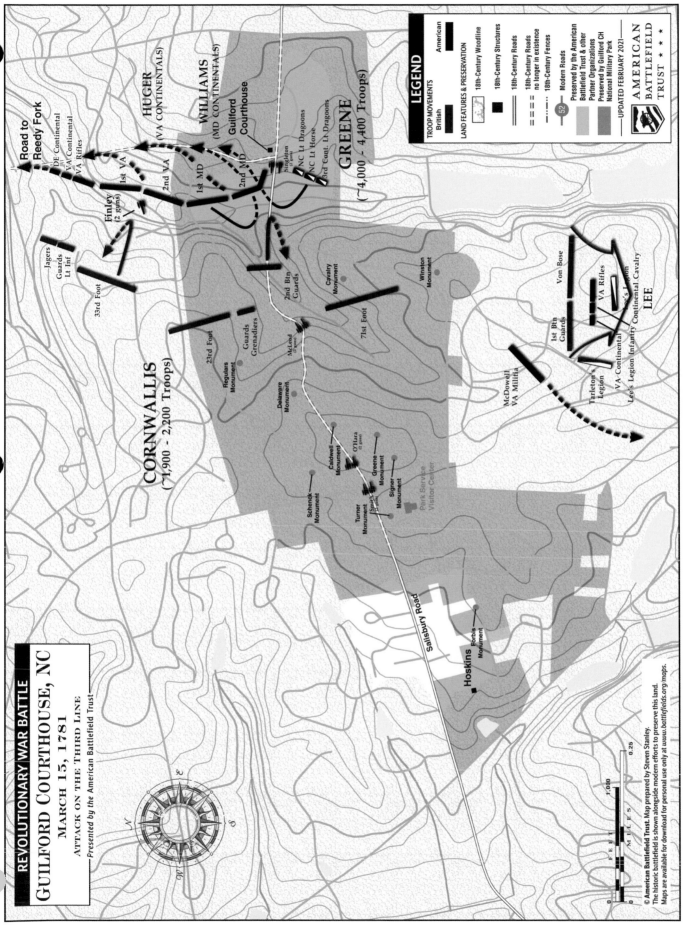

REVOLUTIONARY WAR BATTLE

GUILFORD COURTHOUSE, NC

MARCH 15, 1781

ATTACK ON THE THIRD LINE

Presented by the American Battlefield Trust

AMERICAN BATTLEFIELD TRUST

LEGEND

TROOP MOVEMENTS
British
American

LAND FEATURES & PRESERVATION
18th-Century Woodline
18th-Century Structures
18th-Century Roads
18th-Century Roads no longer in existence
18th-Century Fences
Modern Roads
52
Preserved by the American Battlefield Trust & other Partner Organizations
Preserved by Guilford CH National Military Park

— UPDATED FEBRUARY 2021 —

AMERICAN
BATTLEFIELD
TRUST ★ ★ ★

Road to Reedy Fork

DE Continental
VA Continental
VA Rifles

HUGER
(VA CONTINENTALS)

1st VA

2nd VA

Finley
(2 guns)

Jagers

Guards
Lt Inf

33rd Foot

WILLIAMS
(MD CONTINENTALS)

Guilford Courthouse

1st MD

2nd MD

Singleton
(2 guns)

NC Lt Dragoons

NC Lt Horse

3rd Cont. Lt Dragoons

GREENE
(~4,000 - 4,400 Troops)

CORNWALLIS
(~1,900 - 2,200 Troops)

23rd Foot

Guards Grenadiers

McLeod
(2 guns)

2nd Btn Guards

Cavalry Monument

71st Foot

Winston Monument

Regulars Monument

Delaware Monument

O'Hara
(2 guns)

Caldwell Monument

Greene Monument

Smith
(2 guns)

Signer Monument

Turner Monument

Schenck Monument

Park Service Visitor Center

LEE

Von Bose

VA Rifles

1st Btn Guards

Tarleton's Legion

VA Continental

Lee's Legion Infantry Continental Cavalry

McDowell VA Militia

Salisbury Road

Hoskins

Forbis Monument

101

© American Battlefield Trust. Map prepared by Steven Stanley.
The historic battlefield is shown alongside modern efforts to preserve this land.
Maps are available for download for personal use only at *www.battlefields.org/maps.*

FEET 1,000

MILES 0.25

BATTLE *of* HOBKIRK'S HILL

APRIL 25, 1781

AFTER HIS PYRRHIC VICTORY AT THE BATTLE OF GUILFORD COURT HOUSE, British General Charles Lord Cornwallis began withdrawing towards Wilmington, North Carolina. Initially pursuing Cornwallis's army, General Nathaniel Greene turned south and moved back into South Carolina. Greene hoped to draw his opponent into another battle and defeat him on ground favorable to the Continental Army. Cornwallis, however, refused to take the bait, moving instead into Virginia.

For his part, Greene chose to focus on the British occupying forces that remained in the South. The British held a chain of outposts that ran from Augusta, Georgia, up through South Carolina. Camden, the site of a catastrophic American defeat in the summer of 1780, lay in the center of the British line. The British garrison at Camden was led by Lt. Col. Francis Rawdon, who had been left in effective command of British forces in the Carolinas and Georgia after the departure of Cornwallis.

Although Greene attempted to approach Camden in secret, his arrival did not go undetected. The British forces positioned behind fortifications prepared for an American attack. Nonetheless, Rawdon was in a precarious position. Not only was his position threatened by Greene, but his supply line connecting Camden with Charleston was also under attack by Francis Marion's partisan band. The British commander was forced to dispatch 500 men under Lt. Col. John Watson Tadwell-Watson to seek out and destroy the legendary "Swamp Fox." Rawdon was left with only 900 men to defend Camden.

On April 20, Greene arrayed his forces on a ridge known as Hobkirk's Hill, a mile and half north of town. Greene commanded 1,551 men, most of whom were regular Continental Army soldiers. He hoped to draw out and destroy the British army. The next day, Greene heard that Watson's force was en route back to Camden. In response, the American general detached his artillery and a portion of his infantry to cover the road from Charleston.

On the morning of April 25, a deserter from Greene's army arrived in Camden and informed Rawdon of the division of the American army. With the Patriots on Hobkirk's Hill temporarily outnumbered and unsupported by artillery, the British commander decided to strike. He gathered as many of his men as were fit to bear arms, including his musicians, and advanced on Greene's position.

At around 11 a.m., musket fire from Greene's pickets alerted the Patriots to their peril. As Rawdon advanced on Hobkirk's Hill from the southeast, the American pickets fell back slowly, firing as they went and buying time for Greene to prepare. Suddenly, as the British moved forward, into a hail of grapshot hail of grapeshot. Unbeknownst to Rawdon, Greene had reunited his army early that morning after discovering that the rumor of Watson's approach was false and attacked Rawdon's flanks.

Greene's attack initially went as planned. The British were confused by the unexpected presence of American artillery and suffered heavy losses. Some of Rawdon's men fled before the American attack. Unfortunately for Greene, the Patriots' attack began to unravel. Greene ordered a portion of his force to hold off the British attackers while the rest of the American army retreated. As Greene's army retreated, some of the American gunners abandoned their pieces, leaving the artillery at risk of capture. Greene ordered the guns saved, and after a melee, they were extracted from the field.

As at the Battle of Guilford Court House, Hobkirk's Hill was a pyrrhic victory for the British, who could ill afford heavy losses. Rawdon ultimately concluded that the American army was too strong, and on May 10, he abandoned Camden.

✳ ✳ PRESERVATION ✳ ✳

To date, the **American Battlefield Trust** has not saved any land at Hobrirk's Hill Battlefield.

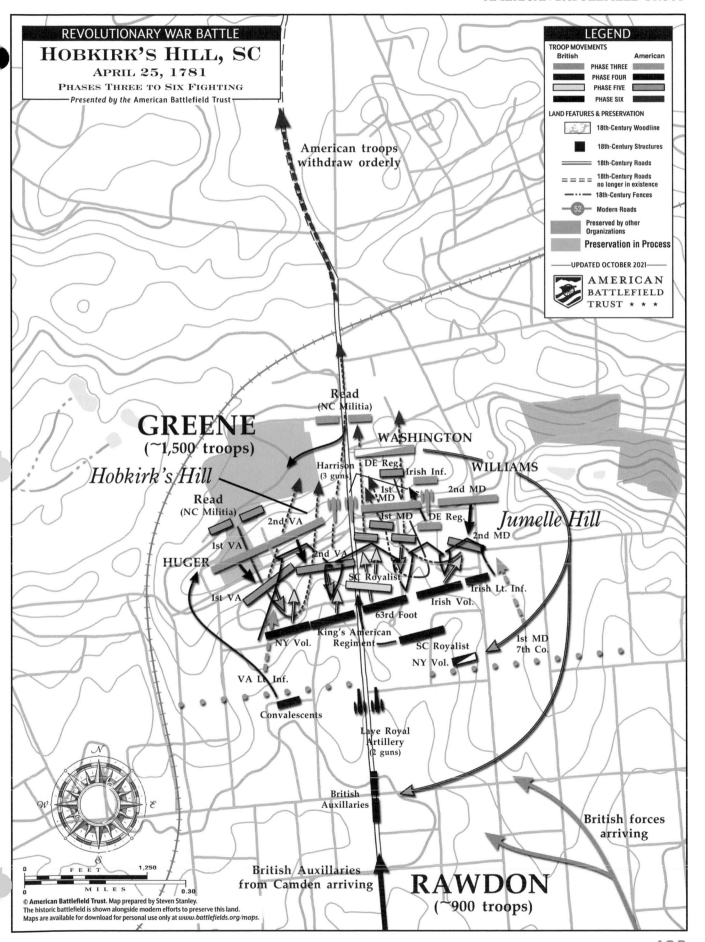

REVOLUTIONARY WAR BATTLE
HOBKIRK'S HILL, SC
APRIL 25, 1781
PHASES THREE TO SIX FIGHTING
Presented by the American Battlefield Trust

LEGEND

TROOP MOVEMENTS

British	American
PHASE THREE	
PHASE FOUR	
PHASE FIVE	
PHASE SIX	

LAND FEATURES & PRESERVATION

- 18th-Century Woodline
- 18th-Century Structures
- 18th-Century Roads
- 18th-Century Roads no longer in existence
- 18th-Century Fences
- 52 Modern Roads
- Preserved by other Organizations
- **Preservation in Process**

—UPDATED OCTOBER 2021—

AMERICAN BATTLEFIELD TRUST ★ ★ ★

American troops withdraw orderly

Read (NC Militia)

WASHINGTON

GREENE
(~1,500 troops)

Hobkirk's Hill

Read (NC Militia)

Harrison (3 guns)

DE Reg.

Irish Inf.

WILLIAMS

1st MD

2nd MD

2nd VA

1st MD

DE Reg.

Jumelle Hill

1st VA

2nd MD

HUGER

2nd VA

SC Royalist

1st VA

Irish Lt. Inf.

Irish Vol.

63rd Foot

1st MD 7th Co.

NY Vol.

King's American Regiment

SC Royalist

NY Vol.

VA Lt. Inf.

Convalescents

Laye Royal Artillery (2 guns)

British Auxillaries

British forces arriving

British Auxillaries from Camden arriving

RAWDON
(~900 troops)

N
W E
S

FEET 1,250
MILES 0.30

© American Battlefield Trust. Map prepared by Steven Stanley.
The historic battlefield is shown alongside modern efforts to preserve this land.
Maps are available for download for personal use only at *www.battlefields.org/maps*.

SIEGE *of* NINETY SIX

MAY 22 – JUNE 19, 1781

THE TOWN OF NINETY SIX, SOUTH CAROLINA, IS ONE OF THE MOST STRANGELY named hamlets in the state. There are numerous accounts as to why the settlement was named Ninety Six. It was supposed to be 96 miles from the nearest Cherokee village—but it was not. The name may have its origins with a Welsh word. Or it may have to do with early notations on maps. Regardless, Ninety Six was the intersection of twelve roads and was the home of two towns and a trading post. It was also the scene of military action throughout the American Revolutionary War.

War came quickly to Ninety Six, where patriots and loyalists were already sharply divided by the struggle with the frontier Cherokee. In July 1775, when patriots suspected that loyalists were supplying the Cherokee, they initiated a three-day battle for control of the town that culminated in an uneasy truce. This, the first major engagement outside of New England, brought a national character to the burgeoning revolution.

Tensions simmered through the 1770s while the British army continued to focus on the war in New England. In the wake of the battle of Guilford Courthouse, General Greene initiated a campaign to wrestle the Carolinas from British control. In May of 1781, Greene set his sights on a British garrison of 550 men defending Ninety Six.

Ninety Six was protected by the formidable Star Fort and the smaller Stockade Fort. Its garrison was made up almost entirely of loyalists from the South and, ironically, from New York. Colonel John Cruger, Jr., the garrison commander, was a New Yorker by birth and a former mayor of New York City.

Greene initiated siege operations, much of which was overseen by Tadeusz Ko ciuszko, a Polish-born officer who had loaned his engineering skills to the patriot cause since the Saratoga Campaign. Patriot soldiers laid siege to the town, cutting trenches that zig-zagged towards the British positions.

Greene's siege lasted from May 22-June 18, one of the longest sieges of the Revolution. The loyalists managed to maintain control of the Spring Branch water supply, thus averting a major crisis. Meanwhile, Greene divided his force and sent Harry Lee and his legion to capture Augusta, South Carolina, which they did, returning on June 8.

Soon after, Greene received word that British troops led by Lord Rawdon were marching from Charleston to relieve Ninety Six. Greene launched an assault on the fortifications. American storming parties captured both forts with supporting fire from sharpshooters in a siege tower on the American lines. The redcoats rallied, however, and retook the forts. Greene broke off the attack and withdrew, ending the siege. The loyalists eventually withdrew, as well, burning the town behind them.

Although Greene failed to take Ninety Six, he had begun his campaign boldly. His continued operations in the Carolinas would prove essential to overall American victory in the Revolution as he drove the tories from their backcountry outposts to the safety of Charleston.

✻ ✻ **PRESERVATION** ✻ ✻

To date, the **American Battlefield Trust** has not saved any land at Ninety Six Battlefield.

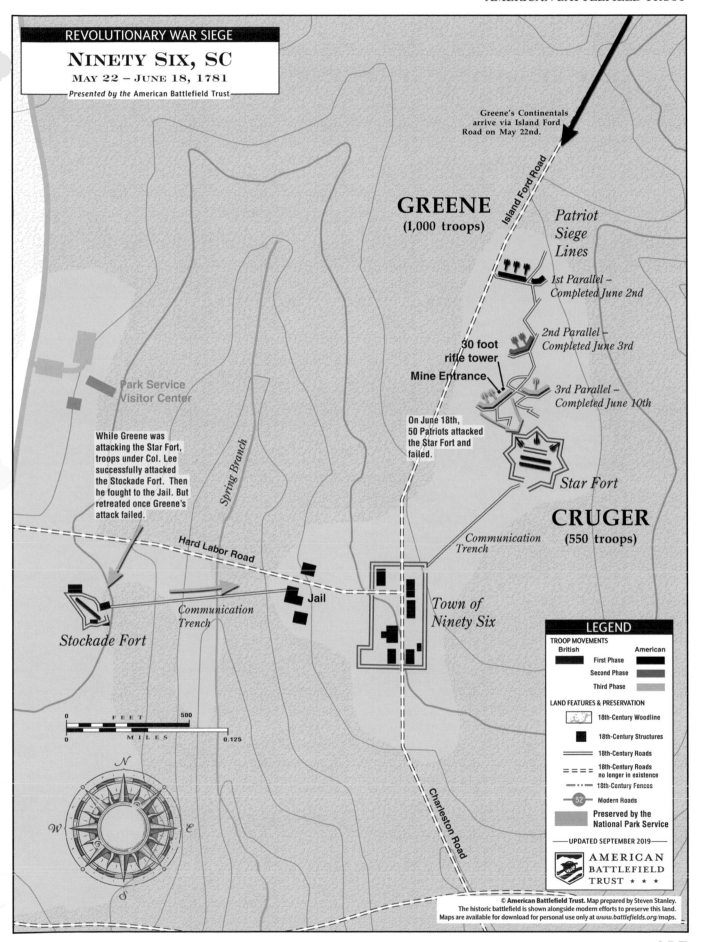

REVOLUTIONARY WAR SIEGE
NINETY SIX, SC
MAY 22 – JUNE 18, 1781
Presented by the American Battlefield Trust

Greene's Continentals arrive via Island Ford Road on May 22nd.

Island Ford Road

GREENE
(1,000 troops)

Patriot Siege Lines

1st Parallel –
Completed June 2nd

2nd Parallel –
Completed June 3rd

30 foot rifle tower

Mine Entrance

3rd Parallel –
Completed June 10th

On June 18th, 50 Patriots attacked the Star Fort and failed.

Star Fort

CRUGER
(550 troops)

Park Service Visitor Center

While Greene was attacking the Star Fort, troops under Col. Lee successfully attacked the Stockade Fort. Then he fought to the Jail. But retreated once Greene's attack failed.

Spring Branch

Communication Trench

Hard Labor Road

Jail

Communication Trench

Town of Ninety Six

Stockade Fort

Charleston Road

FEET 500
0
MILES 0.125
0

N
W   E
S

LEGEND
TROOP MOVEMENTS
British   American
First Phase
Second Phase
Third Phase

LAND FEATURES & PRESERVATION
18th-Century Woodline
18th-Century Structures
18th-Century Roads
18th-Century Roads no longer in existence
18th-Century Fences
52 Modern Roads
Preserved by the National Park Service

— UPDATED SEPTEMBER 2019 —

AMERICAN
BATTLEFIELD
TRUST ★ ★ ★

BATTLE *of* GREEN SPRING

JULY 6, 1781

IN THE SPRING OF 1781, THE AMERICAN REVOLUTIONARY WAR HEATED up in Virginia. Lord Cornwallis shifted his army from Wilmington, N.C., to Virginia. Loyalist forces commanded by the turncoat Benedict Arnold campaigned through the region. Virginia Governor Thomas Jefferson was forced to flee in the face of the British advance. With Washington still fixated on retaking New York City, he dispatched two trusted subordinates to Virginia, Generals Anthony Wayne and the Marquis de Lafayette. The two Patriot officers played a cat-and-mouse game with Cornwallis. Like Greene before them, they eluded the British main force time and again, avoiding a pitched battle, but acting as a shadow.

Withdrawing from Richmond back down the Virginia peninsula between the York and James Rivers, the British continued skirmishing with their pursuers and finally reached the area of Jamestown on July 4, 1781. Having been ordered by General Sir Henry Clinton to send troops to New York City, Cornwallis's plan was to cross the James River at the Jamestown Ferry and then proceed to Portsmouth. However, informed that Lafayette was closing in upon the British, Cornwallis prepared an ambush.

Green Spring was named after the plantation that stood there and was surrounded by marshy ground, dense woods, and valleys. The British positioned their regular regiments in the woods and valleys, concealed from any approaching enemy force. The British baggage train was sent to the south side of the James River, along with the Loyalist Queens Rangers and North Carolina Provincials. The Americans believed the British force was divided and that they could catch their prey in the midst of crossing the wide river.

On the morning of July 6, upon reaching the area of Green Spring, the Americans began skirmishing with pickets from Banastre Tarleton's command. Under the misconception that the British force was vulnerable, Wayne and Lafayette snapped into action. Wayne formed his battle line as Lafayette explored the possibilities of crushing this British force on the north side of the river. As he proceeded forward, he noted large groups of men in red coats formed in lines. Cornwallis had led the Americans right into his trap.

Lafayette galloped back to the advance guard under Wayne, but it was too late. Wayne was advancing with several regiments of Pennsylvania Continentals, light infantry, and Virginia riflemen. Veteran redcoats smashed into Wayne's force. A bayonet charge drove in the American right flank. Lafayette gave the order for the entire American force to withdraw. In an effort to save the army, Wayne made a desperate a bayonet charge straight into the British center. Cornwallis led the British in a countercharge, which drove Wayne's men off of the field. With the Americans in full retreat, Cornwallis chose not to pursue, and instead took the opportunity to safely cross his men to the south side of the James.

The Americans fell back to Richmond. Cornwallis marched to Yorktown, effectively cornering his own army. Seizing the opportunity, Lafayette wrote to Washington, asking his to advance into Virginia. The decisive battle of the war in the South was at hand.

✳ ✳ PRESERVATION ✳ ✳

To date, the **American Battlefield Trust** has not saved any land at Green Spring Battlefield.

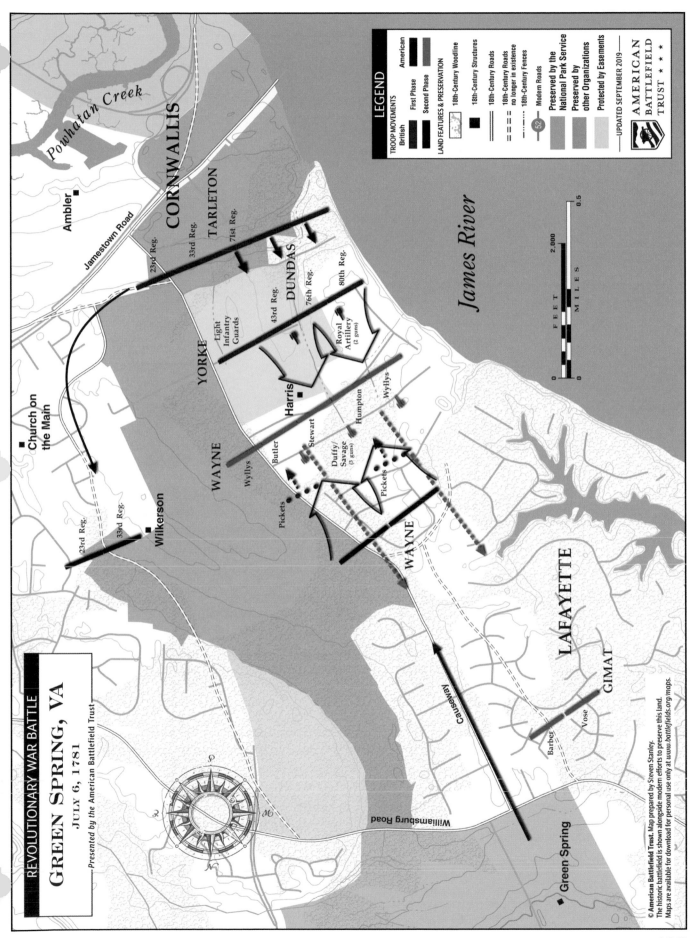

REVOLUTIONARY WAR BATTLE
GREEN SPRING, VA
JULY 6, 1781
Presented by the American Battlefield Trust

Powhatan Creek

James River

CORNWALLIS

TARLETON

DUNDAS

YORKE

WAYNE

WAYNE

LAFAYETTE

GIMAT

Ambler

Church on the Main

Wilkerson

Jamestown Road

23rd Reg.

33rd Reg.

71st Reg.

23rd Reg.

33rd Reg.

43rd Reg.

76th Reg.

80th Reg.

Light Infantry Guards

Royal Artillery (2 guns)

Harris

Butler

Stewart

Wyllys

Humpton

Wyllys

Pickets

Pickets

Duffy/ Savage (3 guns)

Causeway

Williamsburg Road

Barber

Vose

Green Spring

AMERICAN BATTLEFIELD TRUST

LEGEND

TROOP MOVEMENTS
British   American
First Phase
Second Phase

LAND FEATURES & PRESERVATION
18th-Century Woodline
18th-Century Structures
18th-Century Roads
18th-Century Roads no longer in existence
18th-Century Fences
52 Modern Roads

Preserved by the National Park Service
Preserved by other Organizations
Protected by Easements

—UPDATED SEPTEMBER 2019—

AMERICAN BATTLEFIELD TRUST ★ ★ ★

FEET   0   2,000
MILES 0   0.5

BATTLE *of* EUTAW SPRINGS

SEPTEMBER 8, 1781

ALTHOUGH GENERAL NATHANAEL GREENE FAILED TO TAKE NINETY SIX through siege, the British forces in the region decided to consolidate their position and move back toward Charleston. While Greene was not scoring battlefield victories at Guilford Courthouse, Ninety Six, or Hobkirk's Hill (April 25, 1871), his war of exhaustion was wearing down the enemy. Local patriots such as Generals Francis Marion and Thomas Pickens harassed Tory forces at every opportunity. In August of 1781, overall British command in South Carolina fell on the shoulders of Col. Alexander Stewart. In an effort to quell the rebels, Stewart marched a force out of Charleston to do battle and hopefully crush Greene's pesky force once and for all.

Greene had his army up and marching early on the morning of September 8, 1781. His destination was Stewart's camp near the Wantoot Plantation on the banks of Eutaw Creek, a tributary of the Santee River. Lacking supplies, Stewart had detached roughly a quarter of his army to forage for yams near the plantation. There, a group of American cavalrymen surprised a contingent of Loyalist scouts. The tories chased the whigs—only to be ambushed by Greene's vanguard. The Americans continued their counterattack and scooped up more than 400 prisoners of the British foraging party.

Next, Greene deployed his infantry in two lines, militia in front of Continentals, and advanced on the British position. Colonel Stewart hastily threw together a defensive line and managed to counterattack the rebels. Utilizing the bayonet, Stewart's troops pierced Greene's lines. The American line was restored, fractured again, and then rallied once more, finally managing to drive back the British into the camps.

Order in the American ranks was lost as the troops looted the British camp. This brief lull allowed Stewart to rally his men and fortify their position in and around the brick plantation home. A renewal of the American assault failed to dislodge the tories from their new position. In the melee, Col. William Washington was unhorsed, wounded, and captured by the British. The Americans were falling back by the time darkness ended the battle.

In a rare showing, Greene stayed on the field to offer battle the next day. Prior to this, the wily American commander normally slipped away to fight elsewhere another day. Stewart, too, stayed in place. On September 10, Stewart marched for Moncks Corner. Every step he made toward Charleston took the British one step closer to reinforcement and the safety of heavy guns and fortifications.

Stewart later wrote to Cornwallis that he had totally defeated Greene, which was a boastful overstatement of the outcome of the battle. Greene's army remained intact and in fighting shape. The Continental Congress awarded Greene a gold medal for his part in the Battle of Eutaw Springs.

While other minor engagements took place in South Carolina for the next two years, the bulk of the fighting in the Deep South was over. It may not have been pretty, but Nathanael Greene thwarted the British "Southern Strategy" at every turn. Now it was up to George Washington to land the killing blow.

✳ ✳ PRESERVATION ✳ ✳

To date, the **American Battlefield Trust** has saved **14.19 acres** at Eutaw Springs Battlefield.

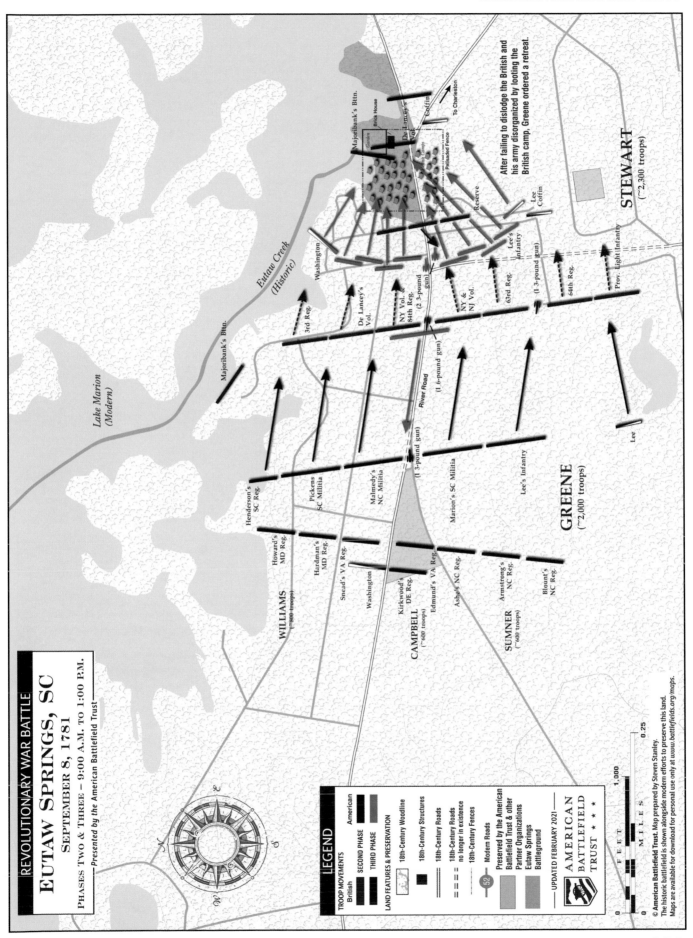

REVOLUTIONARY WAR BATTLE

EUTAW SPRINGS, SC
SEPTEMBER 8, 1781

PHASES TWO & THREE – 9:00 A.M. TO 1:00 P.M.

— Presented by the American Battlefield Trust —

After failing to dislodge the British and his army disorganized by looting the British camp, Greene ordered a retreat.

Lake Marion
(Modern)

Eutaw Creek
(Historic)

Majoribank's Bttn.

Brick House

Garden

De Lancey's Vol.

Coffin

To Charleston

Reserve

Lee Coffin

Lee's Infantry

Washington

3rd Reg.

De Lancey's Vol.

NY Vol. & 84th Reg.
(2 3-pound gun)

NY & NJ Vol.

63rd Reg.

64th Reg.

Prov. Light Infantry

(1 3-pound gun)

River Road

(1 6-pound gun)

(1 3-pound gun)

Henderson's SC Reg.

Pickens SC Militia

Malmedy's NC Militia

Marion's SC Militia

Lee's Infantry

Lee

WILLIAMS
(~800 troops)

Howard's MD Reg.

Hardman's MD Reg.

Snead's VA Reg.

Washington

Kirkwood's DE Reg.

Edmund's VA Reg.

Ashe's NC Reg.

Armstrong's NC Reg.

Blount's NC Reg.

CAMPBELL
(~600 troops)

SUMNER
(~600 troops)

GREENE
(~2,000 troops)

STEWART
(~2,300 troops)

LEGEND

TROOP MOVEMENTS
- British
- SECOND PHASE
- THIRD PHASE
- American

LAND FEATURES & PRESERVATION
- 18th-Century Woodline
- 18th-Century Structures
- 18th-Century Roads
- 18th-Century Roads no longer in existence
- 18th-Century Fences
- 52 Modern Roads
- Preserved by the American Battlefield Trust & other Partner Organizations
- Eutaw Springs Battleground

— UPDATED FEBRUARY 2021 —

AMERICAN BATTLEFIELD TRUST ★ ★ ★

MILES 0.25

FEET 1,000

SIEGE *of* YORKTOWN

SEPTEMBER 29 – OCTOBER 19, 1781

AFTER YEARS OF STAGNATION, GEORGE WASHINGTON'S WAR SPRANG TO LIFE in the fall of 1781. Having kept a close eye on Clinton's army in New York City, and nurturing the new French alliance, Washington was called to action by Lafayette's message that Cornwallis situated his army at Yorktown. If the Franco-American alliance could move quickly enough, the principal British army in the south could be captured or destroyed. A French fleet sailed for the Chesapeake Bay, and Washington and the French General Comte de Rochambeau marched their 20,000-man joint army south to Yorktown.

Cornwallis established a fortified line around Yorktown, bolstered by a series of redoubts. As the combined armies of Washington and Rochambeau arrived onto the field, the French and Americans established a line of circumvallation and engaged in siege operations. The Royal Navy had intended to sail up the Chesapeake Bay in order to provide supplies and much-needed reinforcements for Cornwallis's army; however, no such aid materialized. On September 5, French warships had met the British fleet defeated it at the battle of the Capes.

With the help of French engineers, Allied troops began to dig a series of parallel trenches that brought troops and artillery close enough to inflict damage on the British. On the afternoon of October 9, the Allied barrage began, with the French opening the salvo. On the American side, George Washington touched off the first American cannon to commence their bombardment. For nearly a week, the artillery barrage was ceaseless, shattering British nerves and punching holes in British defenses.

On October 11, Washington ordered men to dig a second parallel 400 yards closer to the British lines. British redoubts #9 and #10 prevented the second parallel from being dug all the way to the York River, allowing the British to still reinforce the garrisons inside the redoubts. Three days later, French and American forces assaulted Redoubts #9 and #10, respectively. Washington chose to launch the attack on a moonless night, adding to the element of surprise. Intense combat followed, but the redoubts were now in Allied hands.

Surrounded on all sides, Cornwallis ordered a futile counterattack on October 15, which failed miserably. On the morning of October 17, a lone British drummer boy, beating "parley," and a British officer waving a white handkerchief tied to the end of a sword appeared on a parapet. Two days later, in a field outside of Yorktown, British troops and their Hessian auxiliaries furled their colors, lay down their arms, and surrendered. Cornwallis feigned illness rather than surrender to Washington, who, in turn, forced the British to surrender to his second in command, Benjamin Lincoln, the man who had surrendered Charleston a year and a half earlier.

Yorktown marks the unofficial end of the American Revolutionary War. Washington's army remained intact, and small engagements flared up from time to time. It was the Treaty of Paris, signed in September of 1783, that marked the official end of the conflict. On Thursday, November 25, 1783, the last British soldier walked up the gangplank and evacuated New York City. Washington led his small but victorious army into the prize he had so long yearned to retake. The long war was over. Independence was won. A new chapter in world history was about to be written.

✳ ✳ PRESERVATION ✳ ✳

To date, the **American Battlefield Trust** has saved **48.76 acres** at Yorktown Battlefield.

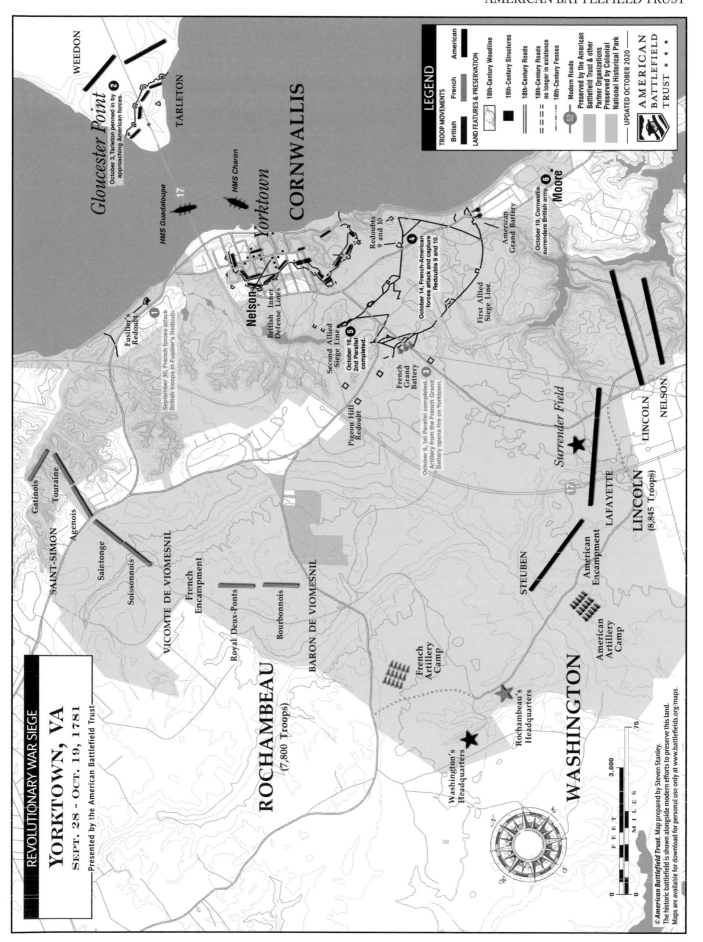

REVOLUTIONARY WAR SIEGE
YORKTOWN, VA
SEPT. 28 - OCT. 19, 1781
Presented by the American Battlefield Trust

LEGEND

TROOP MOVEMENTS

British | French | American

18th-Century Woodline

LAND FEATURES & PRESERVATION

18th-Century Structures

18th-Century Roads

18th-Century Roads no longer in existence

18th-Century Fences

Modern Roads

52 — Preserved by the American Battlefield Trust & other Partner Organizations

Preserved by Colonial National Historical Park

UPDATED OCTOBER 2020

AMERICAN BATTLEFIELD TRUST ★ ★ ★

WEEDON

TARLETON

Gloucester Point
2 October 3, Tarleton penned in by approaching American forces.

TARLETON

HMS Guadaloupe

17

HMS Charon

Yorktown

CORNWALLIS

Nelson

British Inner Defense Lines

Fusilier's Redoubt
1 September 30, French forces attack British troops in Fusilier's Redoubt.

Redoubts 9 and 10
4 October 14, French-American forces attack and capture Redoubts 9 and 10.

American Grand Battery

6 October 19, Cornwallis surrenders British army.

Moore

First Allied Siege Line

Second Allied Siege Line
5 October 16, 2nd Parallel completed.

French Grand Battery
3 October 6, 1st Parallel completed. Artillery from the French Grand Battery opens fire on Yorktown.

Pigeon Hill Redoubt

SAINT-SIMON

Gatinois
Touraine
Agenois
Saintonge
Soissonnois

VICOMTE DE VIOMESNIL

French Encampment

Royal Deux-Ponts

BARON DE VIOMESNIL

Bourbonnois

ROCHAMBEAU
(7,800 Troops)

French Artillery Camp

Rochambeau's Headquarters

Washington's Headquarters

WASHINGTON

American Artillery Camp

STEUBEN

American Encampment

LAFAYETTE

Surrender Field

17

LINCOLN

LINCOLN
(8,845 Troops)

NELSON

FEET
3,000
0

MILES
0   .75

© *American Battlefield Trust.* Map prepared by Steven Stanley.
The historic battlefield is shown alongside modern efforts to preserve this land.
Maps are available for download for personal use only at www.battlefields.org/maps.

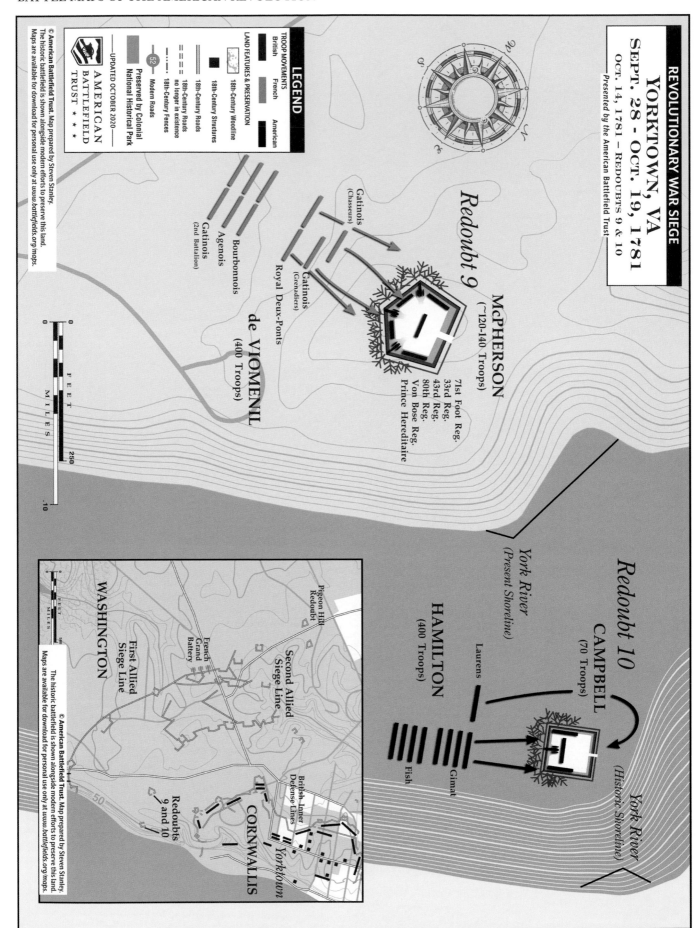

REVOLUTIONARY WAR SIEGE

YORKTOWN, VA
SEPT. 28 - OCT. 19, 1781
OCT. 14, 1781 – REDOUBTS 9 & 10

Presented by the American Battlefield Trust

LEGEND

TROOP MOVEMENTS
British
French
American

LAND FEATURES & PRESERVATION
18th-Century Woodline
18th-Century Structures
18th-Century Roads
18th-Century Roads no longer in existence
18th-Century Fences
Modern Roads
52
Preserved by Colonial National Historical Park

—UPDATED OCTOBER 2020—

AMERICAN BATTLEFIELD TRUST ★ ★ ★

© American Battlefield Trust. Map prepared by Steven Stanley.
The historic battlefield is shown alongside modern efforts to preserve this land.
Maps are available for download for personal use only at www.battlefields.org/maps.

Redoubt 9

McPHERSON
(~120-140 Troops)

Gatinois (Chasseurs)

Gatinois (2nd Battalion)

Agenois

Bourbonnois

Gatinois (Grenadiers)

Royal Deux-Ponts

de VIOMENIL
(400 Troops)

71st Foot Reg.
33rd Reg.
43rd Reg.
80th Reg.
Von Bose Reg.
Prince Hereditaire

FEET
0   250

MILES
0   .10

York River
(Present Shoreline)

Redoubt 10

CAMPBELL
(70 Troops)

HAMILTON
(400 Troops)

Laurens

Gimat

Fish

York River
(Historic Shoreline)

WASHINGTON

Pigeon Hill Redoubt

French Grand Battery

First Allied Siege Line

Second Allied Siege Line

Redoubts 9 and 10

British Inner Defense Lines

CORNWALLIS

Yorktown

50

© American Battlefield Trust. Map prepared by Steven Stanley.
The historic battlefield is shown alongside modern efforts to preserve this land.
Maps are available for download for personal use only at www.battlefields.org/maps.

APPENDIX A
GLOSSARY

BACKCOUNTRY
Sparsely inhabited rural areas; defined in South Carolina as 50 miles or farther inland from the coast.

CONTINENTAL
Another term for Patriots, or those who supported the United States during the American Revolution. The term can also specifically refer to those who fought in the Continental Army, the official standing army of the United States during the war.

CONTINENTAL ARMY
The official army of the United States that was established by the Second Continental Congress in 1775.

CROWN FORCES
Consisted of regiments who served the British in the war..

FEDERALIST
Relating to or denoting a system of government in which several states unite under a central authority.

FUSILIERS
A member of any of several British regiments formerly armed with fusils.

HESSIANS
Name for the professional soldiers from the German land of Hesse hired by the British to fight in America.

LOWCOUNTY
Coastal populated areas urban like Beaufort, Charlestown, and Georgetown and rural areas.

LOYALIST
Those Americans professing loyalty to King George III and England; also called Tories, Royalists, or Kings Men.

MINUTEMAN
One subset of the Massachusetts or New England militia that was prepared to fight at a moment's notice.

PARTISAN
A member of an irregular military force. Partisans formed to oppose control of an area by the British army of occupation by taking part in some kind of insurgent or guerrilla activity like ambushes of supply columns.

PATRIOT
American colonists who rejected British rule during the American Revolution, also called a Whig.

PROVINCIAL TROOPS
American Loyalist troops fighting fulltime for the British. These soldiers armed, equipped, clothed, and paid by the British, and were well trained and led by regular British officers.

REBEL
A term referring to colonists who fought against the British Crown. Also called Patriots, Continentals, Yankees, Whigs, or Colonials.

REGULARS
Term for professional British soldiers sent from England to fight in America.

ROYALIST
Those Americans professing loyalty to King George III and England, also called Tories, Loyalists, or Kings Men.

TORY
Someone who is loyal, or seemingly loyal, to Great Britain. "Tory" was often used as a derogatory term to describe federalists who opposed war with Great Britain. The word is derived from middle Irish words meaning "robber," "outlaw," or "pursued man."

WHIGS
A member of the British reforming and constitutional party that sought the supremacy of Parliament; American colonists who rejected British rule during the American Revolution, also called Patriots.

APPENDIX B
THE LIBERTY TRAIL

FOR MORE THAN THREE DECADES, THE AMERICAN BATTLEFIELD TRUST has worked tirelessly to preserve hallowed ground from the Revolutionary War, War of 1812, and Civil War, resulting in the permanent protection of more than 53,000 acres of battlefield land in 24 states to date. In addition, the Trust has brought historical interpretation to scores of battlefield sites using various tools and techniques, including the installation of on-site interpretive signage and, in more recent years, the development of our Mobile Apps.

As the 250th anniversary of the nation's founding nears, the Trust is exploring a variety of programs designed to ensure that our organization's contributions to this commemoration leaves a powerful and lasting legacy of preservation and education for current and future generations. One such initiative is The Liberty Trail, an innovative driving route designed to connect key Revolutionary War battlefields of the Southern Campaigns of the American Revolution, beginning in South Carolina.

The cornerstone of The Liberty Trail, like so much of the work we do at the American Battlefield Trust, is the preservation of hallowed battlegrounds. Through this project, thousands of acres of battlefield land will be permanently protected. Today, most of these sites are blank slates—quiet fields and forests waiting to tell their stories. While the names of these Southern Campaign battles may not be as well known to many people, the toil and sacrifice that occurred at places like Eutaw Springs, Camden, and Waxhaws played critical and often determinative roles in the winning of American Independence.

Once preserved, these battlefields will be brought to life with innovative on-site interpretation enhanced by cutting-edge digital offerings. An engaging and interactive mobile tour will connect sites along The Liberty Trail—including existing National Park Service, state, and local parks—and guide visitors between these battlefields. Once on-site, the mobile tour will deliver rich content that explains the battles and highlights the many diverse individuals who participated in the Southern Campaigns. Each site on The Liberty Trail, whether a full-scale battlefield park or a roadside pull-off, will be an "outdoor classroom" designed to teach students of all ages and inspire visitors to continue their educational journeys.

The American Battlefield Trust has partnered with the South Carolina Battleground Trust to lead this historic effort to protect The Liberty Trail's battlefields and create new opportunities for visitors to engage with this chapter of American history. Numerous dedicated partners at the federal, state, and local levels have been, and will continue to be, critical to the success of The Liberty Trail. As we continue our work on this initiative, we do so with the goal of creating a unique educational and heritage tourism experience that can serve as a model for future projects undertaken by the Trust and our partners to share the history of America's first century.

To learn more about our efforts to blaze The Liberty Trail, please visit www.TheLibertyTrail.org.

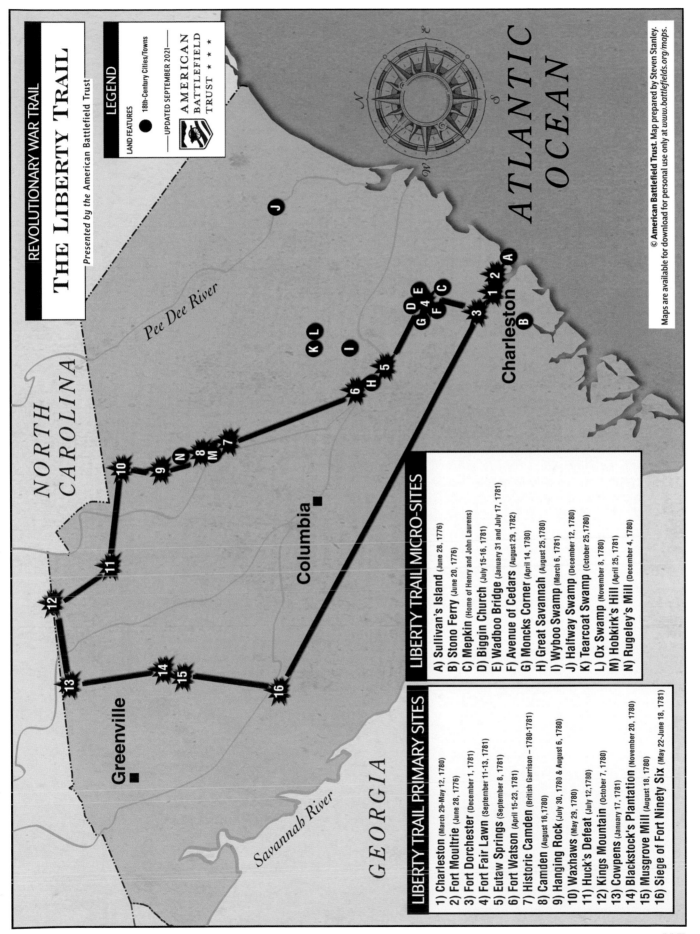

REVOLUTIONARY WAR TRAIL

THE LIBERTY TRAIL

Presented by the American Battlefield Trust

LEGEND

LAND FEATURES

● 18th-Century Cities/Towns

—UPDATED SEPTEMBER 2021—

AMERICAN BATTLEFIELD TRUST ★ ★ ★

ATLANTIC OCEAN

Pee Dee River

NORTH CAROLINA

Charleston

Columbia

Greenville

GEORGIA

Savannah River

LIBERTY TRAIL PRIMARY SITES

1) Charleston (March 29-May 12, 1780)
2) Fort Moultrie (June 28, 1776)
3) Fort Dorchester (December 1, 1781)
4) Fort Fair Lawn (September 11-13, 1781)
5) Eutaw Springs (September 8, 1781)
6) Fort Watson (April 15-23, 1781)
7) Historic Camden (British Garrison – 1780-1781)
8) Camden (August 16, 1780)
9) Hanging Rock (July 30, 1780 & August 6, 1780)
10) Waxhaws (May 29, 1780)
11) Huck's Defeat (July 12,1780)
12) Kings Mountain (October 7, 1780)
13) Cowpens (January 17, 1781)
14) Blackstock's Plantation (November 20, 1780)
15) Musgrove Mill (August 18, 1780)
16) Siege of Fort Ninety Six (May 22-June 18, 1781)

LIBERTY TRAIL MICRO-SITES

A) Sullivan's Island (June 28, 1776)
B) Stono Ferry (June 20, 1776)
C) Mepkin (Home of Henry and John Laurens)
D) Biggin Church (July 15-16, 1781)
E) Wadboo Bridge (January 31 and July 17, 1781)
F) Avenue of Cedars (August 29, 1782)
G) Moncks Corner (April 14, 1780)
H) Great Savannah (August 25,1780)
I) Wyboo Swamp (March 6, 1781)
J) Halfway Swamp (December 12, 1780)
K) Tearcoat Swamp (October 25,1780)
L) Ox Swamp (November 8, 1780)
M) Hobkirk's Hill (April 25, 1781)
N) Rugeley's Mill (December 4, 1780)

APPENDIX C
A SHORT HISTORY OF THE BATTLEFIELD PRESERVATION MOVEMENT

THE IDEA OF PROTECTING AMERICA'S BATTLEFIELD IS NOT NEW. In the mid-19th century, portions of the Revolutionary War battlefields at places like Bunker Hill and Yorktown were set aside as a means of remembrance. Civil War veterans began erecting memorials to their units, actions, and fallen comrades almost as soon as the guns fell silent. Veterans reunions catalyzed battlefield preservation, as, at these gatherings, the men of the blue and the gray discussed creating open-air classrooms where the military could visit and learn the lessons from battles of the past.

By 1900, five national military parks—at Antietam, Chickamauga and Chattanooga, Gettysburg, Shiloh and Vicksburg—had been established under the auspices of the War Department. Gradually, additional parks were created at places like Cowpens, Guilford Courthouse, Fort McHenry, Fort Donelson, and Petersburg, all of which were transferred to the control of the National Park Service in 1933. The so-called "cannonball circuit" continued to grow through the Civil War centennial commemoration in the 1960s, but federal battlefield preservation efforts then began to stall.

In the years following the Second World War, the pace of urban and suburban development in America dramatically escalated, leading to the destruction of battlefield land virtually across the map. The destruction was particularly devastating at battlefields adjacent to major cities. Witnessing commercial and residential construction destroying these historic sites, local preservation and park friends groups began to take shape and advocate for their protection. But there was no unified voice, and success was both scattered and limited; entire battlefields like Chantilly and Salem Church, both Civil War sites in central Virginia, were all but swallowed by sprawl.

In July 1987, twenty or so stalwart souls met in Fredericksburg, Virginia, to discuss what could be done to protect the rapidly disappearing battlefields around them. Calling themselves the Association for the Preservation of Civil War Sites (APCWS), they decided the only way to save these sites for posterity was to buy the physical landscapes themselves. In 1999, seeking to increase the scope of preservation opportunities that could be pursued, that first group merged with another organization sharing its vision to form the Civil War Preservation Trust. On the eve of the war's sesquicentennial commemoration in 2011, the group shortened its name to the Civil War Trust.

By mastering the art of seeking out public-private partnerships to maximize efficiency, and by working with developers to find win-win solutions, the Civil War Trust became the number-one entity saving battlefield land in America, protecting land at a rate four times that of the National Park Service. In 2014, responding to a clear need from the National Park Service, the Civil War Trust launched Campaign 1776, a limited-scope project to lend its considerable expertise and clout to the protection of battlefields associated with the Revolutionary War and the War of 1812. In May 2018, having concluded its 30th anniversary year, the group unveiled a new organizational structure, in which the Civil War Trust and the Revolutionary War Trust would operate as land preservation divisions under the banner of a broader American Battlefield Trust. With the mission to—Preserve. Educate. Inspire —The American Battlefield Trust continues to be the leader in the land preservation community.

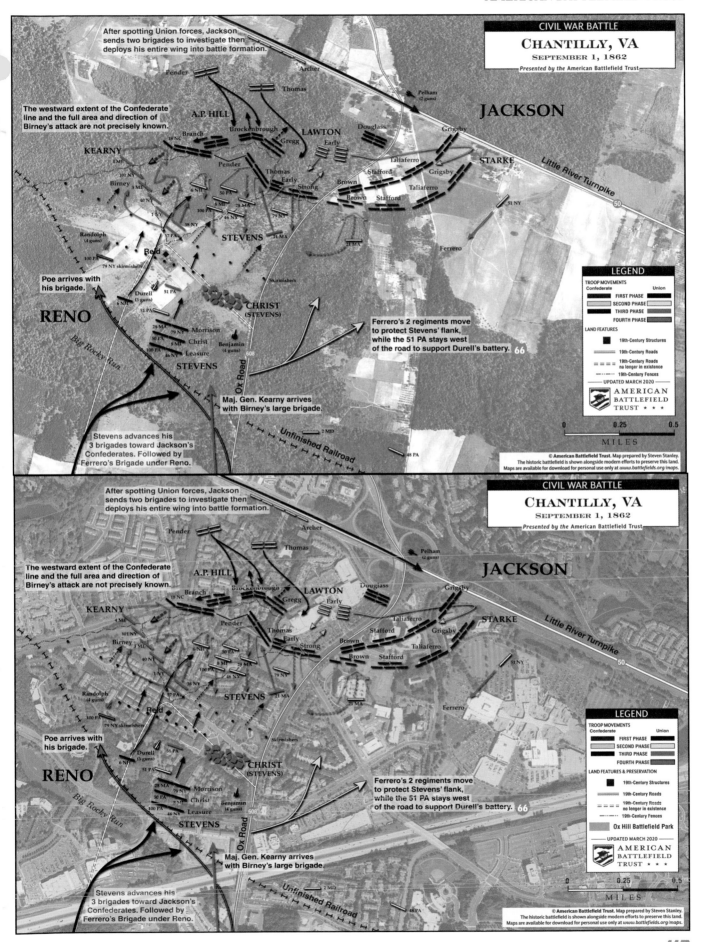

CIVIL WAR BATTLE

CHANTILLY, VA

SEPTEMBER 1, 1862

Presented by the American Battlefield Trust

After spotting Union forces, Jackson sends two brigades to investigate then deploys his entire wing into battle formation.

The westward extent of the Confederate line and the full area and direction of Birney's attack are not precisely known.

JACKSON

Pender
Archer
Thomas
Pelham (2 guns)
A.P. HILL
Branch
18 NC
Brockenbrough
Gregg
LAWTON
Douglass
Grigsby
Early
KEARNY
1 ME
101 NY
Birney
3 ME
Pender
Thomas
Early
Strong
Brown
Brown
Stafford
Stafford
Taliaferro
Grigsby
Taliaferro
STARKE
Little River Turnpike
50
51 NY
40 NY
6 NH
50 PA
8 MI
28 MA
100 PA
46 NY
38 NY
57 PA
STEVENS
21 MA
21 MA
Ferrero
Randolph (4 guns)
100 PA
Reid
79 NY skirmishers
Poe arrives with his brigade.
Durell (3 guns)
51 PA
6 NH
53 PA
Skirmishers
RENO
CHRIST (STEVENS)
Ferrero's 2 regiments move to protect Stevens' flank, while the 51 PA stays west of the road to support Durell's battery.
66
Big Rocky Run
28 MA
79 NY
Morrison
50 PA
8 MI
Christ
100 PA
46 NY
Leasure
Benjamin (4 guns)
608
STEVENS
Ox Road
Maj. Gen. Kearny arrives with Birney's large brigade.
Stevens advances his 3 brigades toward Jackson's Confederates. Followed by Ferrero's Brigade under Reno.
2 MD
Unfinished Railroad
48 PA

LEGEND

TROOP MOVEMENTS
Confederate   Union
FIRST PHASE
SECOND PHASE
THIRD PHASE
FOURTH PHASE

LAND FEATURES
19th-Century Structures
19th-Century Roads
19th-Century Roads no longer in existence
19th-Century Fences

UPDATED MARCH 2020

AMERICAN BATTLEFIELD TRUST ★ ★ ★

0   0.25   0.5
MILES

© American Battlefield Trust. Map prepared by Steven Stanley.
The historic battlefield is shown alongside modern efforts to preserve this land.
Maps are available for download for personal use only at *www.battlefields.org/maps*.

CIVIL WAR BATTLE

CHANTILLY, VA

SEPTEMBER 1, 1862

Presented by the American Battlefield Trust

After spotting Union forces, Jackson sends two brigades to investigate then deploys his entire wing into battle formation.

The westward extent of the Confederate line and the full area and direction of Birney's attack are not precisely known.

JACKSON

Pender
Archer
Thomas
Pelham (2 guns)
A.P. HILL
LAWTON
Branch
18 NC
Brockenbrough
Gregg
Early
Douglass
Grigsby
KEARNY
1 ME
101 NY
Birney
1 ME
Pender
Thomas
Early
Strong
Brown
Brown
Stafford
Stafford
Taliaferro
Grigsby
Taliaferro
STARKE
Little River Turnpike
50
51 NY
40 NY
6 NH
50 PA
8 MI
28 MA
100 PA
46 NY
38 NY
57 PA
STEVENS
21 MA
79 NY
21 MA
Ferrero
Randolph (4 guns)
100 PA
Reid
79 NY skirmishers
Poe arrives with his brigade.
Durell (3 guns)
51 PA
6 NH
51 PA
Skirmishers
RENO
CHRIST (STEVENS)
Ferrero's 2 regiments move to protect Stevens' flank, while the 51 PA stays west of the road to support Durell's battery.
66
Big Rocky Run
28 MA
79 NY
Morrison
50 PA
8 MI
Christ
100 PA
46 NY
Leasure
Benjamin (4 guns)
608
STEVENS
Ox Road
Maj. Gen. Kearny arrives with Birney's large brigade.
Stevens advances his 3 brigades toward Jackson's Confederates. Followed by Ferrero's Brigade under Reno.
2 MD
Unfinished Railroad
48 PA

LEGEND

TROOP MOVEMENTS
Confederate   Union
FIRST PHASE
SECOND PHASE
THIRD PHASE
FOURTH PHASE

LAND FEATURES & PRESERVATION
19th-Century Structures
19th-Century Roads
19th-Century Roads no longer in existence
19th-Century Fences

Ox Hill Battlefield Park

UPDATED MARCH 2020

AMERICAN BATTLEFIELD TRUST ★ ★ ★

0   0.25   0.5
MILES

© American Battlefield Trust. Map prepared by Steven Stanley.
The historic battlefield is shown alongside modern efforts to preserve this land.
Maps are available for download for personal use only at *www.battlefields.org/maps*.

BATTLE MAPS OF THE AMERICAN REVOLUTION
MAPS FROM THE AMERICAN BATTLEFIELD TRUST ⌒ VOLUME 3

PROJECT TEAM

ADMINISTRATION AND MANAGEMENT DEPARTMENT
David Duncan
President
Steve Wyngarden
Chief Administrative Officer

DEVELOPMENT DEPARTMENT
Amanda Murray
Deputy Director of Development

POLICY & COMMUNICATIONS DEPARTMENT
Mary Koik
Director of Communications

DIGITAL OPERATIONS DEPARTMENT
Wendy Woodford
Design Lead

REAL ESTATE DEPARTMENT
Jon Mitchell
GIS Specialist
Catherine Noyes
Liberty Trail Program Director

HISTORY & EDUCATION DEPARTMENT
Kristopher White
Deputy Director of Education

Steven Stanley
Historical Map Designer

Brandywine Battlefield Historic Site
Chadds Ford, Pa.
MEREDITH BARNES

YOU'VE SEEN THE MAPS.
NOW HELP US
SAVE THE LAND.

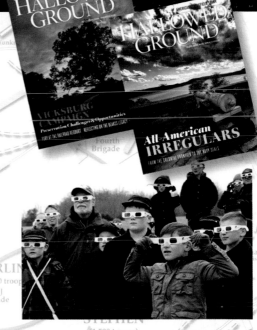

BY PRESERVING our nation's hallowed ground, the American Battlefield Trust provides a means to experience the stories that shaped the nation we have become. We keep alive the memory of our country's formative conflicts — the American Revolution, War of 1812, and Civil War — through a broad range of heritage tourism and education initiatives. Our nonprofit, nonpartisan nature unites many voices to advocate for the future generations on whose behalf we safeguard these resources.

The wars of America's first century — from the shot heard 'round the world at Lexington to the stillness of surrender at Appomattox — established our independence and transformed the fledgling country from a collection of independent states into a cohesive nation. Preserving the lands upon which these defining struggles were contested, whether via outright purchase or conservation easement, creates the opportunity for place-based education, a powerful tool that can make lessons in civics and history come to life. ***www.battlefields.org***

AMERICAN
BATTLEFIELD
TRUST ★★★

PRESERVE. EDUCATE. INSPIRE.

Please mail coupon on flip side to:
1140 Professional Court, Hagerstown, MD 21740

Ninety Six National Hist
Ninety
MARK THOR

PRESERVATION IS PUTTING THIS BATTLEFIELD BACK ON THE MAP

AND YOU CAN HELP SAVE OTHERS BEFORE THEY'RE LOST.

Please send me free information on preserving America's Battlefields.

Name _____

Address _____ State _____ Zip _____

Email _____

Phone _____

AMERICAN BATTLEFIELD TRUST ★ ★ ★

PRESERVE. EDUCATE. INSPIRE.

Mail the coupon to: 1156 15th St. NW, Suite 900, Washington, DC 20005 or go to www.battlefields.org/about